D1345814

ECONOMIC ISSUES, PROBLEMS AND PERSPECTIVES

THE ELUSIVE SEARCH FOR JOB SECURITY

A HISTORICAL INQUIRY INTO DISMISSALS IN THE UNITED STATES WORKPLACE

ECONOMIC ISSUES, PROBLEMS AND PERSPECTIVES

Additional books in this series can be found on Nova's website under the Series tab.

Additional E-books in this series can be found on Nova's website under the E-book tab.

AMERICAN POLITICAL, ECONOMIC, AND SECURITY ISSUES

Additional books in this series can be found on Nova's website under the Series tab.

Additional E-books in this series can be found on Nova's website under the E-book tab.

ECONOMIC ISSUES, PROBLEMS AND PERSPECTIVES

THE ELUSIVE SEARCH FOR JOB SECURITY

A HISTORICAL INQUIRY INTO DISMISSALS IN THE UNITED STATES WORKPLACE

MATTHIAS P. BECK

Nova Science Publishers, Inc.

New York

Copyright © 2012 by Nova Science Publishers, Inc.

For permission to use material from this book please contact us:
Telephone 631-231-7269; Fax 631-231-8175
Web Site: http://www.novapublishers.com

NOTICE TO THE READER

Library of Congress Cataloging-in-Publication Data

The elusive search for job security : a historical inquiry into dismissals in the US workplace / editor, Matthias Beck.
  p. cm.
  Includes index.
  ISBN 978-1-62081-766-7 (hardcover)
  1. Employees--Dismissal of. 2. Employees--Dismissal of--Law and legislation--Great Britain. 3. Employees--Dismissal of--Law and legislation--United States. 4. Labor laws and legislation--United States. I. Beck, Matthias, 1963-
  HF5549.5.D55E48 2011
  331.13'7973--dc23
  2012015287

Published by Nova Science Publishers, Inc. †*New York*

CONTENTS

PREFACE

This book, which is at root an attempt to explain the processes that have led to the absence of a comprehensive system for the regulation of dismissals in the US workplace, is the outgrowth of a range of my interests. It includes some parts of my 1996 PhD dissertation, which I attempted to develop further over the years in light of my growing interest in risk management and risk regulation.

Although the book deals to a large degree with history, and more specifically labor and legal history, it is only fair to warn the reader that I am neither a labor nor a legal historian. My focus on in the history of dismissal regulation is informed by what could broadly be described as a "political economy of management perspective," which means that I am primarily interested in exploring the political and economic processes that have led to different outcomes in terms of the balance between capital and labor across different jurisdictions. It is also worth pointing out that in presenting this monograph, a choice had to be made about the appropriate form of referencing; with US legal citation systems being one of the potential models. In the end, a decision was made to follow some elements of this model but to follow a more conventional referencing style in other areas.

I would like to dedicate this book to the memory of Dr. Caroline Hunter Beck, 1957-2005.

Personal thanks for helping to make the completion of this book possible go to Steven Jones and my colleagues at Queen's University Belfast.

Matthias Beck

Belfast
2012

INTRODUCTION

For the majority of employees—in the US and elsewhere—their jobs are by far their most important properties, with jobs providing not only a principal source of wealth but also being a key source of social status and individual psychological well-being.[1] During recent years, job security has become increasingly tenuous in the United States, making job loss one of the principal risks faced by individuals and families from all walks of life. In 2009, alone, the US economy experienced 11,827 mass layoffs, which left 2.1 million unemployed.[2] This represented the largest number of such events being registered in any one year since the survey was started in 1996. Official figures by the *Bureau of Labor Statistics,* moreover, revealed a rise in unemployment from 5.8 percent in 2008, to 9.3 percent, and a decrease in private nonfarm payroll employment by five percent or by 5,910,000 jobs.[3]

What is more, an insightful article in *The Monthly Review* questioned these figures, suggesting that when the 6.5 million "persons not in the labor force but wanting a job" and the 8.4 million "working part-time but desiring full time work" were added to the 13.5 million workers who are officially defined as unemployed, the figure would rise to 28.4 million,[4] or nearly 20 percent.

The same article cites evidence suggesting that the economic insecurity created by the 2007 downturn had profound negative effects on the US population, which experienced an increase in suicide rates from approximately 11.0 per 100,000 in the early part of the decade to 11.5 per 100,000 in 2007, and a preliminary figure of 11.8 per 100,000 for 2008.[5]

---

[1] See, Barbara A. Lee, "Something Akin to a Property Right" (1989) 8 *Business and Professional Ethics Journal* 63, at 63 (1989) citing Reich, Charles, A., "The New Property" 73 *Yale Law Review* 733 (1964); and Glendon, Mary Ann, and Edward R. Lev, "'Changes in the Bonding of the Employment Relationship," 20 *Boston College Law Review* 457 (1979). See also Ioannis Theodossiou and Efi Vasileiou, "Making the Risk of Job Loss a Way of Life: Does it Affect Job Satisfaction?" 61 *Research in Economics* 71, at 71 (2007), whose investigation of "the relationship between job satisfaction and job security in European countries" showed "workers in jobs with low likelihood of job termination derive higher utility from work compared to the workers in insecure jobs."

[2] See Adam Corey Cross, "Companies Starting to Hire Back after Mass Layoffs," *Fiscal Times,* January 27 (2011). The Bureau of Labor Statistic's Mass Layoff Survey defines a mass layoff as an event involving the layoff of 50 or employees.

[3] See Bureau of Labor Statistics, "Extended Mass Layoffs in 2009," *Report* 1025 1 (2010).

[4] See Fred Magdoff, "The Jobs Disaster in the United States," 63 *Monthly Review-An Independent Socialist Magazine* 1 (2011).

[5] Magdoff, ibid., at para 7, citing Jacob S. Hacker, Philipp Rehm and Mark Schlesinger, *Standing on Shaky Ground: America's Experience with Economic Insecurity* (2010). These findings are echoed by other recent studies including Timothy J. Classen and Richard A. Dunn, "The Effects of Job Loss and Unemployment Duration on Suicide Risk in the United States: A New Look Using Mass-Layoffs and Unemployment Insurance Claims," 21 *Health Economics* 338, at 338 (2012) finding that "unemployment duration" is "the dominant force in the

That the financial crisis of 2007 and the successive recession would have led to job losses is perhaps not surprising; even though the extent of these job losses probably is.[6] What is perhaps more astonishing is that significant levels of mass levels do occur, and have occurred, in the US with some regularity during periods of relative economic stability and prosperity. Accordingly, a February 1996 Editorial in the *New York Times* reported "that between 1991 and 1995, nearly 2.5 million had lost their jobs due to corporate restructuring" yet "top pay for corporate executives had soared to nearly 200 times that of the average worker."[7]

As one of many examples of corporate restructuring of this time, between 1993 and 1995, Kodak eliminated 14,100 jobs, Westinghouse 4,900 jobs, Scott Papers 10,500 jobs, and IBM 36,000 jobs.[8]

For many companies of the 1990s, downsizing was a fashion,[9] and only too often—with dismissals being far too easy—this fashion harmed both companies and employees alike.

Between 1986 and 1994, for instance, IBM reduced its payroll from 406,000 to 209,000, which saw the company's share price increase significantly. However, by 1997, both IBM's research and development expenditure and net worth had shrunk by more than 15 percent.[10]

In many ways, these labor market outcomes are the result of concrete institutional and political choices, which concern the way employment is regulated and economic policy is conducted. More specifically, they are due to the fact that while the US political system provides extensive protection to capital, it paradoxically offers only very limited protection to labor.[11] This lack of protection is evidenced, above all, by the fact that the job protection afforded to US workers is amongst the weakest of all industrialized nations—even though the protection of other forms of property in the US is amongst the broadest.[12]

---

relationship between job loss and suicide," while "mass-layoffs may be powerful localized events where suicide risk increases shortly afterward." See also David J. Roelfs, Eran Shor, Karina W. Davidson, Joseph E. Schwartz, "Losing Life and Livelihood: A Systematic Review and Meta-analysis of Unemployment and All-cause Mortality," 72 *Social Science and Medicine* 840, at 840 (2011) finding that "unemployment was associated with an increased mortality risk for those in their early and middle careers, but less for those in their late careers" while "the risk of death was highest during the first 10 years of follow-up, but decreased subsequently."

[6] See, e.g., Nicholas Kulish, "Defying Others, Germany Finds Economic Success," *The New York Times,* August 13 (2010) noting that, in contrast to the U.S., Germany has continued to experience job growth during this period by relying extensively on counter-cyclical interventions and stimulus measures.

[7] Anonymous, "Editorial: Downsizing," *New York Times* 14, 25 February (1996).

[8] See also Anonymous, "Learning to Cope" *The Economist* 13, 6 April (1996) and Anonymous, "Fire and Forget" *The Economist* 51, April 20 (1996).

[9] Wally Seccombe, "Contradiction of Shareholder Capitalism: Downsizing Jobs, Enlisting Savings, Destabilizing Families," 35 *Socialist Register* 76 (1999) notes that a 1992 survey of 530 firms found two-thirds of these to have downsized, often in spite of being profitable within current arrangements.

[10] Seccombe, ibid., at 83. By the end of 2011, IBM's value was less than two-thirds of that of Apple.

[11] See, e.g., Andrew Thompson, "A View from Abroad," in *U.S. Industrial Relations 1950 to 1980* 297 (Jack Stieber, Robert B. McKersie, and D. Quinn Mills, eds., 1981), whose radical critique of U.S. employment law argues that that the only property rights effectively recognized in the U.S. are those of capital.

[12] See, e.g., Jay E. Grenig, "The Dismissal of Employees in the United States" 130 *International Labor Review* 569 (1991). Canada, France, Germany, Italy and the UK established comprehensive systems for adjudicating disputes arising in dismissal matters in the 1950s and 1970s. These provisions have been based on a wide variety of rationales, including, especially in the case of public sector employees concerns over their loyalty, integrity, or autonomy, or the fact that such employees make substantial job-specific human capital investments in order to perform their jobs. See, e.g., Matthias P. Beck, "The Law and Economics of Dismissal Regulation: A Comparative Analysis of U.S. and UK Systems," in *Law and Economics and the Labour Market* 92 (Gerrit de Geest, Jacques J. Siegers, Roger van den Bergh, eds., 1999); and also Matthias P. Beck, "Union Agendas and the Disintegration of Job Stability—an Institutional Perspective," 5 *Journal of Interdisciplinary Economics* 79 (1994).

The observation of this discrepancy of management rights as compared to labor rights has caused a number of observers to be highly critical of the current system of US labor law. Among more recent works, James Cross's 2010 book *A Shameful Business: The Case for Human Rights in the American Workplace*, for instance, suggests that:[13]

> ... the clash of the right of freedom of association with management rights and the unregulated market philosophy that constitutes the business creed ... has been resolved judicially, legislatively, and otherwise in ways that facilitate employer resistance to workers' exercise of their freedom of association, give management rights dominance over workers' rights, leave workers dependent and powerless to protect themselves, promote and protect the rights and freedoms of employers, and enable employers to retain unilateral control over workers and workplaces.

Cross' views, interestingly, echo those of earlier writers who similarly observed a lack of balance in the way US society regulated its labor force. This is exemplified by Glenn W. Miller's 1948 book *American Labor and the Government*, which noted that:[14]

> ... the judiciary has tended to bulwark the existing economy and protect it from rapid change. It seems clear that the tone of the decisions rendered come more from conservatism than from precedent. ...
>
> Whatever the reason for the general conservatism of the judges, their decisions influence strongly the extent and type of government controls. This influence is exercised strongly through the approval or disapproval of legislation coming before the courts. As examples of the retarding influence of the courts, minimum-wage legislation for women was delayed by fifteen years by adverse rulings of the Supreme Court; federal regulation of child labor was held up by twenty years by the opinion of the same body; and attempts to guarantee the right of workers to join unions if they so desired were delayed by an even longer period.
>
> Indirectly, the Court has a further effect on the economic controls of the nation. Legislators realize that any controversial legislation which they enact must pass the scrutiny of the Supreme Court. Thus, adverse rulings on some law may discourage the enactment of a control until a way is found which it is hoped will justify the new legislation in the eyes of the court.
>
> In still another way, opinions of the Supreme Court influence the decisions of lower courts, and, thus, many cases that never come before the echelons of the judiciary are remotely controlled.

The primary purpose of this monograph is not to add to the already substantial body of work that criticizes US employment law, and in particular its lack of provisions for the protection of workers from unfair or unnecessary dismissals.[15] Rather it is the intent of this

---

[13] James A. Cross, *A Shameful Business: The Case for Human Rights in the American Workplace*, at 4 and 5 (2010).

[14] Glenn W. Miller, *American Labor and the Government*, at 88 (1948).

[15] This lack of protection of workers from unfair, arbitrary or unnecessary dismissals is due to a number of factors that are described in some detail in subsequent chapters of this book. Among the more obvious factors, it is worth noting that most collective bargaining agreements include clauses that prohibit the discharge of employees except for "good cause." Yet the effect of these provisions on the U.S. workforce as a whole are limited: i) because of the limited and declining coverage of workplaces by union contracts; ii) union discretion, which allows union representatives to refuse arbitration to an individual; and iii) most importantly, the court's traditional support for managerial prerogatives, which tend to render dismissals for alleged economic reasons largely untouchable. Lastly, the dismissal protection available through court actions alleging violation of federal law or state law exemptions is contingent on the availability and affordability of legal representation.

monograp to draw out the historical circumstances that can be used to explicate how this situation has come about and to highlight some of the key themes that help us understand why, despite long-standing dissatisfaction with the *status quo*, the US has not engaged in fundamental reforms of workplace governance, which would bring the country in line with other advanced industrialized nations. The book then is about dismissal regulation, or more precisely, the regulation of employment termination; and, more specifically, about a particular form of US exceptionalism—namely the absence of comprehensive dismissal regulation in the US—its origins, and its consequences.

In the narrow, legal sense, a dismissal is the typically isolated incident of the discharge of an employee for various reasons. The topic of this book is not dismissal in this sense, but rather the termination of employment relationships more generally. Such terminations include: a) "classical" dismissal, that is the discharge of an individual employee because of her personal characteristics, who is then replaced with another worker; b) "strategic dismissal," that is the discharge of workers based on the adoption of a particular managerial strategy or policy (such as subcontracting, the prevention of overstaffing, etc. ...); and c) redundancies, that is the discharge or permanent layoff of workers for economic reasons, including plant closings. While these distinctions are of some importance in legal contexts, this book does not focus on these differences but rather views dismissal as a unified phenomenon. This is based on the observation that there is much blurring among categories, which is particularly apparent in the context of a legal historical analysis. The just-cause standard of the unionized workplace, created to prevent arbitrary discharges, for instance, became, once a formal arbitration apparatus had been developed, a much more general mechanism for the protection of workers whose dismissal was based on alleged skill mismatches or even economic reasons.

The primary agenda of this book is to trace how institutional choices, which have prevented a comprehensive, European-style regulation of dismissal in the United States, have been made,supported, modified and maintained against attempts by US workers to secure greater job security. The relevance and the viability of this research agenda is premised on two working hypotheses or assumptions. The first of these working assumptionsis relates to the author's belief that much of the experience of job insecurity of US workers can be directly attributed to the country's lack of a comprehensive and effective system of dismissal regulation, which has, over time, blocked any serious investigation—at the national, state or local level—of codetermination, active labor market policy or corporatist collaboration as a means for securing greater job security for the US workforce (while encouraging its very opposite—namely an extremely casual attitude towards the very real suffering frequent job loss imposes on members of the working population).

My second working assumption is that the absence of comprehensive dismissal regulation is a historical *explanandum* of some social and political relevance. The presence of US exceptionalism has been asserted in perhaps too many areas to maintain its usefulness as a historiographical concept. There are, however, within the field of industrial relations relatively few areas where "exceptionalism" is, over a prolonged time frame, more clearly discernible than within the institutional rules that govern the dismissal of US employees. In

---

Accordingly, Lee, *supra* note 1, at 64, has described the job protection available to U.S. workers as a "complex web of legal theories that differs from state by state and changes with each new court opinion" that "tends to destabilize employment relations and to make the current law governing employment relations unpredictable."

this sense, this book is not purely about an exceptional outcome in terms of weak dismissal protection in the US workplace,[16] but rather it is about more fundamental questions about the processes that have, over time, sustained this anomaly and that seem to make its reversal impossible.

The following chapters of this book examine these processes in a roughly historical order. Chapter One takes a historical look at the common law as a source of dismissal protection and suggests that the adoption of the at-will doctrine in the United States of the late nineteenth century—which allowed for the dismissal of employees at any time and for any reason—marked a crucial departure of the US form the legal practices of other countries of the common law family. This analysis of the at-will regime forms the basis for Chapter Two, which examines how, following a period of regulatory inertia, some restrictions on the dismissal of employees were introduced in the 1930s alongside legislation that was primarily aimed at regulating collective bargaining processes. Chapter Three, next, discusses the evolution of plant-level bargaining and "bartering" for job security, which evolved partly as a consequence of restrictions imposed by the courts on legal challenges (by unions) to employer decision to close or relocate plants. Chapter Four concludes the review of attempts to restrict the right of management to dismiss workers by looking at the evolution of unjust dismissal litigation, which commenced in the last decades of the twentieth century. The concluding section addresses some conceptual questions associated with dismissal protection and argues that there are significant reasons as to why societies should restrict the right of employers to dismiss workers. This is followed by a brief Afterword, which discusses the obstacles to, and possibility of, fundamental reform of US employment legislation in this area.

---

[16] Indeed, it has been argued that the question as to why the U.S. has at this point in time no comprehensive system of dismissal regulation, severance pay or industrial adjudication is of limited relevance—if only because neoliberal reforms have undermined earlier gains by organized labor in many regions. This view, however, ignores the relatively limited scope of these neoliberal reforms in so much as key employment rights are concerned.

Chapter 1

THE COMMON LAW OF EMPLOYMENT TERMINATION

I am not speaking of conscious impartiality; but the habits you are trained in, the people with whom you mix, lead to you having a certain class of ideas of such nature that, when you have to deal with other ideas, you do not give as sound and accurate judgments as you would wish. This is one of the great difficulties presently with labour. Labour says: "Where are your impartial Judges? They all move in the same circles as the employers, and they are all educated and nursed in the same ideas as the employers? How can a labor man or a unionist get impartial justice?" It is very difficult ... to be sure that you have put yourself into an impartial position between disputants, one of your own class and one not of your class.

Lord Justice Thomas E. Scrutton, "The Work of the Commercial Courts,"1
Cambridge Law Journal, 6, at 8 (1921)

This chapter, which focuses on the common law of employment termination, forms the first part of an explanatory framework for the lack of a comprehensive framework for the regulation of dismissals in the US.

The lack of a comprehensive system for the regulation of dismissals in the US is the product of complex and overlapping historical processes. Historically speaking, these processes originated in the mid-nineteenth century, when the US common law of employment termination started to gradually depart from older British standards; or in other words, when what could be loosely described as US labor law came into being. Prior to the late nineteenth century, the common law of employment inherited from the colonial era posed significant obstacles to the dismissal of employees.

These restrictions were largely eliminated with the adoption of the employment at-will doctrine in the late nineteenth century US workplace, which allowed for the dismissal of employees at any time and for any reason, and in so doing marked a crucial departure of the US from the legal practices of other countries of the common law family.[17]

The following sections of this chapter look in some detail at the influence of British colonial inheritance on US labor law, key departure points, and the processes that supported the creation of the new at-will regime. This analysis of the at-will regime, in turn, forms the

---

[17] See Sanford M. Jacoby, "The Duration of Indefinite Employment Contracts in the U.S. and England: A Historical Analysis," 5 *Comparative Labor Law* 85 (1982), which highlights the significance of the adoption of the atd-will doctrine to U.S. legal developments.

basis for a consecutive chapter, which examines how, following a period of regulatory inertia, some restrictions on the dismissal of employees were introduced 1930s as part of legislation that was primarily aimed at regulating collective bargaining processes.[18]

Today, common law exemptions to at-will employment, which emerged from the late 1970s and early 1980s, onwards, are at times invoked by plaintiffs in unjust dismissal litigation in conjunction with other regulations such as statutes that govern the unionized or union-contract covered workplace, or rules that apply to individuals on account of their special status.[19] In focusing on the rise of the at-will doctrine, this chapter examines the "common law of dismissal" in isolation of other statutory and legal sources of employment rights that represent, in any case, much later developments of the twentieth century.

THE COMMON LAW OF EMPLOYMENT TERMINATION

The origins of American employment law can be traced to eighteenth and nineteenth century English and Scottish legal doctrine. In the eighteenth century, English and Scots law viewed the employment of individuals as a sub-category case of the common law contract; commonly described as the "law of master and servant."

The law of master and servant set stringent limits on dismissals of, and quits by, employees. Thus, as regards dismissals in the absence of contractual termination provisions (or "indefinite contracts"), key legal sources such as Sir William Blackstone's *Commentaries on the Laws of England* (1765-1769) explicitly stated that, where there was no evidence to the contrary, an indefinite hiring was to be interpreted as extending to a full year.[3]

Although several authors describe eighteenth and early nineteenth century English and Scots law as a means for the subjugation of labor—whereby numerous obligations where placed on laborers without corresponding obligations being placed on employers—legal writing of the time does provide some evidence that this law offered some protection against

---

[18] Cynthis L. Estlund, "The Ossification of American Labor Law," 102 *Columbia Law Review* 1527, at 1552 (2002), correctly notes that "The NLRA represents a very early and important wrongful discharge law. It was the first major inroad into what had been, in the Lochner era, employers' constitutional right to fire for good reason, bad reason, or no reason at all." Yet it must be kept in mind that neither the common law of employment nor the NLRA were primarily concerned with regulating dismissals. The common law of employment was, by and large, the by-product of contract law. Statutory provisions on dismissals, such as those contained in the NLRA, meanwhile, were the outgrowth of legislation whose stated policy goal was the extension of orderly collective bargaining.

[19] The following analysis of the English Law of Master and Servant prior to its *de facto* elimination through wartime and postwar government legislation is based on numerous sources including F. Raleigh Batt, *The Law of Master and Servant,* especially at 40-58 (3rd edition, 1939); John MacDonell, *The Law of Master and Servant: Part I-Common Law and Part II-Statute Law,* especially at 167-175 (1883); and Charles Manley-Smith, *A Treatise on the Law of Master and Servant,* especially at 108-173 (7th edition, 1922). In addition, information has been obtained from more general sources such as the contract law books by Joseph Chitty, *Chitty's Treatise on the Law of Contracts,* especially at 863-909 (19th edition, 1937); and Ralph Sutton and Norman P. Shannon, *Sutton and Shannon on Contracts,* especially at 231-316 (4th edition, 1933). Comparisons of English and Scottish law draw on James Patterson, *A Compendium of English and Scotch Law Stating their Differences,* especially at 272-289 (2nd edition, 1865), who notes significant similarities between English and Scots' law in this area. Some historical American sources wrongly describe Scottish decisions as "English" case law, and the inclusion of some references to Scots law in this analysis is based on that observation.

wrongful discharge for at least certain groups of employees.[20] In this context, several sources suggest that, although focusing on the duty of the "servant to serve" and providing numerous and draconic penalties for non-compliance, the law of master and servant also entailed an element of dismissal protection, which arose primarily from the fact that employees hired for an indefinite time, who were dismissed prematurely, could seek compensation for breach of contract under various legal doctrines.

The origins of the one-year rule itself are largely undisputed, being attributed to an oft-cited passage of Sir William Blackstone's *Commentaries on the Laws of England*, written in the late eighteenth century, which stated that:[21]

> If the hiring be general, without any particular time limit, the law constitutes it a hiring for one year; upon a principle of natural equity, that the servant shall serve and the master shall maintain him, throughout all the revolution of the respective seasons; as well as when there is work to be done as when there is not.

---

[20] This interpretation of eighteenth and nineteenth century English Common Law as being a source of protection contradicts a branch of scholarship that suggests that this law was primarily repressive and exploitative in nature. Expanding on the earlier argument mde in Karen Orren's, *Belated Feudalism: Labor, the Law and Liberal Government in the United States,* at 70 (1991) that the law of master and servant inherited from the feudal period "was the foundation of capitalist development" in that it codified labor as unfree, Marc W. Steinberg, "Capitalist Development, the Labor Process, and the Law," 109 *American Sociological Review* 445, at 451 (2003), for instance, suggests that "the law drawn on by English capitalists was not a mere remnant of feudalism" but rather a "particular development of the eighteenth and nineteenth centuries," which was aimed at providing a "form of advanced formal subsumption of labor in the absence of other institutional and technical forms of control in the workplace." Steinberg's argument, and particularly the implication that law existed virtually exclusively in order to deprive employees of rights rather than conferring any rights on them, is problematic in its sweeping generality. Thus, Kahn-Freund, "Blackstone's Neglected Child: The Contract of Employment," 93 *Law Quarterly Review* 508, at 518 (1977) provides a nuanced analysis of early English employment law, which notes that Blackstone distinguished between four categories of servants. The most distinctive of these categories was a fourth group of servants whom Blackstone described as being in "superior or ministerial capacity" and among whom he included stewards, factors, and factors. Unlike menial servants, apprentices or laborers, Blackstone considered these servants as "*pro tempore*," implying that there was no general compulsion for them to work and by implication suggesting that the law bestowed contractual right upon these employees. Kahn-Freund (1977, at 522-23) concludes that "there was in the eighteenth century an enormous gulf between, say a factor or other commercial employee and an agricultural labourer or domestic servant ... it was incongruous to treat their relationship to their employers as belonging to the same categories. The steward or bailiff who Blackstone mentions could not possibly be in the same category as the labourers under his control." Given this analysis, it is perhaps more useful to conceptualize eighteenth and early nineteenth century contract of employment as one that was not unwilling to bestow employment rights on distinct groups of upper level employees, while serving as a means of tying lower level "servants" to master/employers, without imposing,as Caunce documents, significant obligations on the employer; see Stephen Caunce, "Farm Servants and the Development of Capitalism in English Agriculture," 45 *Agricultural History Review* 49 at 57 (1997). This interpretation would match more closely the assumptions of Marxian class analysis, which has inspired much of this literature; if only because this very theory would lead us to expect the superstructural law of employment to mirror the contradictions of a dynamic society in which new prosperous classes assert utilize existing and novel legal doctrine in order to obtain or assert employment rights; see also the subsequent discussion of Burn (1831) in this chapter; and Louis E. Wolcher, "The Privilege of Idleness: A Case Study of and the Common Law in Nineteenth Century America," 36 *American Journal of Legal History* 237, at 243 (1992), which discusses the potential role of class sympathy of the judiciary with articulate and educated employees as a potential cause of employee friendly decisions.

[21] Sir William Blackstone, *Commentaries on the Laws of England,* Book 1, Chapter 14 (1769), cited here from the first edition (made available in electronic form by the University of Adelaide Library) provides an analysis of the indefinite employment contract, which appears to have been widely accepted in nineteenth century English courts. There is a significant literature that highlights the repressive application of these provisions in terms of the criminal prosecution of non-compliant laborers, rather than its grounding in principles of natural equity or mutual obligation. Accordingly, Caunce, *supra* note 20 at 58, notes that in 1854, as many as 3,000 workers were imprisoned for leaving or neglecting their work.

Through custom and the legal endorsement of the one-year rule, contracts of less than one year were deemed objectionable by employers and several occupational groups in pre-industrial England. This virtual ubiquity of the yearly contract was arguably defensible prior to industrialization because few occupations were unaffected by seasonal fluctuations, and even early mining was highly seasonal due to flooding in winter and difficulties of moving goods on muddy roads. However, this was no longer the case in the first decades of nineteenth century England, when technical advances, such as the improvements in transport through the building of canals, etc., reduced the impact of seasonal changes. At this time, marginal adjustments to legal doctrine heralded a gradual sidelining of the one-year rule. [22] These modifications initially focused on domestic servants and employees of comparable status, while the position of higher-status employees appears to have been preserved or even strengthened. This novel understanding of the indefinite contract was summarized in one of the early nineteenth century editions of the widely read manual, *The Justice of the Peace and Parish Officer* by Robert Burn, which it is cited here in its 1831 edition:[23]

> II. Contract of Service, and putting an end to
> The contract of service need not in general be in writing ...
> If a person retains a servant generally, without expressing any time, the law shall construe it to be for one year, for that retainer is according to the law. ...
> And so of clerks and servants in general; and the service, except of domestic servants, cannot be put an end to before the end of the current year. Beeston v. Collyer, 4 Bing.389, 2 C. and P.607, S.C.; Hutton v. Bullnois, 2 C.andP.510; Aitkin v. Acton, cor. Tenterden, at

---

[22] This discussion of seasonality follows Caunce, *supra* note 20, at 53. Kahn-Freund, *supra* note 20, at 519 suggests that the contract of employment atrophied in nineteenth century England in that "the presumption of yearly hiring was very early on extended far beyond agricultural work to conditions which it did not fit at all, and, however outmoded, it lingered on until in 1969 the Court of Appeal gave it the *coup de grâce*." My own reading of historical sources would suggests that this interpretation is only partially correct in that the rules compensating prematurely or wrongfully dismissed employees had already undergone significant changes during the early decades of the nineteenth century. In line with the evolving class society, these modifications weakened the position of lower level workers, while strengthening that of the newly evolving middle class of clerical and managerial employees.

[23] See Richard Burn, *The Justice of the Peace and Parish Officer,* Volume V at 360 (26th edition, 1831). Eblen Moglen, Taking the Fifth: Reconsidering the Origins of the Constitutional Privilege Against Self Incrimination," 92 *Michigan Law Review* 1086, at 1098 (1992) highlights the crucial influence of Justice's manuals on legal developments in Great Britain and British North America. As regards the succession of these manuals, Moglen notes that Michael Dalton's *The Country Justice* (1690) was the key authority of the English JP throughout the 17th century, when it was replaced by Giles Jacob's, *The Modern Justice: The Business of a Justice of the Peace* (1716) and William Nelson's *The Office and Authority of a Justice of the Peace* (1710). Both works were replaced by Burn's *Justice of the Peace and Parish Officer,* which was originally published in two volumes in 1755, which was probably the most influential of these manuals. As concerns the cases cited in this passage of Burns the 1827 case of Beeston v. Collyer, 4 Bing. 389 involved the clerk of an army agent who was hired in June 1811 and had been paid a quarterly salary of 125l on a monthly basis (500l per year) for a period of six years, until September 1826, when he was paid in advance until January 1827. "On the 23rd of September, 1826, he received a letter which was written by the defendant to the plaintiff, declining any interview with him, and stating that he would give him intimation when he had any thing for him to do. Matters continued in this state until the 23rd of December, 1826, when the defendant wrote again that the plaintiff, stating, that as the business of the office did not require further assistance, he was under the necessity of informing him that the salary must cease at the time to which it had been paid;" See Frederick A. Carrington and Joseph Payne, *Reports of Cases Determined at Nisi Prius, in the Courts of King's Bench and Common Pleas and on the Circuit, From the Sittings in Easter Term 1825 to the Sittings in Trinity Term, 1827, Volume II,* at 608 (1827). The court affirmed that Beeston's contract was for a yearly hire, even though payment had been received more frequently and awarded him the 83l (being the remaining balance of his annual wage of 500l).

Westminster, 16th April, 1830; unless upon some ground of misconduct on the part of either party. ...

By express agreement, either in writing or otherwise, the hiring may be for more or less than a year.

A hiring at 6s per week for the winter, and 9s per week for the summer, is not a yearly hiring ...

By the general understanding on the subject, and without an express agreement or understanding to the contrary, it should seem that domestic servants, who are hired by the year, are subject to be dismissed or to depart at any time on a month's notice, given by either, or a month's pay by the master.

But this does not apply to a person in the situation of a clerk of an army-agent, or the like, receiving a yearly salary. Beeston v. Collyer, 4 Bing.389, 2 C. and P.607, S.C.

This early nineteenth summary of the English law on dismissals marked a significant departure from Blackstone's original exposition of the indefinite contract of master. This deviation centered on the now explicit revocation of the one-year rule for domestic servants through the provision that these could be dismissed "at any time on a month's notice, given by either, or a month's pay by the master" and the parallel re-assertion of the dismissal protection implied in the rule for higher-status employees; the latter being underpinned by the precedent of *Beeston v. Collyer* (1827), which is mentioned twice in this short passage. In terms of its legal implications, this modification of the one-year rule established a differentiation of the "duties of the master" with regard to different classes of employees, which, of course, also was more in tune with the social realities of the time and which helped adapting the law to ongoing social changes that accompanied the rise of a new middle class.

From the 1820s, onwards, the contracts of masters with servants and workmen in England were subject to extensive statutory regulation—which until 1875, failed to treat manual workers and employers as equal contracting parties and which gave magistrates summary jurisdiction to enforce contracts through fines and penal measures. Parliamentary Acts passed under George IV (1820-1830) and in the first decades of Queen Victoria's rule (1837-1901) regulated contract length, notice requirements, as well as damages and compensation to be paid to if an employee quit before the contract was worked out or if she or he was dismissed prematurely without cause.[24]

---

[24] Kahn Freund, *supra* note 20, at 523, describes how the Conspiracy and Protection of Property Act of 1875 (38 and 39 Vic, c 90) "abolished the rule by which it was a criminal offence for the worker, but not for the employer, to break a contract." Following Denis Nowell Pritt, *Law Class and Society. Book I: Employers, Workers and Trade Unions*, at 38 (1970), Caunce, *supra* note 20, at 59, suggests that the Statute of Labourers (1563, 5 Eliz. I c. 4 Artificers and Apprentices Act) "was designed to regulate employment in favour of employers, not to raise the status of labour" and that this "basic anti-servant bias of the original legislation survived extensive changes made by two amending acts passed under George II, and another under George IV," including 20 Geo II, c 19; 31 Geo II, c 2; and 4 Geo IV, c 34. These Georgian Acts abolished the compulsory recruitment of labor mandated by the earlier Elizabethan Act and its amendments. Sepcifically the 1747 Regulation of Servants and Apprentices Act (20 Geo II, c. 19) gave summary jurisdiction to justices of the peace on disputes between masters and servants hired for one year or longer; which was extended to those hired for less than a year in 1757 (31 Geo II, c 2); and the Master and Servants Act of 1824 (4 Geo IV, c 34) limited terms of imprisonment of servants for breach of contract to three months while imposing a fine, and where applicable a duty to compensate for lost wages, on employers. The Master and Servant Act of 1867 (30 and 321 Vic, c 141) also improved the position of employees by limiting imprisonment to breaches of an "aggravated character." See also David Hoseason Morgan, *Harvesters and Harvesting, 1840-1900: A Study of the Rural Proletariat*, at 124 (1982). English law originally did not require a master to state grounds for a dismissal. If a servant alleged insufficient cause in court, the master was expected to prove a sufficient unpardoned cause for the dismissal. Orren, *supra* note 20, at 100, cites Ridgway v. Hungerford Market Co.

On the whole, neither statutes nor common law precedent posed significant obstacles to the dismissal of most domestic employees or menial servants who were paid monthly and whose dismissal required either a month's notice or the payment of a month's wages.[25] Thereafter, matters became more complicated, with the courts disagreeing on the principles that should guide the award of compensation.

In early nineteenth century, in wrongful discharge suits, the plaintiff typically had to prove "readiness and willingness" to continue in the service of the master. If this claim was accepted by the court, and no credible evidence for misconduct by the employee was at hand, the courts provided several courses of action.

According to the 1840 version of John W. Smith's compendium *Selection of Leading Cases on Various Branches of the Law*, a leading mid-nineteenth century legal textbook, English courts allowed employee to sue either for that part of the wages for which they had already worked on a *quantum meruit* basis or to wait until the duration of the contract had passed and claim "constructive service" and sue for the whole period's wages in an action of *indebitatus assumpsit*:[26]

> ... if the dismissal be unjust, the master cannot by his wrongful discharge prevent the servant from recovering due compensation. ... [I]f .. [t]he master has absolutely refused to perform his contract with the servant, and it is apprehended that the servant has thereupon a right to rescind it, and to sue upon a *quantum meruit* for what he has already done under it. But though he *may* rescind the contract, he is not, it would seem, obliged to do so. He has a right, it would seem, to consider it still in existence, to treat the wrongful dismissal as no dismissal at all, and to demand, at the expiration of the time for which he was hired, the whole

---

(1835), 3 A. and E. 171, 4 N. and M. 797, Lord Denman stated that "it is not, in my opinion, necessary that a master having good ground for dismissal, should either state that ground, or be actuated by it in dismissing his servant. It is sufficient that the master has a justifiable cause for dismissing his servant. Suppose a master intended to dismiss his servant without sufficient cause and the servant, learning this, grossly insults his master, surely this would entitle the master to dismiss the servant. ... It is sufficient for the master to show (in answer to an action by the servant for his wages) that a good ground for dismissal exists."

[25] Manley-Smith, *supra* note 19, at 113, states that the "amount of damages which a servant would recover in an action for wrongful discharge must, of course, depend on the nature of the contract, and the wages agreed to be paid. So in the case of a domestic or menial servant, or where there was an express agreement for a month's notice, it would be a month's wages," citing Fewings v. Tisdal, (1870) 1 Ex. 295 as authority for the first issue and Hartley v. Harman, (1840) 11 A. and E. 798 for the second. A preceding passage of the same textbook, at 38, notes that a "general rule can be laid down as to who do and who do not come within the category of domestic or menial servants. Each case must depend upon its own circumstances;" with evidence being cited of a farm bailiff to whom a year's wages were awarded following a dismissal on a month's notice (Louth v. Drummond, Kingston Spring Assizes, 1849, Times, March 28), a governess where a similar decision was made (Todd v. Kellage, 1853, 22 L. J. Ex. 1), as well as a housekeeper to a large hotel (Lawler v. Linden, 1876, Ir. Rep. 10 C. L. 188). See also the earlier analysis in Charles Manley-Smith, *A Treatise on the Law of Master and Servant, including therein Masters and Workmen in Every Description of Trade and Occupation*, at 168 (from the 4th English edition, 1886), published in Philadelphia, which cites Goodman v. Pocock, (1850) 15 Q. B. 576; 19 L. J., Q. B. 410 as establishing that an employee could sue either for damages for breach of contract or sue on a quantum meruit for the value of the work that he has actually performed.

[26] See John W. Smith, *A Selection of Leading Cases on Various Branches of the Law*, Vol II at 20 (3rd edition, 1840) which is quoted here with dates added to cases. This passage is virtually identical with the 4th American edition (1852) of Volume II of Smith's compendium, which is described on the cover sheet as drawing on "the 3rd English edition ... with additional notes and references to American cases by J.I. Clark Hare and H.B Wallace." A number of later English textbooks such as Batt, *supra* note 19, at 192; and Sutton and Shannon, *supra* note 19, at 253-255, also closely follow Smith's analysis. Arthur L. Corbin, *Cases on the Law of Contracts: Selected from Decisions of English and American Courts*, at 796 (1921), suggests that the notion of the entire contract "was first announced by Lord Ellenborough in Gandell v. Potigny ... a *nisi prius* case decided in 1816, in which he held that a servant employed for a quarter and wrongfully discharged before the end thereof might recover upon an *indebitatus assumpsit* count for wages for the entire quarter."

of his stipulated wages,— not on a *quantum meruit*, but by virtue of the special contract, his own part of which he may then safely aver that he has performed, his readiness to serve during the rest of the term being considered equivalent in law to actual service; and it has been thought that he may sue in *indebitatus assumpsit*, that being no more than any creditor may do upon an executed special contract, and his action, though not special in its form, being still upon the special contract and supported by the same evidence by which a special count would be substantiated. *Gandell v. Pontigny*, [1816] 4 Campb. 375, is a direct authority in favor of these positions.

That was an action brought by a clerk for his whole quarter's salary against his master, who had wrongfully dismissed him in the middle of a quarter; the declaration only contained the common count for work and labour. Lord Ellenborough: "If the plaintiff was discharged without a sufficient cause, I think this action maintainable. Having served a part of the quarter, and being willing to serve the residue, in contemplation of law he may be considered to have served the whole. The defendant was therefore indebted to him for work and labour in the sum sought to be recovered."

Interestingly, the subsequent paragraph suggests that the authors of this legal compendium were uncomfortable with such a broad application of the doctrine of constructive service. This is evident, above all, in their attempt to link the application of the doctrine to a special form of a "whole contract," the nature of which is not further specified by the authors:[27]

This peculiarity in the case of servants and agents wrongfully dismissed, results altogether from the doctrine of constructive service, which originated in decisions on the law of settlement; and though it may be applicable to some other cases (see *Collins v. Price*, [1828] 5 Bingh.132), it seems difficult to understand how it can be rationally applied to most other cases of special contract. For instance, in *Planche v. Colburn* [1831] it would have been impossible for Mr. Planche, with much show of reason, to contend that he had *constructively* written the whole treatise on armour, when, in point of fact, he only had finished half of it. It has, however, been applied to cases of servants, clerks, and agents;

Nonetheless, Smith's popular compendium concluded its section on wrongrul dismissal by stating that an action for *indebitatus assumpsit* was one of the options available to wrongfully dismissed employees, provided that they waited until the expiration of the term:

---

[27] See Smith (1840), ibid., at 20, whose discussion of the potential courses of action was replicated in twentieth century textbooks such as Sutton and Shannon, *supra* note 19. The textbook seems to mistakenly emphasize the special nature of the apportionable contract as giving rise to the presumption of constructive service, rather than the fact that an indefinite contract was historically assumed to be as a one-year duration. This dissatisfaction with the doctrine of constructive service was echoed by several writers. Accordingly, a U.S. textbook by Henry Dwight Sedgwick, *A Selection of American and English Cases on the Measure of Damages,* at 410 (1878), notes that "Mr. Smith had very properly expressed himself with hesitation as to this second proposition; and Erle, J., in referring to it, said, 'I think the servant cannot wait till the expiration of the period for which he was hired, and then sue for his whole wages, on the ground of a constructive service after dismissal. I think the true measure of damages is the loss sustained at the time of dismissal.' In Whitaker v. Sandifer (1 Duval [Ky.] 261), and in Chambertine v. McAllister (6 Dana [Ky.] 352), C. J. Robertson, a very eminent judge, held that readiness and willingness to perform, after a wrongful discharge, was not equivalent to full performance, and that all the employee was entitled to recover was the actual damages he sustained for the disappointment and loss of equally profitable employment. ... I might pursue this examination by citing many cases, both in this country and in England, that are, by analogy, inconsistent with this doctrine of constructive service, and reasons might be adduced to show that there never was any foundation for it; but I deem it sufficient to rely upon the authority of the cases above cited, to show that it is now wholly repudiated." Sedgwick's argument then goes on to run over more than four pages.

... therefore, the result of the authorities on this subject may be, that a clerk, servant, or agent, wrongfully dismissed, has his election of three remedies: viz., that,

1. He may bring a special action for his master's breach of contract in dismissing him, and this remedy he may pursue immediately. *Pagani v. Gandolfi*, [1826] 2 C.and P. 370.

2. He may wait till the termination of the period for which he was hired, and may then perhaps, sue for his whole wages, in indebitatus assumpsit, relying on the doctrine of constructive service, *Gandell v. Pontigny* [1816]; and see *Collins v. Price*, [1828] 5 Bingh. 132 ...

3. He may treat the contract as rescinded, and may immediately sue, on a quantum meruit, for the work he actually performed, *Planche v. Colburn* [1831]; but, in that case, as he sues on an implied contract arising out of actual services, he can only recover for the time that he actually served. ...

Assuming the position to be correct, that a servant or agent wrongfully dismissed,

may wait till the expiration of the term, and then maintain for his whole wages, questions may arise as to his conduct in the intermediate time, and how far it may afford the master a defence; as, for instance, if he have before the expiration of his term hired himself to another master, and how far the first master may be entitled to his intermediate earnings, by virtue of the doctrine asserted in T*hompson v. Havelock*, [1808] 1 Campb. 529; *Diplock v. Blackburn*, [183?] 3 Camp. 43. See *Patmore v. Colburn*, [1834] 4 Tyrwh. 840.

Despite the reservations of major textbooks such as Smith's *Leading Cases* and those of other writers against allowing actions for *indebitatus assumpsit* in these contexts, the doctrine of constructive service continued to inform a number of key English decisions as well as several US authorities.[28] Thus, the 1834 ruling on *Fawcett v. Cash* reiterated the view that an employee was entitled to treat a wrongful dismissal as no dismissal at all, and subsequently recover on a general "*indebitatus* count." The facts of the case and the court's decision were reported by a contemporary writer as follows:[29]

The first count of the declaration stated, that on the 5th March, 1832, in consideration that the plaintiff would enter into the service of the defendant for a year, in the capacity of a warehouseman, at a salary then agreed between plaintiff and defendant at the rate of 12l. 10s. per month for the first year, and an advance afterwards of 10l. per year until the salary should amount to 180l., the defendant undertook to retain and employ him ... in this capacity for *one whole year* from the day aforesaid; that the plaintiff served the defendant until 28th January, 1833, and was willing to continue to serve for the month for the remainder of the year: Yet the defendant refused to suffer first him to continue in his service, and without cause discharged him therefrom:

At the trial before Denman, C.J. at the London sitting after Michaelmas term, 1833, it appeared that the plaintiff had, on 5th March, 1832, entered the service of the defendant, who on that occasion signed the following memorandum of agreement:—

---

[28] See, e.g., Anonymous, "Note: Remedies and Measure of Damages in Employment Contracts," 7 *Columbia Law Review* 408 (1907) which discuss Smith's (1840) third remedy—an action for *indebitatis assumpsit*. Here the author notes that this rule "severe upon the defendant, was employed in a recent case in Louisiana, Thurmond v. Skannal (1907) 42 So. 577, where the court awarded damages, as of course, to the amount of the full contract wages for the whole term," but then suggests that this seemed to be an exception to the "general rule of contract damages."

[29] See Sandford Nevile and William Montagu Manning, *Reports of Cases Argued and Determined in the Court of King's Bench, in Hilary, Easter and Trinity Terms, In the Fourth Year of Will IV*, Volume III, at 17 (1835).

"W. Cash engages to pay Thomas Fawcett 12/. 105. per month for the first year, and advance 10/. per annum until the salary is 180/."

"From 3 mo. 5 (i.e., 5th March), 1832."

The plaintiff continued in the defendant's service until the middle of January, 1833, when he was discharged by the defendant. The plaintiff's wages had been paid monthly up to the 5th January, 1833. This action was brought in Hilary term, 1833, to recover 25l., being the wages of 12l. 10s. a month from 5th January to the 5th March, 1833, the time at which a hiring for a year from the date of the agreement, supposing it to operate as such a hiring, would expire. ... A verdict was entered by consent for 25l. leave being given to move to enter a nonsuit.

The decision to interpret Fawcett's contract as being for one year was supported by four judges against the contention of the defendant's counsel that it was an established practice that servants could be dismissed on a month's notice or the payment of a month's wages.[30]

Actions for *indebidatus assumpsit* were likely to result in greater damage awards than those for *quantum meruit*.[31] However, the judiciary's support for the doctrine of constructive service did not necessarily imply a desire to support the position of employees. Rulings such as *Beeston* and *Fawcett*, above all, were steeped in formalistic conceptions of contract law; with the analysis of employment contracts being influenced by earlier interpretation of sales contracts (which had been transposed into the sphere of employment).[32]

---

[30] See Nevile and Manning, ibid., at 179. The question as to which employees were to be counted as domestic servants elicited considerable debate. See Manley-Smith, *supra* note 25, discussing, Nowlan v. Ablett, 1835, 2 Cr. M. and R. 54. R. 320, as reported in Charles John Crompton, Roger Meeson, and Henry Roscoe, *Reports of Cases Argued and Determined in the Courts of Exchequer, From Easter Term, 5 Will. IV. to Michaelmas Term, 6 Will IV. Volume II*, at 55 (1836), where the court affirmed a judgment that had classed as a domestic servant a "head gardener, having the management and superintendence of the hot-houses, pineries," and "the privilege of taking in apprentices" with "five undergardeners employed for his assistance in the gardens" on grounds that he lived "he lived in the grounds within the domain." There is some indication that Scottish courts were less willing to class a wide range of employees as domestic servants with limited dismissal rights. Thus, William Campbell, *Treatise on Master and Servant, Employer and Workman, and Master and Apprentice According to the Laws of Scotland*, at _ (1881, 3rd edition) cites the case of Maclean v. Fyfe (4 Feb 1813) F.C., where the court found that a gardener, engaged by the year, who was dismissed nine days after a new term started was entitled to the full years' wages. Wages and board for a year were also awarded to a farm overseer who was dismissed improperly without warning at the start of a new term; see Finlayson v. McKenzie (1829) 7 S. 717. In Anderson v. Wishart (1818) 1 Mur. 429 and 442 a farm overseer, hired yearly at 42 pounds and allowances, was improperly dismissed at the end of term without sufficient warning, and the jury gave him 95 pounds. In Morrison v. Allardyce (27 June 1823) 2 S. 387, a domestic servant dismissed without due notice was awarded wages and board wages for the ensuing half year. See also the similar judgments in Gunn v. Ramsay (1801) Hum. Dec. 384 involving a cook and Thomson v. Douglas (1807) Hum. Dec. 392 involving a servant.

[31] See, e.g., the quantum meruit decision of Turner v Robinson and Sanford, (1833) 6 Car. and P. 15, 172 ER 1126, which is discussed in Frederick A. Carrington and Joseph Payne, *Reports of Cases Determined in the English Courts of Common Law*, Volume XXV, at 257 (published in Philadelphia in 1835). This involved a "young man" who was employed by a silk manufacturer in January 1831, and dismissed in June 1831. Following a discussion about the rightfulness of the dismissal, the court supported compensation of the plaintiff on *a quantum meruit* basis.

[32] Calvin W. Corman, "The Partial Performance Interest of the Defaulting Employee—Part One," 38 *Marquette Law Review* 61, at 69 (1954) discusses the growth of *assumpsit* in English law, alongside early English cases such as Weston v. Downes (1778) 2 Doug. 23, which involved the rescission of a contract of sale. Notwithstanding the initial tendency of English courts to support the application of the *assumpsit* doctrine from a perspective of contract law, there appear notable differences in the willingness to apply this interpretation. This is exemplified by the relatively liberal stance taken by Thomas Denman, later 1st Baron Denman, who was appointed Lord Chief Justice of King's in 1832 on employment matters (see, e.g., Fawcett v. Cash) and the conservative stance of James Scarlett, later 1st Baron Abinger, who was appointed Lord Chief Baron of the Exchequer in 1834 (see, e.g., Nowlan v. Ablett, 1835, 2 Cr. M. and R. 54. R. 320).

Perhaps surprisingly, the notion of constructive service found a further extension in the 1853 case *Hochster v. De La Tour,* in that this judgment allowed the plaintiff to claim damages before the term of contract had expired. However, this decision was based on rather special circumstances: Hochster had signed a declaration with De La Tour that he would enter service as a courier on June 1, 1852. He further agreed to travel with De La Tour for three months, at the rate of 10 shillings per month. The declaration stipulated that Hochster would be in employ for the contract period "until the time when [he] ... wrongfully refused to perform his duty."In early May, De La Tour contacted Hochster and informed him that he would not employ him. Hochster issued a writ for breach of contract on May 22, 1852. De La Tour's defense contended that Hochster could not sue until the 1st of June when the contract took effect and could not receive damages before three months thereafter.

The court awarded Hochster wages for the three months in question, even though the employment never commenced. Further details are presented here by drawing on the 4th English edition of Charles Manley-Smith's *A Treatise On Law of Master and Servants*, which was published in Philadelphia in 1886:[33]

> And where a person has entered into a binding agreement to take another into his service on a future day, but before that day arrives, announces his intention not to do so, he is entitled to be believed, and the servant day may thereupon immediately bring an action against him, and is not bound to wait till the day arrives to see if the master will change his mind. In a case therefore, in which a gentleman in April engaged a courier to accompany him on a tour for three months on the continent of Europe, to commence on the 1st of June, but in May wrote to say he had changed his mind, and declined the courier's services, and the courier there upon in May commenced an action against him, and afterwards, before the 1st of June obtained another engagement, on equally good terms, but not commencing till 4th of July; it was held that the courier was entitled to recover, although it was objected, and very powerfully contended, that the plaintiff was bound to remain ready and willing to perform the contract till the day when the actual employment was to begin, and that there could be no breach of the contract before the 1st of June. And Lord Campbell, C. J., said: "The man who wrongfully renounces a contract into which he has deliberately entered, cannot justly complain if he is immediately sued for a compensation in damages by the man whom he has injured; and it seems reasonable to allow an option to the injured party either to sue immediately or to wait till the time when the act was to be done, still holding it as prospectively binding for the exercise of this option, which may be advantageous to the innocent party and cannot be prejudicial to the wrongdoer. An argument against the action before the 1st of June is urged from the difficulty of calculating the damages; but this argument is equally strong against an action before the 1st of September, when the three months would expire. In either case the jury, in assessing the damages, would be justified in looking to all that had happened, or was likely to happen, to increase or mitigate the loss of the plaintiff down to the day of trial."

Applying the same formalistic logic as earlier courts, the court's *Hochster* decision thus suggested that an employee could sue for the full wages over the whole contract length, even before a contract had expired or commenced, as long as there was clear evidence that the master would prevent the completion of the term.[34]

---

[33] See Manley-Smith, *supra* note 25, at 161, discussing Hochster v. De La Tour, (1853) 2 E. and B. 678.

[34] Samuel Williston, "Note: Repudiation of Contracts" 14 *Harvard Law Review* 421, at 432 (1900), suggested that, having been "apparently mislead by the argument of counsel, Lord Campbell drew the conclusion that the plaintiff must have an immediate right of action; and also drew the conclusion from the earlier cases already

Chief Justice Lord (John) Campbell justified this reasoning as follows:[35]

> The defendant's counsel very powerfully contended that, if the plaintiff was not contended to dissolve the contract and to abandon all remedy upon it, he was bound to be ready and willing to perform it till the day when the actual employment as courier in the service of the defendant was to begin, and that there could be no breach of the agreement till the day for doing the act has arrived. But it cannot be laid down as a universal rule ... [that] no action can be brought for a breach of the argument till the day for doing the act has arrived. If a man promises to marry a woman on a future day and before that day marries another woman he is instantly liable for breach of promise of marriage: *Short v. Stone* (1846). If a man contracts to execute a lease on and from a future day for a certain term, and, before the day he sells and delivers them to another, he is immediately liable to an action: *Bowell v. Parsons* (1808) ... it is surely much more rational, and more for the benefit of defendants, that the plaintiff should be at liberty to consider himself absolved from any future performance of it ... Thus, instead of remaining idle, and laying out money in preparations which must be useless, he is at liberty to seek service under another employer ...

While the willingness of the court to allow an employee to treat a contract as whole and to seek redress for anticipatory breach before the contract period was expired could be construed as being employee friendly, the decision was probably based on a desire to maintain a unified framework of contract law; with the treatment of contracts of employment bearing as close as possible a resemblance with other types of contracts.[36] In any case, in as far as contracts of employment were concerned, *Hochster* did not lead to growth in employee-friendly decisions that could have theoretically emerged from existing notions of "constructive service" and the much later notion of "constructive dismissal."[37] This "failure"

---

referred to that incapacity before the time for performance had already been settled by decision to be a breach, neglecting to notice the distinction, hereafter adverted to, between a fixed future day and a day which may be fixed at any time in the present or future. These two misapprehensions of Lord Campbell, for as such they must be regarded, make the case an unsatisfactory one. It has, however, settled the law in England,' and the doctrine for which it stands has been adopted in Canada, in this country either by dictum or decision in the federal courts, and in the courts of a majority of the states in which the question has arisen."

[35] See Smith, *supra* note 26, Volume II at 33. Despite its seeming formalism and pragmatism, the wording of Lord Campbell's judgment suggests that his views might also have been influenced by the plaintiff's social class as well as the recklessness of the defendant.

[36] Keith A. Rowley, "A Brief History of Anticipatory Repudiation in American Contract Law," 69 *University of Cincinnati Law Review* 565, at 575 (2001) cites a number of cases that anticipated Hochster, most of which did not involve contracts of employment. These include Jones v. Barkley. 99 Eng. Rep. 434 (K.B. 1781)—which involved the redemption of a loan; Bowdell and Parsons, 103 Eng. Rep. 811 (K.B. 1808)—involving the purchase of hay; Newcomb v. Brackett, 16 Mass. 161 (1819)—a U.S. case involving the transfer of a deed; Ford v. Tiley, 108 Eng. Rep. 472 (K.B. 1827)—involving the lease of a building; and Planche v. Colburn, 131 Eng. Rep. 305 (C.P. 1831)—involving the employment of an author.

[37] The English notion of constructive dismissal, where an employee resigns because his employer's behavior makes it impossible to stay dates from the 1970s, and it can be argued that a broad interpretation of Hochster eventually served as one of the underpinning of this concept. Accordingly, Douglas W. Crump, William M. Rees and Paul N. Todd, "Constructive Dismissal Construed: The Court of Appeal Digs for Clarity," 41 *Modern Law Review* 581, at 583 (1978), notes that the presence of constructive dismissal involves two tests: "First the contract test: is it dismissal if the employee terminates when the employer's conduct amounts to a significant breach going to the root of the contract [see Mersey Steel and Iron Co. v. Naylor Benzon and Co. (1884) 9 App.Cas. 434]; or shows that the employer no longer intends to be bound by one or more of its essential terms? [Hochster v. De la Tour (1863) 2 E. and B. 678]" and "Secondly, the unreasonableness test," which suggests that "the employer behaves so unreasonably that the employee cannot fairly be expected to tolerate it, the employee is justified in leaving." As regards the U.S., Dena De Noyer, "Comment: Remedying Anticipatory Repudiation—Past, Present, and Future?" 52 *Southern Methodist University Law Review* 1787, at 1789 (1999), suggests that in the U.S., the notion of anticipatory repudiation or breach narrowed early on so as

to expand on the potential of Hochster was due to a number of factors. These included, firstly, a complex unpredictable set of requirements imposed with regards to the evidence needed to confirm an employee's willingness to serve and, secondly, the increasing reluctance of the courts to allow contract to be treated as "absolute." As concerns the former aspect, the US edition of Charles Manley-Smith's *Treatise On Law of Master and Servants* (1886) noted that: [38]

> In order to enable a servant to maintain this action, he must be ready and willing to continue in his master's service at the time he is discharged. Ready does not imply willing, but ready and willing implies disposition, capacity and ability, i.e., not physical ability, but freedom from any other inconsistent engagement. For if the servant enters the service of another before his discharge, and is thereby disabled from serving his first master in the manner contracted for, he could not be said to be ready to serve him, and upon a traverse of that averment, his action would be defeated. But although it is necessary that he should be ready and willing and able to serve his master in order to enable him to sue his master for a wrongful discharge, it is not necessary that he should offer to do so, if he can prove his readiness, in any other way. It is obvious, however, that an offer to discharge his duty is the best proof of his readiness to do it. And as readiness and willingness is a matter that is within his own mind only, the master ought at least to have notice of it.

As regards the issue of when a contract should be treated as absolute, Manley-Smith similarly stressed that "… where the contract of hiring is defeasible, either by express agreement or by the custom of the trade, business or occupation to which it relates …, care must be taken not to sue upon it as upon an absolute contract, or the action may be defeated on a plea of the general issue."[39]

During the latter half of the nineteenth century, English and Scottish courts gradually imposed additional restrictions on the amount of damages employees could recover in such actions. This was achieved by introducing the idea that a plaintiff was obliged to mitigate the damages that arose in the context of actions in relation to constructive service. One of the first cases to suggest that damages for wrongful discharge had to be assessed in relation to losses associated with the time it took to find new employment was the 1849 House of Lords judgment in *Beckham v. Drake*, in which Erle J (probably Sir William Erle), one of the judges who advised the House, stated: [40]

---

to require "the words or conduct creating anticipatory repudiation" to "be distinct, unequivocal, and absolute. Given these stringent requirements, anticipatory repudiations are atypical." DeNoyer further suggests that "Even when a party intends to repudiate a contract before time of performance, he generally refuses to be distinct, unequivocal, or absolute in order to anticipatorily repudiate. Thus, anticipatory repudiation cases require unique facts involving uncommon conduct by both buyers." Rowley, *supra* note 36, at 603 (2001), observes that Williston, *supra* note 34, was particularly critical of the English rule of "permitting promise to increase its damages by electing not to treat a repudiation as a breach," which, in any case, was rarel followed by American court rulings on employment contract.

[38] See Manley-Smith, *supra* note 25, at 169.

[39] Manley-Smith, *supra* note 25, at 169, cites two cases in support of the notion that custom overrides the presumption of a yearly hiring. Metzner v. Bolton, 1854, 9 Exc. 518 involved an agreement to continue for a year the employment of a commercial travel who was paid a yearly salary; which was held invalid by the court on account of an admission by the plaintiff that "there was a usage in the trade to dismiss with three month's notice." Parker v. Ibbetson, 1858, 27 L. J., C.P. 236 involved an agent of a woolen-merchant on a yearly contract who was paid monthly and had received a month's notice to quit. The plaintiff's claim was rejected on the presumption that there was a custom to terminate such hirings on a month's notice.

[40] See Macdonell, *supra* note 19, at 192, citing Beckham v. Drake (1849) 2 HL Cas 579, at 606.

The measure of damages for the breach of promise now in question is obtained by considering what is the usual rate of wages for the employment here contracted for, and what time would be lost before a similar employment could be obtained. The law considers that employment in any ordinary branch of industry can be obtained by a person competent for the place, and that the usual rate of wages for such employment can be proved, and that when a promise for continuing employment is broken by the master, it is the duty of the servant to use diligence to find other employment.

Although wrongfully discharged employees could still recover some damages, such awards were now increasingly assessed with reference to the time likely to elapse before an employee obtained another suitable post.[41] The courts, moreover, demanded that a wrongfully dismissed servant use "diligence" to seek other employment and stipulated that the offer of a suitable post should be taken into account in assessing damages. [42] In addition, the 1909 House of Lords decision in *Addis v. Gramophone Co* radically restricted damages for non-pecuniary losses for wrongful dismissal—which is said to have had lasting repercussions in terms of the restriction of damages available to wrongfully dismissed employees within jurisdictions following English precedent.[43]

THE AMERICAN RULE OF EMPLOYMENT AT-WILL

If the old law of master and servant had been viewed as inappropriate in nineteenth century England and Scotland, it was even more so in the United States, where the transformation of the labor force had been particularly rapid and radical. Accordingly, Louis Wolcher notes that "while most of the free labor force was self-employed in 1800, by century's end 61.8 percent of all workers were employees," forming part of a labor force that had "swelled more than fifteen-fold ... from 1.9 million to 29 million," while the "share of workers employed in nonfarm jobs went from 25 to 60 percent."[44]

---

[41] See also Hartland v. The General Exchange Bank (1866), 14 L. T. N. S. 863, which is discussed in Macdonell, *supra* note 19, at 191.

[42] On the diligence standard and the role of job offers see *Reid v. Explosives Co.* (1887) 1 Q. B. D. 264; and Brace v. Calder (1895) 2 Q. B. 253.

[43] See Addis v. Gramophone Co. [1909] A. C. 488. Judy Fudge, "The Spectre of Addis in Contracts of Employment in Canada and the UK," 36 *Industrial Law Journal* 51, at 51 (2007), suggests that "These distinctive features of the employment relationship made it difficult to rationalise within a concept of contract modeled on a commercial transaction. This difficulty was particularly acute when courts had to deal with claims by middle-class and salaried workers to have their expectations met. Courts began to develop a 'contractual model based upon reciprocity and mutuality' for higher status workers, and by the early 1900s, this model was gradually extended to industrial workers, agricultural labourers, and domestic servants." In 1909, in *Addis v Gramophone*, the House of Lords "impose[d] a firmly free market transactional approach to the termination of contracts of employment, and resist[ed] the encroachment of, at that time tort-based, relational obligations upon the employing entity which would vindicate the dignity and autonomy of the individual employee." See also Mark Freedland, *The Personal Employment Contract*, at 360 (2003).

[44] See Wolcher, *supra* note 20, citing Carl N. Degler, *The Age of the Economic Revolution, 1876--1900*, at Preface (2nd edition, 1977); David Gordon, Richard Edwards, and Michael Reich, *Segmented Work, Divided Workers*, at 230 (1982); Joyce Appleby, *Capitalism and a New Social Order*, at 89 (1984); and William W. Bratton, Jr., "The New Economic Theory of the Firm: Critical Perspectives from History Bratton," 41 *Stanford Law Review* 1471, at 1483 (1989); and Stanley Lebergott, "Labor Force and Employment, 1800-1960," in 30 *Output, Employment, and Productivity in the United States After 1800: Studies in Incomes and Wealth* 117, 118 (1966). Wolcher's work marks a key departure from the earlier analyses of Orren and Steinberg (both *supra* note 20) in that he recognizes the rapid growth during the second half of a new urban middle class—that

This rapid transformation of the workforce was destined to create tensions with remnants of the old law of master and servant that had developed against a background of agricultural or seasonal production. In reviewing these developments, Philip Selznick's pioneering analysis of nineteenth century American labor law highlights the initial efforts made by the courts to adhere to inherited interpretations of the labor contract when settling employment disputes; with William W. Story's mid-nineteenth century *Treatise on the Law of Contract* closely paraphrasing Blackstone by saying that "where there is a general hiring, nothing being said as to its duration, and no stipulation as to payments being made, which may govern its interpretation, the contract is said to be for a year."[45] Story's adherence to English legal doctrine is hardly surprising, given that a large number general legal textbooks as well as specific works on the law of master and servant written by English authors continued to be published throughout the nineteenth century in the US; and that US authors continued to base much of their analysis on English precedent.

Adherence to the one-year rule, however, created problems, both in cases where employers sued workers who quit and in cases where employees sought compensation for being dismissed prematurely. One issue faced by early American courts was whether to interpret contracts as "entire," allowing the injured party to recover the entire value of the contract, or whether the injured party was to recover on a *quantum meruit* basis.

In his widely read work on the transformation of American law, Morton Horwitz suggests that the main focus of nineteenth century US courts was on employees who quit and the subsequent application of the doctrine of the "entire" contract to the detriment of employees.[46] Implicit in Horwitz's analysis is the assumption that practices were widespread whereby US courts refused the recovery of wages to employees who had not completed the full spell of their contract. In other words, it is assumed that US courts effectively assisted employers in tying workers to their jobs, and/or in expropriating malcontents by subjecting them to the risk of losing everything if they left before the contract ended.[47]

One sided as some court decisions may have been, there is evidence that American courts also protected workers who were dismissed in violation of contractual agreements or the one-year rule. Thus, the legal historian Peter Karsten reports that up until 1880, forty-one state court cases were recorded in which employers were found to have unjustly dismissed

---

was able to increase its social status at the very time at which the position of the blue collar labor force was eroding; see, Wolcher, *supra* note 20, at 255.

[45] See Philip Selznick, *Law, Society and Industrial Justice*, at 133 (1969), citing William W. Story, *A Treatise on the Law of Contracts*, at 1041 (1851). In the colonial period, English precedents had been binding. Although there was apparently antipathy toward a ubiquitous adherence to English precedent after 1776, U.S. lawyers and judges apparently continued to rely on English case law into the late nineteenth century and beyond. Frederick Hicks, *Material and Methods of Legal Research*, at 92 (1923), states that a survey by the Boston Book Company in 1894 noted that, among the reports cited by judges in 44 states, the order of preference in citation was as follows: first their own respective state reports, second U.S. Supreme Court reports, and third English reports (with reports of other U.S. states and other sources following).

[46] Morton J. Horwitz, *The Transformation of American Law, 1780-1860*, at 186 (1978).

[47] Horwitz's work is part of what has now become known as the "subsidy thesis," whereby it is argued that nineteenth century U.S. law subsidized economic growth by giving a privileged position to employers. Current scholarship has generally adopted a more nuanced view on these matters, by recognizing *inter alia* the sympathetic attitude of some courts showed in particular towards members of the new middle classes, as well the widespread divergence of legal doctrine within U.S. jurisdictions; see also Melvin I. Urofsky, "State Courts and Protective Legislation during the Progressive Era: A Reevaluation," 72 *The Journal of American History* 63 (1983).

workers.[48] In each of these 41 cases, awards to employees were upheld. The cases included plasterers in Maine and Kentucky, drivers and factory superintendents in Pennsylvania, ministers in Connecticut, mail carriers and agents in Illinois, ship stewards in California, hire hands in Vermont, Missouri, Minnesota and North Carolina, seamen and a railroad superintendent in New York, painters in Minnesota, lumber jacks and wood cutters in Ohio, Pennsylvania and Maine, overseers in Arkansas, Georgia and South Carolina, engineers in Missouri, salesmen in Maryland, riverboat pilots in Indiana, and sharecroppers in Kentucky, Vermont, Pennsylvania and Massachusetts.[49] In most of these cases, the employees were reimbursed on a *quantum meruit* basis for their wrongful dismissal. In ten cases, the employee was awarded the full wages for the entire contract period.[50]

Like Karsten, Philip Selznick's earlier analysis of US employment law leads him to conclude that rather than following any clearly discernible trends, the rules governing the dismissal of employees had been in a state of confusion by the second half of the nineteenth century.[51] This confusion pertained in particular to the interpretation of the indefinite contract and arose from the fact that US writers were reluctant to support the universal application of English standards, while being unwilling to break with the common law tradition altogether. This ambivalence was exemplified by a new generation of US legal works, such as James Schouler's *Treatise on the Law of Domestic Relations* (1870), which is cited by Selznick as follows:[52]

> If the hiring be general, without any particular time limited, the old law construes it into a year's hiring. But the equity of this rule applied only to such employment as the chance of seasons affected; as when the servant lived with the master or worked in agriculture. By custom, such contracts have become terminable in the case of domestic servants, upon one

---

[48] Peter Karsten, "'Bottomed on Justice': A Reappraisal of Critical Legal Studies Scholarship Concerning Breaches of Labor Contracts by Quitting or Firing in Britain and the U.S.," 34 *The American Journal of Legal History* 208 (1990).

[49] According to Karsten, ibid., pp. 250-251 successful cases included Adams v. Hill, 16 Me (4 Shep.) 215 (1839); Chamberlain v. McCallistar and Sanders, 6 Dana. (36 Ky.) 352 (1838); Steward v. Walker, 14 Pa. 293 (1850); Green v. Hulett, 22 Vt. 188 (1850); Williams v. Anderson, 9 Minn. R. 50 (1864); Madden v. Porterfield, 53 N.C. 166 (1860); Williams v. Chicago Coal Co, 60 Ill. 149 (1871); Colburn v. Woodsworth, 31 Barbour (N.Y.) 381 (1860); Mackabin v. Clarkston, 5 Minn. R. 247 (1860); Newman v. McGregor, 5 Hammond (Ohio) 349 (1832); Alexander v. Hoffman, 5 Watts and S (PA) 382 (1843); Wright v. Morris, 15 Ark. 444 (1855); Meade v. Rutledge, 4 Tex. 44 (1853); Hassell v. Nutt, 14 Tex. 260 (1855); Nations v. Cudd, 22 Tex. 550 (1858); Gordon v. Brewster, 7 Wis. 355 (1858); Rogers v. Parham, 8 Ga. 190 (1850); Cox v. Adams, 1 Nott and McCord (S.C.) 284 (1818); Rankin v. Darnell, 11 B. Monroe (50 Ky.) 30 (1850); Swift v. Harriman, 30 Vt. 607 (1858); Williams v. Bemis, 108 Mass. 91 (1871); Given v. Charron, 15 Md. 502 (1860); Jenkins v. Long and Byrne, 8 Md. 132 (1855); Rick v. Yates, Adm. 5 Ind. 115 (1854); Cf. Howard v. Day, 61 N.Y. 362 (1875); Bull v. Schuberth, 2 Md. 38 (1852).

[50] Karsten, ibid., pp. 251-252 cites the following cases in which the defendants were awarded the full wage for the contract: Nears v. Harbert, 25 Mos. 352 (1857); King and Graham v. Steiren, 44 Pa. St. 99 (1862); Webster v. Wade, 19 Cal. 291 (1861); Lawrence v. Gullifer, 38 Me 582 (1854); Hoyt v. the Wildfire, 3 Johns. (N.Y.) 518 (1808); Costigan v. Mohawk and Hudson Rrld., 2 Denio (N.Y.) 609 (1846); Whitney v. Brooklyn, 5 Ct. 405 (1824); Hoy v. Gronoble, 34 Pa. St. 9 (1859); Walworth v. Pool, 9 Ark. 394 (1849). Additionally, New York courts enforced the one-year rule and awarded damages for the entire contract period up until the 1890s. See, e.g., Bleeker v. Johnson, 51 How. 380 (1876) involving the case of a clerk paid $1,500 p.a.; Tucker v. Philadelphia and R. Coal and Iron Co., 53 Hun. 138, 6 N.Y.S. 1134 (1889) involving a sales agent paid $4,500; Douglass v. Merchants' Insur. Co., 118 N.Y. 484, 23 N.E. 806 (1890) involving a corporate officer; Adams v. Fitzpatrick, 125 N.Y. 124, 26 N.E. 143 (1891) involving a clerical employee paid $3,000.

[51] See Selznick, *supra* note 45, at 127.

[52] See Selznick, *supra* note 45, at 127, citing James Schouler, *Treatise on the Law of Domestic Relations; Embracing Husband and Wife, Parent and Child, Guardian and Ward, Infancy, and Master and Servant*, at 606 (1870).

month's notice, or, what is equivalent, payment of a month's wages. Laborers are hired frequently by the day, and to hire by the week is not unusual. ... Custom modified this principle [meaning the one-year rule], and the date and frequency of periodical payments are material circumstances in this case.

Schouler's discussion of the indefinite contract closely paralleled discussions by English legal authorities, who also felt inclined to limit the applicability of the one-year rule but were reluctant to do so in a radical fashion that would deprive middle class employees of their status.

It has conventionally been argued that, unlike in English law where confusion continued about the interpretation of indefinite contracts, a definitive end was put to this ambiguity and vacillation in US law through Wood's rule of employment at-will; and this account will—for the sake of brevity—follow this conventional narrative while providing a more detailed information account in the footnotes. Wood's rule, then, originates from Horace Gay Wood's 1877 *Treatise on the Law of Master and Servant*, in which the author proposed a radical departure from older English doctrine. With regard to the indefinite contract of employment, Wood specifically argued that, since no term of employment was specified none should be infered by the courts. Said Wood:[53]

> With us, the rule is inflexible, that a general or indefinite hiring is, prima facie, a hiring at will, and if the servant seeks to make it out a yearly hiring, the burden is upon him to establish it by proof. A hiring at so much a day, week, month or year, no time being specified, is an indefinite hiring, and no presumption attaches that it was for a day even, but only at the rate fixed for whatever time the party may serve. It is competent for either party to show that the mutual understanding of the parties was in reference to the matter; but unless their understanding was mutual that the service was to extend for a certain fixed and definite period, it is an indefinite hiring and is determinable at the will of either party, and in this respect there is no distinction between domestic and other servants.

Wood's rule indeed forcefully stipulated that since all indefinite employment was "at-will," either party was entitled to terminate employment at any time and for any reason. In making this assertion, Wood no longer required the justifications English courts had employed in voiding the older one year rule—be it by expanding the definition of what a domestic servant was or by deriving exemptions to the one-year rule for specific occupational groups from loosely defined customs. and What is Wood's rule seemed to simplify the law by making redundant any need to distinguish between different classes of servant.

Even though Wood's analysis of case underpinning this interpretation was apparently largely mistaken, his approach appears to have had found wide acceptance across several state jurisdictions within a relatively short time period.[54] Accordingly, most turn–of-the-century

---

[53] The rule first appeared in Horace G. Wood, *A Treatise on the Law of Master and Servant, Covering the Relation, Duties and Liabilities of Employers and Employees* §134, at 272 (1877). Joey Feinman, "The Development of the Employment-At-Will Rule," 20 *American Journal of Legal History* 118, at 126(1976) suggests that little is known about Wood. Wood apparently was a practicing Albany lawyer, but not a member of the New York State Bar, and a prolific writer of legal treatises. In addition to this work, Wood (1831-1893) edited and authored treatises on nuisances, tort, and evidence, among authors.

[54] J. Peter Shapiro and James F. Tune, "Implied Contract Rights to Job Security," 26 *Stanford Law Review* 335, at 341 (1974), note that Wood was not a contract theorist and that his work in the field consisted of case collections. Wood appears to ground his view not on notions of freedom of contract, as many later analysts

textbooks acknowledge the widespread acceptance of Wood's rule and the at-will doctrine in general but continue to refer to the English one-year rule, alternative approaches to the interpretation of the indefinite contract (based, e.g., on custom), and the practices of other jurisdictions such as Louisiana, Scotland and Quebec. This is exemplified by Charles Bagot Labatt's 1913 *Commentaries on the Law of Master and Servant*, which commences its section on the duration of contract by highlighting the deviation of US law from English doctrine in line with Wood's rule—but then moves on to discuss an alternative contractual approach:[55]

> The English doctrine as to the presumptive yearly duration of a general hiring has been recognized more or less explicitly in American cases and textbooks. But the doctrine applied by the great majority of the courts which have so far expressed an opinion on the subject consists essentially in a complete repudiation of the presumption that a general or indefinite hiring is a hiring for a year, and the substitution of another presumption, viz., that such a hiring is a hiring at will, under which either party may at any time determine the employment, for a year rests upon the party who seeks to establish that the contract covered that period.
>
> Under another theory as to the juridical situation, the notion of a presumption as a specific element is entirely discarded, and the contract is construed with reference to the broad principle that, "where a person is hired to serve another without any agreement as to the duration of the service, there is no inflexible rule of law as to the length of time the hiring is to continue." * In this point of view, the duration of the hiring is treated as an open question, to be determined from the circumstances in each particular case, or as one which is dependent upon the "understanding and intent of the parties" to be ascertained "by inference from their

---

did, but rather on mistaken precedent; whereby none of the four American cases he cites genuinely support his analysis. Perhaps unsurprisingly, modern legal scholarship has been highly critical of Wood's legacy. Clyde W. Summers, "Individual Protection against Unjust Dismissal. Time for a Statute," 62 *Virginia Law Review* 481, at 485 (1976), for instance, notes that "The American rule apparently was announced a hundred years ago by a treatise writer who cited as authority four cases, none of which supported him. Despite its doubtful antecedents, the rule was embraced by American lawyers and judges. Within thirty years, the employer's unrestrained freedom to discharge was transmuted into a constitutional right." Despite the wide acceptance of Wood's rule, it is important to note that it may have taken up until the first decade of the twentieth century before rule became universally cited across U.S. jurisdictions; see Ken Matheiny and Marion Crain, "Disloyal Workers and the Un-American Labor Law," 82 *University of North Carolina Law Review* 1705, 1710 (2003-2004).

[55] See Charles Bagot Labatt, *Commentaries on the Law of Master and Servant,* in Eight Volumes, Volume 1, at 516 (1913). It is interesting to note that, despite recognizing the near-universal acceptance of the doctrine, Labatt, at 519, appears to oppose its general application on account of a mix of contractual and social arguments: "The preponderance of American authority in favor of the doctrine that an indefinite hiring is presumptively a hiring at will is so great that it is now scarcely open to criticism. But a commentator may perhaps be permitted to point out that, in many instances—more especially those in which the compensation is specified as being a certain sum per annum—it cannot be applied without entailing results different to those which may reasonably be supposed to have been within the contemplation of the parties. Having regard to the ordinary course of affairs in the business world, the higher the position to which the contract relates the more certainly may it be inferred that the employer and employed expect their relationship to continue for a considerable period. It seems questionable whether a doctrine resting on a presumption which ignores that expectation as an element indicative of intention can with propriety be treated as one of general application. Assuming that the social and economic conditions which prevail in the United States are such as to require the rejection of the English rule regarding the presumptive yearly duration of an indefinite hiring, it is by no means self-evident that those conditions, when viewed as a whole and with relation to the various descriptions of employment, afford a sufficient justification for going to the opposite extreme involved in the adoption of an unvarying presumption that such a hiring is not binding for any fixed period at all. It is at least fairly open to argument whether the more reasonable doctrine is not that which treats the duration of the engagement as an entirely open question of fact, unencumbered by any presumption whatever, and determinable with reference to the various elements discussed in the next subtitle."

written and oral negotiations, the usages of the business, the situation of the parties, the nature
of the employment, and all the circumstances of the case."

There is an extensive literature discussing the factors that may have contributed to the
popularity of the at-will doctrine in US courts, which is too vast and complex to be discussed
here in any detail.[56] Suffice it to say, that ideologically, the at-will doctrine complemented the
spirit of *laissez faire*, by allowing courts to "stay out" of the employment relationship.
Intellectual underpinning for the new rule, meanwhile, was provided by a generation of legal
scholars who viewed the at-will doctrine as matching the requirements of a newly evolving
rational legal system based on the principles of "freedom of contract." On a purely material
basis, the rule, moreover, provided significant advantages to a new class of employers and
entrepreneurs who had come to economically and politically dominate US society.

As concerns the direct implications of Wood's Rule, Selznick attributes particular
significance to its structural or power implications by arguing that the broad application of the
at-will rule effectively led to the elimination of any significant legal limits to the authority of
the employers, on the very key issue of dismissal; and in so doing undermined the position of
labor as bargaining agent in a fundamental way. Not only could employers in most
jurisdictions now hire and fire workers unconstrained by the legal requirement of a just-cause
for rescinding a contract not yet expired, but also could they modify many terms of
employment contracts at any time without notice. According to Selznick, this transformation
of the labor contract marked the successful, and largely, unopposed culmination of a sequence
of judicial efforts aimed at disempowering labor. Said Selznick: [57]

> The contract at-will went hand in hand with absolute managerial discretion. The
> employer is free to hire and fire unconstrained by the legal requirement that he have just cause
> for rescinding a contract not yet exposed ... the contract at-will is not a device for framing

---

[56] The contemporary literature appears to provide three principal explanations for the popularity of the at-will rule.
Lawrence M. Friedman, *A History of American Law*, at 532 (1985) views the dissemination of the rule as part
of a "golden age of contract" during which nineteenth century U.S. courts focus on the elimination of
feudalistic and moralistic restrictions on contracting in line with the emerging doctrine of freedom of contract.
Alternatively, Feinman, *supra* note 53, at 132, suggests that the at-will rule emerged as a move to prevent
white-collar employees from asserting their positions in the capitalist system. Lastly, Jacoby, *supra* note 17, at
102, attributes the adoption of at-will terminability, among other factors, to the weakness of trade unionism in
the U.S.. An older branch of the literature, exemplified by the socialist writer and activist James ONeal's, *The
Workers in American History*, at 139 and 191 (1912), lastly, attributes the harsh attitudes toward employment
in the U.S. to the subservient status of a significant portion of the laboring population (including slaves and
indentured white workers) during the colonial and early post-colonial decades.

[57] See Selznick, *supra* note 45, at 134. As part of an earlier generation of writings on nineteenth century U.S. labor
law, Selznick's work probably overestimates the level of acceptance of Wood's rule. Thus, it took until 1916,
that a Virginia court refused to apply the doctrine of constructive service to a school teacher who came to work
after having been dismissed; see Jameson v. Board of Education, 78 W. Va. 612, L. R. A. 1916F, 926.
However, in rejecting the validity of contractual justification of Wood's rule and specifically the idea that the
right of the employer to dismiss for whatever reason merely mirrors that of the employee to quit (see, e.g.,
Adair v. United States, 208 U.S. 161, 1908), Selznick was able to conclude that Wood's rule allowed
employers to dominate the workplace while abrogating any long-term responsibility for their workforce; until
such time as other systems of workplace governance came into operation in some areas of the U.S. economy.
This view of an evolving, but ultimately unstable, legally supported managerial hegemony appears to mirror
subsequent developments of U.S. labor law more closely than the claims by Orren (*supra* note 20) and
Tomlins, according to which nineteenth century courts consciously constructed new social roles within the a
republican state in and effort distance to English precedent; see Christopher L. Tomlins, *Law, Labor and
Ideology in the Early American Republic*, (1993).

day-to-day activities. Since there is no definite duration, the terms of the contract are not binding for the future ...

The main economic significance of this contract at-will was the contribution it made to ease the layoff of employees in response to business fluctuations. But it also strengthened managerial authority. By the end of the nineteenth century, the employment contract had become a very special sort of contract, in large part a legal device for guaranteeing to management the unilateral power to make rules and to exercise discretion.

In its final analysis, Selznick's work suggests that recourse to the at-will rule allowed employers to manipulate employment contracts into legal tools for the unilateral exercise of their power over virtually all aspects of workplace governance. This unilaterality of management power appears to have indeed pervaded the American workplace from the late nineteenth century onwards.It is perhaps best exemplified in the oft-cited 1884 case of *Payne v. Western and Atlantic Railroad*, in which a Tennessee court stated that:[58]

All may dismiss their employees at-will, be they many or few, for good cause, for no cause, or even for cause morally wrong without being guilty of legal wrong. A *fortiori* they may "threaten" to discharge them without thereby doing an illegal act, per se. The sufficient and conclusive answer to the many plausible arguments to the contrary, portraying the evil to workmen and to others from the exercise of such authority by the great and the strong, is: They have the right to discharge their employees. The law cannot compel them to employ workmen, nor to keep them employed. If they break contracts with workmen they are answerable only to them; if in the act of discharging them, they break no contract, then no one can sue for loss suffered thereby. Trade is free; so is employment. The law leaves employer and employee to make their own contracts; and these, when made, it will enforce; beyond this it does not go. Either the employer or employee may terminate the relation at-will, and the law will not interfere, except for contract broken. This secures to all civil and industrial liberty. A contrary rule would lead to a judicial tyranny as arbitrary, irresponsible and intolerable as that exercised by Scroggs and Jeffreys ...

Following *Payne*, US legal history has been rife with blatant abuses of human rights resulting from the unquestioning application of the at-will rule. For instance, in the 1932 case of *Comerford v. International Harvester*, an employee was discharged because his wife

---

[58] Payne v. Western and Atlantic R.R. Co. 81 Tenn 507, at 519-520 (1884). During the last twenty years of the nineteenth century, the at-will rule coexisted with other interpretations of the indefinite contract, such as a) the one-year rule, b) the analyses of circumstances to determine intended duration, and c) the rule that dismissal was possible with each payment period. Pauline T. Kim, "Cynicism Reconsidered," 76 *Washington University Law Quarterly* 193, at 194 (1998), suggests that by the turn of the century, the application of rules other than the at-will rule had become increasingly rare; with employees the courts ignoring evidence that the parties intended a more permanent relationship, Skagerberg v. Blandin Paper Co., 266 N.W. 872 (Minn. 1936); Rape v. Mobile and O.R. Co., 100 So. 585 (Miss. 1924); and requiring additional consideration by the employee for contracts to be interpreted as being permanent, Harrington v. Kansas City Cable Ry. Co., 60 Mo. App. 223, 228 (1895). Interestingly, the dissenting opinion in Payne anticipated future criticisms of the at-will rule in arguing: "Employment is the means of sustaining life to himself and family to the employee, and so he is morally though not legally compelled to submit. Capital may thus not only find its own legitimate employment, but may control the employment of others to an extent that in time may sap the foundations of our free institutions. Perfect freedom in all legitimate uses is due to capital, and should be zealously enforced, but public policy and all the best interests of society demands, it shall be restrained within legitimate boundaries, and any channel by which it may escape or overleap these boundaries should be carefully but judiciously guarded. For its legitimate uses, I have perfect respect, against its legitimate use I feel bound, for the best interests both of capital and labor to protest."

refused to sleep with the man's supervisor. The husband's challenge was rejected by the court because of his at-will status, which, in the court's view, made his termination legal, "regardless of the motive or malice which actuated it."[59] What is more, support for the principles underlying Woods extended to the highest echelons of the US legal establishment. In *McAuliffe v. Mayor of New Bedford City*, a policeman was discharged for expressing political views. Upholding this discharge, Oliver Wendell Holmes stated for the Massachusetts Supreme Court that:[60]

> The petitioner may have a constitutional right to talk politics, but he has no constitutional right to be a policeman. There are few employments for hire in which the servant does not agree to suspend his constitutional rights of free speech as well as of idleness by the implied terms of his contract. The servant cannot complain, as he takes the employment on the terms which are offered him. On the same principle the city may impose any reasonable condition upon holding offices within its control. This condition seems to us reasonable, if that be a question open to revision here.

With the adoption of the at-will rule, the US law of employment had largely severed ties with its older English or even more broadly, its European heritage. Employment law, as a source of social order, had lost much of its relevance; and when some employment rights were eventually re-established, it was through the intervention of statutory law within the changed political context of the New Deal. Nonetheless, the at-will rule was seen by many as a matter of contention, and it was contention with the status of labor regulation as a whole that instigated new debates around the appropriate role of the state in regulating economic affairs. Initially primarily academic in nature, these debates focused on two key themes; namely, the need for the legal protection of the individual worker and the protection of collective bargaining rights.

---

[59] Comerford v. International Harvester Co., 235 Ala 376, 178 So 894 (1938).

[60] See McAuliffe v. Mayor of City of New Bedford, 29 N.E. 517, 517 (1892) which had an enduring impact on employment relation in the U.S. public sector. In the early years of the McCarty witch hunt, J. Edgar Hoover published a comment on an article on loyalty of government employees, which had criticized the FBI's practices; See J. Edgar Hoover, "Comment on the Article Loyalty among Government Employees," 58 *Yale Law Journal* 401, at 409 (1948). Hoover wrote: "Shortly after the President's Loyalty Order was issued, I appeared before the Loyalty Review Board and frankly discussed the problems of sources of information … I outlined the alternatives to the Loyalty Review Board and asked what that Board wanted us to do. I offered to submit reports with no confidential sources appearing therein and I offered to adopt the policy of not accepting any information if the source had to be concealed. The Board refused this offer because they put the interests of the Government and the security of the nation above the whims and convenience of the individual. In fact, the Board did no more than to follow the wise words of that great liberal, the late Associate Justice Oliver Wendell Holmes, who ruled in McAuliffe vs. New Bedford (155 Mass. 216) that, 'The petitioner may have a Constitutional right to talk politics, but he has no constitutional right to be a policeman. There are few employments for hire in which the servant does not agree to suspend his constitutional rights of free speech as well as of idleness by the implied terms of his contract.' As to the sources of information, if the responsibility were given the authors, I dare say that the confidential informants who provided us with Communist cards No. 36485, No. 46854, No. 46734, No. 76577, and the numerous others we have secured and forwarded to the appropriate authorities would never be disclosed. Unlike a criminal case, these informants are sources of information in many cases. So far as Loyalty proceedings are concerned, they do not have the protection of subpoena nor can they be required to testify. Then, too, there is the individual who will furnish information only on condition that his identity be protected. Is the Government to be deprived of this information? I dare say the majority of the citizens of this nation if given the right to vote would say, 'No!' The authors kindly referred to the record of the FBI in preventing sabotage and espionage during the war. This was made possible in a large measure because of sources of information both in this country and abroad, whose identity must be protected so long as they or their immediate families survive."

CRITICS OF AT-WILL EMPLOYMENT

By the beginning of the twentieth century, many progressive legal scholars argued in favor of a restriction of employers' right to dismiss. At the time, criticisms of the at-will doctrine took several forms, focusing, *inter alia*, on the inappropriateness of the court's preoccupation with the "freedom of contracts" and on the need to address the inequality of the parties forming the employment contract via statutory legislation.

Taking the first approach, Roscoe Pound highlighted the misapplication of legal formalisms to the employment relationship in line with a more general opposition to the widespread application of the doctrine of freedom of contract. In several of his writings, Pound argued that by the late nineteenth century, US courts had come to routinely misuse notions of "freedom of contract" in order to prevent necessary and socially beneficial regulatory measures. This he attributed to the nation's individualistic idea of justice, a mechanistic jurisprudence that deferred to fixed rules, the influence of eighteenth century philosophy on legal training, and the great vogue of the theory of natural rights. According to Pound, insistence on the principles of freedom of contract now created obstacles to the passage of necessary labor legislation, which, in his view, involved issues of fact rather than principle and could not be resolved by recourse to abstract principles. In his 1909 essay *Liberty of Contract*, Roscoe Pound argued specifically that:[61]

> Rate laws, in the investigation of which it may prove that a rate is confiscatory, at one time and not at another, are compelling courts to recognize that the constitutionality of a statute may depend upon questions of fact to be investigated and determined as such. Hence they are likely to induce a change of judicial attitude towards other legislation, the reasonableness of which might depend on questions of fact which only those who have investigated special industrial situations can fairly determine. As it is in the ordinary case involving constitutionality, the court has no machinery for getting the facts ... The court is driven to deal with the problem artificially or not at all, unless it is willing to assume that the legislature did its duty and to keep its hands off on that ground. More than anything else, ignorance of the actual situation of fact for which legislation was provided and supposed lack of legal warrant for knowing them, have been responsible for the judicial overthrowing of so much social legislation.

In Pound's view, cases like *Frorer v. People* (1892) and *Ramsey v. People* (1892)[62] were evidence for the courts' misconception of economic realities.[63] In these cases, the Illinois

---

[61] Roscoe Pound, "Liberty of Contract," 18 *Yale Law Journal* 454, at 469 (1909). Roscoe Pound was Dean of Harvard Law School from 1916 to 1936, during which time he advocated legal reforms in support of the New Deal, which many senior members of the legal establishment opposed. Stephen H. Norwood, *The Third Reich in the Ivory Tower: Complicity and Conflict on American Campuses*, at 36 (2009) reports that Pound was awarded a medal by Nazi Germany in 1934.

[62] Frorer v. People, 141 Ill. 171 (1892), voided an act requiring wages to be paid in money and prohibiting those engaged in mining and manufacturing from having "truck stores" for selling furnishing to laborers groceries, clothing, tools, etc., while Ramsey v. People, 142 Ill. 380 (1892) held unconstitutional an act requiring coal to be weighed before screening and the mining to be paid for on such weight; see Henry Brannon, *A Treatise on the Rights and Privileges Guaranteed by the Fourteenth Amendment to the Constitution of the United States*, at 205 (1901).

[63] The ideological roots of this opposition to employment regulation have been discussed in great detail elsewhere. See, e.g., Daniel R. Ernst "Free Labor, the Consumer Interest and The Law of Industrial Disputes, 1885-1990," 36 *The American Journal of Legal History* 19, at 24 (1992), argues that these views were ideologically

Supreme court had held void statutes forbidding the payment of wages in token money, which had been passed on the basis of the police powers vested in the state or county authorities.[64] Pound expressed his dismay at the courts' sublime disregard of reality, which he attributed to a deep-rooted misunderstanding of the power relationships that were prevalent within contemporary capitalist society. Expanding on Pound's views, the constitutional historian Edward R. Lewis cited case law where a court stating that "there is no inferior class other than those degraded by crime or other vicious indulgences of the passions, among our citizens" and declared that due process does not mean "a law passed for the purpose of righting the wrong."[65] Similarly, a Kansas court had overthrown a token money statute arguing that "freedom of action—liberty—is the cornerstone of our governmental fabric" and that the token money law classified the workmen "with the idiot, the lunatic, or the felon in the penitentiary." "As between persons *sui juris*," the court had asked, "what right has the legislature to assume that one class has the need of protection against another?" It is "our boast," the court concluded "that no class distinctions exist in this country."[66] Like many progressive members of legal establishment, Pound and Lewis saw these, and similar attitudes, as symptomatic of a judiciary that, adhering to antiquated principles, had prevented the creation of necessary statutes protecting workers from the vicissitudes of the industrialized economy.

These observations were well grounded in fact. By the 1920s, conservative Supreme Court judges had opposed nearly every attempt by state legislatures to impose regulatory protection on workers. The constitutional historian Charles Warren recorded that between 1889 and 1918 inclusive, the Supreme Court had decided 790 cases in which state statutes were attacked under the due process and equal protection clauses.[67] Over 400 of these cases involved the use of police power. Over 50 cases were held wholly unconstitutional, 14 of these involved rights and liberties of individuals, including issues that touched on issues of employment rights.

Pound and other progressive legal scholars were severe in their criticism of judicial review, particularly as it concerned its application to labor legislation; which involved, at times, even suggestions for the elimination of judicial review. However, due to the intransigence of the courts, little progress was made in strengthening the power of legislatures to pass the requisite statutes. Despite the initial prowess of the debate, reformist zeal soon died down, mostly on account of the start of World War I. Apart from scattered decisions such as the pre-Holden case of *Mugler v. Kansas* (1887), very little headway had been made

---

legitimized by the assumption that there were no permanent social classes. Ernst cites a 1884 editorial in the Philadelphia record, which expresses this belief in the following way: "This is the country of the workmen, ... in it there are no classes except good and bad. Even the capitalists are only workingmen who display superior energy and intelligence. Most have once been hired or were the sons of men who started their lives as employees. So it must always be unless our workingmen degrade themselves and pull away the ladder upon which they are to rise by classifying themselves as a sort of inferior part of the whole."

[64] These and similar decisions were widely criticized in the legal press of the time for a failure to expand police powers to allow for socially necessary regulations; see, e.g., Darius H. Pingree, "The Anti-Truck Laws, and Some Other Laws-A Legal Criticism," 3 *The American Lawyer* 386 (1895) and Charles Bagot Labatt, "State Regulation of the Contract of Employment," 27 *American Law Review* 857 (1893).

[65] See Edward R. Lewis, *A History of American Political Thought From The Civil War To The World War*, at 95 (1937)

[66] See Lewis, ibid., at 95, discussing State v. Haun, 61 Kans. 146, 162.

[67] See Charles Warren, *The Supreme Court in United States History*, Volume 3 (1922) at 468.

toward extending police power to the protection of employees. [68] Pound's critique nevertheless had a profound impact on future generations. If nothing more, Pound's writings had encouraged a critical attitude toward "freedom of contract" as an abstract and absolute concept of limited merit, and in that sense provided the groundwork for a debate that resurfaced in connection with New Deal legislation in the 1930s.

The second and, perhaps ultimately more influential, set of arguments opposing the notion of at-will employment and state non-interference in matters of dismissal, focused on the recognition, by Institutionalist economists, that the employment contract and other common law contracts differed in fundamental ways. Instead of highlighting the inadequacy of existing legal principles, as Pound had done, these arguments focused on the proposition that employment contracts should legally be treated differently than conventional sales contracts. In one of the most prominent analyses of employment regulation of its time, the 1916 book *Principles of Labor Legislation,* John R. Commons and John B. Andrews argued that, since slavery had been abolished and restrictions on the sale of labor were already imposed, the labor contract too differed and no longer could be viewed within the narrow confines of contract law. Said Commons and Andrews:[69]

> Not until the enactment of the Thirteenth Amendment, following the Civil War, did slavery and involuntary servitude, except as a punishment for crime, become everywhere illegal. The labor contract hence has its peculiar significance. Although in theory it is like other contracts, yet it cannot in fact be enforced. The laborer cannot sell himself into slavery of into involuntary servitude ... Business contracts, if violated, are ground for damages ... The labor contract also, if violated, is ground for damages, but for the court to order damages paid out of labor property would be to order the laborer to work out the debt. This is involuntary servitude.

Commons and Andrews further suggested that the "peculiar relation" between a property-less seller of himself, and a prosperous buyer, necessitated a legal conception of the labor contract different from other contracts, that is a "... legislation [which] goes behind the legal face of things and looks at the *bargaining power* which precedes the contact."[70] In *Principles*

---

[68] In Mugler v. Kansas, 123 U.S. 623 (1887) the Supreme court upheld a ruling of the Supreme Court of Kansas, affirming the State's uncompensated taking of Mugler's brewery property on ground of health safety and moral grounds. Mugler has been interpreted as a predecessor to Holden v. Hardy, 169 U.S. 366 (1898) where the Supreme Court upheld a Utah State law restricting the working hours for miners and smelters. See Ray A. Brown, "Police Power. Legislation for Health and Personal Safety," 42 *Harvard Law Review* 868 (1929), in which, after exploring the Supreme Court's willingness to support the concept of police power more widely, the author argues that "The minimum wage case is today the only unrepudiated decision in which, the facts being undisputed and the factors of health and safety apparent, the Court has denied to the state the power to do what it deemed necessary for the protection of the health and safety of its people." See also William E. Forbath, "Ambiguities of Free Labor: Labor and the Law in the Gilded Age," 1985 *Wisconsin Law Review* 767 (1985) for a detailed analysis of the legal and political struggles during this time period.

[69] John R. Commons and John B. Andrews, *Principles of Labor Legislation,* at 504 (4th revised edition 1936, 1st edition, 1916). Bruce E. Kaufman's "Labor Markets and Employment Regulation: The View of the 'old' Institutionalists," in *Government Regulation of the Employment Relationship* 11, (Bruce E. Kaufman, ed., 1997) highlights the influence Commons had as leader of the Wisconsin School of Labor relations on the enactment of statutes pertaining to workers compensation, unemployment insurance, minimum wages, maximum hours, prohibition of child labor, restrictions on injunctions against labor disputes and the protection of collective bargaining rights.

[70] Commons and Andrews, ibid., at 503, emphasis added.

of Labor Legislation, Commons and Andrews, moreover, characterized the employment contract as an exchange of property rights:[71]

> ... property and liberty change places and merge their meanings when industry changes from the agricultural stage of production for self to the modern stage of bargaining with others. The wage earner's "property" becomes his right to seek an employer and acquire property in the form of wages ... The employer's "property" is, in part, his right to seek laborers and acquire their services; his property in the sense of "liberty" is his right to ... discharge the laborer if the bargain is unsatisfactory.

According to Commons and Andrews, the right to discharge was to be constrained, firstly, through the qualification that the bargain was unsatisfactory which implied the need for a cause for dismissal. Secondly, Commons and Andrews suggested that broader regulatory intervention by the state was justified on account of the public's legitimate concern with the preservation of the employee's property—i.e., the worker's "labor power."

Commons and Andrews argued that, as a consequence of the already established rights of the state to exercise police power, "the liberty of both the employer and the employee to make a labor contract may be restricted and regulated, if it is found that the contract is injurious to the laborer." The notion of police power, of course, had gained prominence with the Supreme Court's ruling in *Holden v. Hardy,* which had stated that the "proprietors lay down the rules and the operators are practically constrained to obey them" because they "are induced by fear of discharge to conform to regulations which, if their judgment was fairly exercised, they would pronounce detrimental to their health."[72] Commons and Andrews suggested that further restrictions to the freedom to contract in labor matters had become justified primarily because "employers and their laborers do not stand upon an equality." As long as employment at-will governed the workplace, market mechanisms gave an insufficient protection to workers, or as Warren had commented earlier, "inequality of bargaining power

---

[71] Commons and Andrews, ibid., at 528. This analysis of the labor contract closely mirrored Commons's theoretical works such as; John R. Commons, *Legal Foundations of Capitalism* (1924) and John R. Commons, *Institutional Economics* (1934). Both works are characterized by efforts to introduce legal concepts into economic analysis, with a view towards creating an alternative perspective to prevailing *laissez faire* and Social Darwinist ideologies.

[72] See also John R. Commons, "Institutional Economics," 26 *The American Economic Review* 237, at 245 (1936), where the author states that "There is an evolutionary principle within the Anglo-American common-law idea of willingness corresponding to the evolution of sovereignty from the time of William the Conqueror. The idea started in warlike and feudal times when only the wills of martial heroes were deemed worthwhile; then was extended to unwarlike merchants in the law of the market overt; then to serfs and peasants; then to the most timid of people, for whom not only actual violence or trial by battle, but even the merest subjective apprehensions of inferiority created fear which deprived them of their freedom of will (Galusha v. Sherman, 105 Wis. 263, 1900.) Then towards the end of the nineteenth century this simplified formula of a freewill was extended to the relations between employers and employees, the economic assumption that employers, being owners of property, were in a stronger economic position than property-less laborers, such that laborers were deprived by fear of unemployment of their freedom of will in bargaining. (Holden v. Hardy, 169 U.S. 366, 1898.) Further variations were partly allowed where women and children were deemed economically unequal to the superior managers, merchants, lawyers, or employers; so that the agreements which they made respecting the price of labor were not contracts between willing buyers and willing sellers. Many other complexities arise with the incoming of large-scale production, collective action, and the cycles of prosperity and depression; and these also are among the variabilities that must be taken into account in the evolutionary application of the basic principle of the willing buyer and willing seller."

between employees and employer gave the latter the power to drive a harsh bargain."[73] Commons and Andrews advocated that labor legislation address both issues of health and dismissal simultaneously; by providing police powers to protect workers from health hazards and by redressing economic imbalances though the protection of workers from unjust dismissal.[74]

While Commons and Andrews appear to have been reluctant to propose detailed legislative measures for protecting employees from arbitrary dismissals, they repeatedly stressed the logic and legitimacy of such restrictions; usually on grounds that the existing inequality of power disfavored the worker. Said Commons and Andrews:[75]

> Inequality of bargaining power has long been a ground for legislative and judicial protection of the weaker party to the bargaining even though the courts found other grounds on which to base their opinion. It was early conceded as a justification of usury laws, protecting the weak debtor against the strong creditor, latterly utility laws, protecting the weak consumer, farmer, or shipper against the powerful corporation; and now it only needs the recognition of facts to justify labor legislation to protect the weak wage earner against the more powerful capitalist. Such legislation could be held to deny equal protection of the law only where the facts showed that both parties were actually equal. But where the parties are unequal (and a public purpose shown), then the state which refuses to redress the inequality is actually denying the weaker party the protection of the law.

This analysis of power asymmetries, which was rooted in the tenets of institutionalist economics, anticipated much of the economic and political nexus on which some of the exemptions from employment at-will, such as the public policy exemption, have been based. Commons and Andrews recognized that their thinking stood in contrast to established doctrine, which still tended to classify statutes protecting the interest of labor as class legislation. Their key argument was that reasonable legislation, based on observable economic realities, should no longer be viewed within antiquated standards of judicial review. Specifically, they noted that "It is by recognizing this *inequality of bargaining power*, coupled with a *public purpose*, that the courts pass over, in any particular case, from the theory of class legislation to the theory of reasonable classification."[76]

The notion that state legislation should remedy existing inequalities in bargaining power was shared by a number of policymakers, particularly in mid-western states. Thus, William L. Huggins, who had been instrumental in the creation of the Kansas Court of Industrial

---

[73] Commons and Andrews, *supra* note 69, at 528. See also Charles Warren, "*Volenti Non Fit Injuria* in Actions of Negligence," 8 *Harvard Law Review* 457 (1895), where a similar argument is presented in opposition to the assumption that workers would be compensated for dangers by market forces.

[74] These views were expanded by William L. Prosser, *Handbook of the Law of Torts*, at 516 (1941), where Prosser argued that nineteenth century legal doctrines on labor, including employment-at-will, were based on an intentionally constructed mythical conception of the labor market, which allowed judges to consistently favor employers. He describes this myth as follows: "The cornerstone of the common law edifice [on employment law] was the economic theory that there was complete mobility of labor, that the supply of work was unlimited, and that the workman was an entirely free agent, under no compulsion to enter into the employment."

[75] Commons and Andrews, *supra* note 69, at 529. Bruce E. Kaufman, *supra* note 68 at 33, notes that Commons advocated a three-pronged approach to improve employment practices, which centered on the introduction of progressive employment practices, the extension of collective bargaining and relevant legal enactments.

[76] Commons and Andrews, *supra* note 69 at 529 and also Kaufman, *supra* note 69, at 35-36.

Relations in 1920, and acted as its Presiding Judge from 1920-26, closely echoed the institutionalist views:[77]

> The business corporation, by means of which very many individuals may safely invest their savings or their capital in a single enterprise, is a modern necessity. Correspondingly, the great number of workers employed, because of their individual weakness and lack of personal touch with their powerful employer, are compelled to organize in their own protection. And so the labor union, its place in industry as a correlation of the corporation. In the essential industries the undivided employer who knows his employees by name, who is in constant touch with them and understands them, has almost disappeared. Practically, all of the big business of the country is done through the medium of the corporation, whose stock capital is owned by large numbers of people. Now, the management and direction of the tremendous business enterprises owned by corporations places far-reaching powers in the hands of a small number of directors or of the president or manager of the institution. In the presence of such immense power, the individual worker is helpless. Only by mass action can he meet his employer upon anything approaching a plane of equality. Therefore, the labor union is legitimate and, in fact, necessary.

Viewed by some as a national model for dealing with labor disputes, the Kansas Industrial Act mapped out a framework for future legislation and for the extension of collective bargaining. Section 9 of the Act stipulated that workers engaged in specified industries "shall receive at all times a fair wage and have healthful and moral surroundings while engaged in such labor." The same section recognized "the right of every person to make his own choice of employment and to make or carry out fair, just and reasonable contracts and agreements," giving the Court the right to modify terms and conditions.[78] Perhaps even more radical, section 14 stated that "any union or association of workers" in the specified industries was to be "recognized in all its proceedings as a legal entity" that may appear before the Court. Further to this, section 15 outlawed the dismissal of employees on account of them acting as witness to the Court or bringing a case before the Court.[79] The Kansas experiment, unsurprisingly, failed after five years, when it was found to be unconstitutional by the US Supreme Court, and the Court itself was merged with the Public Utilities Commission and the State Tax Commission to form the Public Service Commission.[80]

---

[77] William L. Huggins, *Labor and Democracy*, at 22-23 (1922). The Kansas court was created through the Court of Industrial Relations Act of January 23, 1920, ostensibly with the purpose of ensuring continuity of operation in coal mining and other businesses, whose operation was thought to be in the public interest.

[78] See Huggins, ibid., at 147. The industries to which the law was to apply were broadly specified as including the manufacture or preparation of food products, wearing apparel, mining, transportation and public utilities.

[79] See Huggins, ibid., at 149-50. This clause implicitly introduced a ban on the dismissal of employees on account of them joining a union. Earlier legislation to this effect had been declared unconstitutional in Coppage v. State of Kansas, 236 U.S. 1 (1915).

[80] Dan Hopson, "Kansas Labor Law and District Court Injunctions," 6 *University of Kansas Law Review* 1 (1957-1958) summarizes the history of the act as follows: "After World War I, the organized coal miners in southeast Kansas requested a greater share of the profits. Unrest and violence followed their demands. Fearful of complete chaos, the Kansas Legislature, called to special session in 1920, passed the Court of Industrial Relations Act. ... This act, a forerunner of Mussolini's corporate state concept, attempted to vest control of all important industry and agriculture, and their labor relations, in an administrative court. This court had the power to settle all problems of wages and prices in a 'fair' manner. In effect, it provided for compulsory arbitration and prevented all strikes or lockouts. The multitude of litigation that followed centered on three factual situations. The first was the Dorchy and Howat cases arising out of a series of strikes in the southeastern Kansas coal fields. The second was the Wolff Packing Co. cases, resulting from an attempt by the Court of Industrial Relations to set wages and hours at a Kansas City packing company [Howat v. Kansas, 258

With experiments such as the Kansas Court of Industrial Relations being doomed to failure on account of a predominantly conservative state and federal justiciary, legislation protecting employees from arbitrary dismissals like that protectiong employee welfare more generally, was slow in the making. By 1912, thirty-eight states had established child-labor laws and 28 had restricted hours worked by women. Further to this, by 1918, thirty-five had passed worker compensation laws that required employers to make payments to workers injured on their job.[81]

Despite these enactments, the law offered little or no protection to employees who were dismissed on account of union membership, organizing activities or participation in industrial action. Indeed, in a series of cases, state courts held void statues passed by the state legislatures of Missouri, Illinois, New York and Minnesota and those of other states, to protect workers from signing yellow dog contracts or from being fired on account of union membership.[82]

In its 1915 ruling on *Coppage v. State of Kansas*, the US Supreme Court crucially voided a statute passed in 1903, by the state of Kansas for the same purpose.[83] *Coppage* involved the imposition of a fine on a superintendent of Frisco Lines who had discharged a switchman after he refused to sign a form agreeing to withdraw from the Switchmen's union. Writing for the majority, Justice Mahlon Pitney's opinion argued that: [84]

> There is neither finding nor evidence that the contract of employment was other than a general or indefinite hiring, such as is presumed to be terminable at the will of either party. The evidence shows that it would have been to the advantage of Hedges, from a pecuniary point of view and otherwise, to have been permitted to retain his membership in the union, and at the same time to remain in the employ of the railway company. In particular, it shows (although no reference is made to this in the opinion of the court) that as a member of the union he was entitled to benefits in the nature of insurance to the amount of fifteen hundred dollars, which he would then have been obliged to forego if he had ceased to be a member. But, aside from this matter of pecuniary interest, there is nothing to show that Hedges was

---

U.S. 181, 184; Wolff Packing Company v. Court of Industrial Relations, 262 U.S. 522, 542; Dorchy v. Kansas, 264 U.S. 286, 288]. And the third was the Personett case, triggered by a strike on the Santa Fe Railroad [Dorchy v. Kansas, 264 U.S. 286, 288]. In these cases, the Kansas Supreme Court upheld the validity of the Act, but the United States Supreme Court ruled otherwise. The Court said that a state could not regulate an industry not affected with the public interest and that forcing an arbitration award and destroying freedom of contract were prohibited by the fourteenth amendment."

[81] Aleine Austin, *The Labor Story: A Popular History of American Labor*, 1786-1949, at 161 (1949).

[82] See Clarence E Bonnett, "The Yellow Dog Contract in Its Relation to Public Policy," 7 *Tulane Law Review* 315, at 330 (1932-1933), where it is noted that "Anti-yellow dog contract legislation has been declared to be unconstitutional by state courts, in the following cases: Coffeyville Tile Co. v. Perry, 69 Kansas 297, 76 Pac. 848, 66 L. R. A. 185 (1904); Atchison, T. and S. F. Ry. v. Brown, 80 Kansas 312, 102 Pac. 459, 23 L. R. A. (N. s.) 247, 133 Am. St. Rep. 213, 18 Ann. Cas. 346 (1909), but reversed itself in the Coppage case; State ex rel Zillmer v. Kreutzberg, 114 Wis. 530, 90 N. W. 1098 (1902); People v. Marcus, 185 N. Y. 257, 77 N. E. 1073, 7 L. R. A. (N. s.) 282, 113 Am. St. Rep. 902 (1906); State v. Daniels, 118 Minn. 155, 136 N. W. 584 (1912); State v. Julow, 129 MLo. 163, 31 S. W. 781, 29 L. R. A. 257, 50 Am. St. Rep. 443 (1895); Gillespie v. The People, 188 Ill. 176, 58 N. E. 1007, 52 L. R. A. 283, 80 Am. St. Rep. 176 (1900)."

[83] Bonnet, ibid., at 328 observed that "The Kansas statute differed from the model bill, of the anti-yellow dog section of the Norris Act, in that while the former provides a penalty of a fine of not less than $50 or imprisonment of not less than thirty days for any violation; the latter merely outlaws the yellow dog contract and denies it all legal or equitable protection. In the Coppage case, a number of unfavorable features were present which might not arise in a constitutional test of the model bill."

[84] Mahlon Pitney was appointed to the U.S. Supreme Court by President William Howard Taft, where he served as Associate Justice from 1912 to 1922. The following quotes are from his majority opinion in Coppage v. State of Kansas, 236 U.S. 1, at 8 and 12 (1915).

subjected to the least pressure or influence, or that he was not a free agent, in all respects competent, and at liberty to choose what was best from the standpoint of his own interests.

Moving from the sublime to the bizarre, Pitney thereafter queried the practicality of the provisions entailed in the Kansas statute:

> The constitutional right of the employer to discharge an employee because of his membership in a labor union being granted, can the employer be compelled to resort to this extreme measure? May he not offer to the employee an option, such as was offered in the instant case, to remain in the employment if he will retire from the union; to sever the former relationship only if he prefers the latter? Granted the equal freedom of both parties to the contract of employment, has not each party the right to stipulate upon what terms only he will consent to the inception, or to the continuance, of that relationship? And may he not insist upon an express agreement, instead of leaving the terms of the employment to be implied? Can the legislature in effect require each party at the beginning to act covertly; concealing essential terms of the employment—terms to which, perhaps, the other would not willingly consent—and revealing them only when it is proposed to insist upon them as a ground for terminating the relationship? Supposing an employer is unwilling to have in his employ one holding membership in a labor union, and has reason to suppose that the man may prefer membership in the union to the given employment without it—we ask, can the legislature oblige the employer in such case to refrain from dealing frankly at the outset? And is not the employer entitled to insist upon equal frankness in return? Approaching the matter from a somewhat different standpoint, is the employee's right to join a labor union any more sacred, or more securely founded upon the Constitution, than his right to work for whom he will, or to be idle if he will? And does not the ordinary contract of employment include an insistence by the employer that the employee shall agree, as a condition of his employment, that he will not be idle and will not work for whom he pleases but will serve his present employer, and him only, so long as the relation between them shall continue? Can the right of making contracts be enjoyed by all, except by parties coming together in an agreement that requires each party to forego, during the time and for the purpose covered by the agreement, any inconsistent exercise of his constitutional rights?

Having established the impracticality of such statutory interference, Pitney's opinion ultimately revealed a deeply rooted anti-union animus, which was, if anything, rather typical of the conservative judiciary of the time:[85]

> When a man is called upon to agree not to become or remain a member of the union while working for a particular employer, he is in effect only asked to deal *openly* and *frankly* with his employer, so as to retain the employment upon terms to which the latter is not willing to agree. And the liberty to procure employment from an unwilling employer, or without a *fair understanding* (emphasis added).

Pitney and his fellow conservative judges, despite their rhetorical confidence, hardly walked on solid judicial ground. US unions had earlier defended their right to organize collectively by citing the Thirteenth Amendment giving support of "labor liberty," and this interpretation was not without merit. In the 1911 case of *Bailey v. Alabama*, the Supreme

---

[85] Holmes' dissent on Coppage found the statute to fall within the legitimate exercise of police power and is well known for recognizing the significance of financial coercion.. Coppage was eventually overruled in Phelps Dodge Corp. v. NLRB, 313 U.S. 177 (1941).

Court, for instance, had invalidated Alabama's debt peonage law on account of its infringement of Thirteenth Amendment rights.[86] The *Bailey* Court had specifically noted that it had been the purpose of the Amendment "to make labor free by prohibiting that control by which the service of one man is disposed of or coerced for another's benefit."[87] Based on this interpretation, some labor representatives argued that coercion could only genuinely be prevented if workers were allowed to organize collectively. Ultimately, most courts were unwilling to depart from their anti-labor stance, and by 1922, a special committee report by the American Federation of Labor on the decisions of the courts, concluded that "a judicial oligarchy is threatening to set itself above the elected legislatures, above the people itself:"[88]

> What confronts the workers of America … Is not one of several court decisions favoring the interests of property as against human rights of labor, but a series of adjudications of the highest tribunal of the land, successively destroying a basic right or cherished acquisition of organized labor each forming a link in a fateful chain consciously designed to enslave the workers of America.

In the view of some labor leaders, there was an urgent case for action. The freedom of labor, and more generally democracy, required a restriction on the Supreme Court's right to invalidate legislation. Accordingly, the 1922 report concluded, with reference to six decisions handed down between 1917 and 1922, that "by six decisions the United States Supreme Court, composed of nine men without clear mandate by the people and without responsibility to the people, has set aside a congressional enactment which clearly expressed the will of the people, and all but outlawed the rights of organized labor."[89]

Following the defeat of legislative initiatives by conservative courts of the early two decades of the twentieth century, the 1920s proved to be too volatile a period to allow for significant advancements in labor legislation on account of union action. In the early 1920s, witch hunts and the often brutal suppression of strikes had taken a severe toll on the labor movement, American Federation of Labor membership had been forced down from 4,078,740 in 1920, to 1,926,468 by 1923. Added to this, a series of confrontations, starting with the Pittsburgh US Steel strike of 1918, and culminating in the Bonus March of June 1932, had created an atmosphere of anti-left hysteria that made it difficult for progressive politicians to secure advances. [90]

As an impassionate observer, the labor economist Robert Hoxie, concluded that, given the weakness of unions in affecting significant changes, the position of American workers depended largely on the future actions of the courts. Said Hoxie:[91]

---

[86] See Bailey v. Alabama, 219 U.S. 219 (1911), which is discussed in James G. Pope, "Labor's Constitution of Freedom" 106 *Yale Law Review* 941, at 943 (1997).

[87] Bailey v. Alabama, ibid., cited in Pope, ibid., at 943.

[88] American Federation of Labor, Proceedings, at 371, cited in Charles G. Haines, *The American Doctrine of Judicial Supremacy*, at 450 (1932).

[89] American Federation of Labor, ibid., at 372, cited in Charles L. Haines, ibid., at 450. The cases referred to are Hitchman Coal and Coke Co. v. Mitchell, 245 U.S. 229 (1917); Duplex Printing Press Co. v. Deering, 254 U.S. 443 (1917); Truax v. Corrigan, 257 U.S. 312 (1912); American Steel Foundries v. Tri-City Central Trades Council, 257 U.S. 184 (1918); Hammer v. Dagenhart, 247 U.S. 251 (1918); United Mine Workers v. Coronado Coal Co., 259 U.S. 344 (1922).

[90] See, e.g., Anthony Bimba, *The History of the American Working Class*, at 359-369 (1936).

[91] See Robert F. Hoxie, *Trade Unionism in the United States*, at 233 (1923), cited in Albion G. Taylor, *Labor Problems and Labor Law*, at 213 (1938).

In general the courts have the power ... to hold the balance of power between the worker and the employer. They can make or mar any effort of the organized worker to better their relations with unwilling employer. They hold the practical destinies of militant unionism in their hands. If, as judges, they are closely identified in viewpoint with the employers, they can destroy any practical equality of legal relationship between the two forces.

Up until the 1930s, US courts largely reiterated their earlier conservative stance.[92] For individual workers, this meant that protection against arbitrary and unnecessary dismissals, be it either via individual employment law or through collective bargaining, remained elusive. This discontent with the conservative judiciary was capitalized on by a new Progressive party, which in 1924, nominated Robert La Follette as presidential candidate and who promised to protect from judicial veto Laws re-enacted by Congress after having been nullified by the Supreme Court. The Progressives also called for the election of federal judges for limited terms, the abolition of labor injunctions and public ownership of the railroads and water power.[93] The Progressive plan was subject to severe criticism by both the Attorney General, Harlan Stone and by the Secretary of State, Charles Auges, who had once served on the Supreme Court, and who, in 1930, succeeded Taft as Chief Justice.[94] Congress nonetheless discussed the various approaches to limiting the power of the Supreme Court, with much of the debate focusing on the nullification of legislation through five to four decisions. Amongst the proposals, one Senator introduced a bill that required the concurrence of seven members of the Court for declaring an Act of Congress illegal.[95]

With the appointment of Chief Justice Hughes and Justice Roberts, a conservative majority was restored to the Supreme Court, which only weakened with the appointment of Justice Cardozo in 1932. By 1933, when the Roosevelt administration came to power, events had overtaken the old debates on the rightful place of organized labor. The issue of labor rights now had to be re-examined, not so much because previous administrations had left many matters unresolved, but rather because the new imperative of economic re-construction required the orderly participation of organized labor. Despite this new agenda, up until 1937, the Supreme Court continued to block legislative initiatives that would have strengthened organized labor.[96] Why and how the New Deal was eventually supported by the Court has remained a matter of historical debate. Historical details notwithstanding, it stands to reason that even for conservative members of the judiciary, the partial legalization of organized labor's activities was preferable to the threat of their own marginalization.[97]

---

[92] See, e.g., Texas and N.O.R. Co. v. Brotherhood of R.Y. and S.S. Clerks, 281 U.S. 548 (1930) upholding a permanent injunction against, and the dismissal of, members of the Brotherhood.

[93] Carl B. Swisher, *American Constitutional Development*, at 772 (1943).

[94] Swisher, ibid., at 773.

[95] Swisher, ibid., at 773-74, referring to a widely criticized proposal by Senator Borah.

[96] The case breaking the impasse was, of course, NLRB v. Jones and Laughlin Steel Co., 301 U.S. 1 (1937), in which Justice Owen Roberts switched to the progressive side, allowing the NLRA to be upheld by a five to four vote.

[97] Some Marxist scholars have argued that the defeat of the Hooverites was associated with misleading "leftist" campaign promises by Roosevelt to give "greater assurance of security," which were grounded in statements such as "old age, sickness and unemployment insurance are the minimum requirements in these days;" see Bimba, *supra* note 90, at 370. These claims notwithstanding, there is credible evidence that, given Roosevelt's pluralist predilections, a strengthening of labor rights played at best a peripheral role in the successful 1932 campaign of the Democrats, which would at least partially explain the administration's patience with the conservative judiciary.

Chapter 2

THE FAILED PROMISE OF STATUTORY PROTECTION

> The subject of the legal regulation of labor is one of great complexity. Up to the present time *a priori* objections to such regulations have delayed their introduction, and only gradually, as experience has demonstrated their usefulness, have they been extended to situations which seem to require them. In ... the United States the notion that the legislative power should not be used ... to regulate conditions of employment has been abandoned by most thoughtful persons, but the prejudice against interference ... is as strong as ever.
>
> Henry R. Seager, *Introduction to Economics*, at 431 (1904)

Subsequent to a period of legislative inaction during the late nineteenth and early twentieth century, the largely unrestricted right of employers to dismiss at-will was subject to selective statutory restrictions during the late 1920s and early 1930s, which emerged largely as a by-product of efforts to regulate collective bargaining. The introduction of limitations to the at-will rule within the emerging New Deal legislation, in particular, marked the long overdue recognition that, as long as employers had the right to dismiss employees at-will, public policy goals, such as industrial peace and the extension of orderly collective bargaining, were unattainable.

Following a roughly historical chronology, this chapter explores how, from the 1920s, onwards, restrictions to the at-will doctrine were constructed around notions of orderly collective bargaining.

Thematically, the focus of the chapter is on the creation of new institutional structures and their impact on the status of workers in terms of job security and employment rights. Underlying this analysis is the tentative hypothesis that the Natinal Labor Relations Act, and the practices that evolved from it, provided unions and their members with a sense of control over dismissal rights, which ultimately proved to be largely illusionary. This mistaken sense of control, in turn, encouraged unions to put efforts into job security-enhancing measures at the plant and company level, which did not effectively constrain managerial power. This lack of real control became apparent in the mid-1960s, when the Supreme Court handed down several decisions that reaffirmed the right of management to close branches and discharge employees without union interference.

Apart from excluding a host of specific categories of workers as well as those not covered by a union contract, the NLRA system, perhaps against the intentions of its original sponsors, also severely circumscribed the right of unions to bargain over job security at the very time when such protection was needed.

THE PROMISED LANDS OF PROTECTED BARGAINING

At the turn of the century, many US industrial relations scholars questioned the assumption that injustices in the labor market could be remedied through legislative acts and, more generally, via a strengthening of individual employment rights. This opposition to legislative approaches was grounded primarily in the belief that solutions to the "labor problems of industrial societies" could be created more easily by strengthening the standing of organized labor as collective bargaining agent rather than by creating a host of specific employment regulations.[98]

Representative of this view, the Harvard economist Frank Taussig suggested in his popular 1920 economics textbook that the most urgent task in reforming US employment relations was the protection of bargaining representatives:[99]

> The workmen clearly gain by having their case in charge of chosen representatives, whether or not these be fellow employees; and collective bargaining and unionization up to this point surely bring no offsetting disadvantages to society. As to the immediate employees, there is often a real danger that he who presents a demand, or a grievance, will be "victimized." He will be discharged and perhaps blacklisted; very likely on some pretext, but in fact because "he has made trouble."

In the 1930s, Albion Taylor's influential monograph *Labor Problems and Labor Law* similarly suggested, very much along the lines of earlier reform advocates, that individual workers had been deprived of their ability to bargain effectively primarily because of the increasing professionalization and centralization of management and a corresponding loss of power by organized and unorganized labor.[100]

To remedy this situation, Taylor argued, the state had to facilitate the creation of structures that would enable workers to bargain collectively, both for wages and for the protection of their jobs. Said Taylor:[101]

> Legally free to dispose of his services at any price he deems just, immediate necessity in the face of an oversupply of labor reduces that freedom to empty words. His [meaning the worker's] inferior bargaining position is not wholly due to economic inequality, but in part to a lack of knowledge of labor conditions, and a bargaining skill less effective than that of his employer. The injustices growing out of the individual bargaining burden affect not only the individual worker but the entire group to which he belongs. Unregulated competition resulting from individual bargaining tends to pull down the terms of employment to the level of the weakest employer...

---

[98] The term "labor problems of industrial societies," can be found among others in John A. Fitch, *The Causes of Industrial Unrest* (1924). Fitch identified individualized bargaining as a prime cause of industrial unrest, but his analysis also remained critical of collectivist approaches.

[99] See Frank W. Taussig, *Principles of Economics*, at 293 (4th edition, 1921).

[100] Albion G. Taylor, *Labor Problems and Labor Law*, (1938) expanded on arguments the author had made earlier in his book *Labor Policies of the National Association of Manufacturers* (1928). Taylor used historic examples of collective bargaining to argue that a stabilization of employment could be achieved via arbitration. Taylor's view countered an older tradition of writer who had opposed collective solutions to labor problems, such as the sociologist Sumner. William Graham Sumner, "Industrial War," 2 *Forum* (1886), for instance, argued that the problem of how this "wage-class" was to conduct itself was not a "class question ... but the most distinctly individual question that can be raised."

[101] Taylor, *supra* note 100, at 182.

Taylor's notion that inequalities of labor were due to the exposure of workers to individual, rather than collective, bargaining echoed the opinions of some of the nation's leading judges of the time. Thus, Oliver Wendell Holmes Jr. had earlier opposed bans on union activity on account of the fact that union activity merely counterbalanced the combination of capitalists.[102] Despite the gradual acknowledgement of the legitimacy of strike action by some courts, up until the 1920s, few judges had been willing to offer protection to those workers who had been discharged for union membership or strike activity. In theory, collective bargaining could serve to reduce the power disequilibrium between the employer, who, as Holmes says "is free to discharge the worker, and the worker who depends on his job for his livelihood."[103] In practice, however, the relationship between job security and collective action had remained largely antonymous. Post-World War I, workers who participated in collective action, be it as organizers or as strike participants, often faced retaliatory discharges or even blacklisting; with estimates indicating that 30,000 of the 365,000 workers who had participated in the 1919 steel strike had been discharged and blacklisted.[104] The first congressional statute addressing issues of dismissal and organizing activity, the Erdman Act, had attempted to prohibit the retaliatory discharge of union members working on the railroads at a time when the railroads were one of the few areas where the Federal Government had the authority to intervene in such matters. Passed by Congress in 1898, Section 10 of the Erdman Act made it an offense to threaten an employee "with discharge" or to blacklist the employee after a discharge because of membership in a labor organization. Specifically, the Act stated: [105]

> That any employer subject to the provisions of this act and any officer, agent or receiver
> of such employer who shall require any employee, or any person seeking employment, as a

---

[102] Holmes' opinion in Vegelhahn v. Guntner, 167 Mass. 92, 44 N.E. 1077 (1896), is part of a set of well-known court decisions that have come to be known as the Massachusetts doctrine; see Charles O. Gregory, *Labor and the Law*, at 52 (1946). The Massachusetts doctrine on trade unions and conspiracy dates back to Justice Shaw's decision in Commonwealth v. Hunt, 4 Metc. 111 (1842), where the Boston Journeymen Bootmakers Society stood accused of criminal conspiracy because it had forced an employer to fire a worker who had refused to become a union member. Overruling an earlier decision, Shaw decided in favor of the union, arguing that the union's actions were "perfectly justifiable" in light of its goals to further the welfare of its members. Massachusetts cases following Hunt held some strike actions legal, depending on the purpose and the actions taken. If an association had achieved the near-impossible task of doing nothing, which fell within any established category of tort or crime, the harm it inflicted on the plaintiff in the pursuit of economic gain was in theory not actionable but rather seen to be justified as an element of competition. The New York state Supreme court similarly   ruled that unions causing harm to others while in pursuit of gain were behaving lawfully unless they conducted specific tortuous or criminal acts such as assault or trespass. In contrast to Massachusetts' decisions, courts following the New York doctrine at times refused to judge the purposes of union activity when holding a strike action legal or otherwise; see, Curran v. Galen, 152 N.Y. 33 (1897); National Protective Assn. v. Cumming, 170 N.Y. 315 (1902); and Jacobs v. Cohen, 183 N.Y. 207 (1905).

[103] Gregory, *supra* note 102, at 62.

[104] See John Steuben, *Strike Strategy*, at 205 (1950). Other notable strikes that resulted in mass dismissals included the Homestead strike of 1892 and the Pullman strike of 1894. In the Boston police strike of 1919, in which the policemen struck for the right to organize with an AFL affiliate, more than one third of the police force, or 1,100 officers, were permanently discharged and "entry standards were lowered to allow the department to quickly recruit replacement officers;" see Larry K. Gaines and John L. Worrall, *Police Administration,* at 325 (3rd edition, 2012).

[105] Cited in Taylor, *supra* note 102, at 188. The Erdman Act was narrower than the Wagner Act in that it covered railroad workers only. Prior to the passage of the Act, some state legislatures, including Massachusetts, Connecticut, New York, Pennsylvania, New Jersey, Ohio, Illinois, Indiana, Wisconsin, Minnesota, Kansas, Missouri, California, Colorado, Idaho and Georgia, had passed laws prohibiting employers from discharging employees on the ground that they were members of registered labor organizations—which had typically failed to withstand judicial review; see Philip Taft, *Organized Labor in American History*, at 162 (1964).

condition of such employment, to enter into an agreement, either written or verbal, not to become or remain a member of any labor corporation, association, or organization; or shall threaten any employee with loss of employment, or shall unjustly discriminate against any employee because of his membership ... or who shall, after having discharges an employee, attempt or conspire to prevent such employee from obtaining employment or who shall after the quitting of an employee, attempt or conspire to prevent such employee from obtaining employment, is hereby declared to be guilty of a misdemeanor, and ... shall be punished for such offense by a fine of not less than one hundred dollars and not more than one thousand dollars.

In 1908, section 10 of the Erdman Act was declared in violation of the Fifth Amendment by the Supreme Court in *Adair v. United States*. This rather predictable decision again rendered members of labor organizations unprotected from retaliatory discharges.[106]

Unionized workers were given some support by the courts in the Brandeis and Holmes Supreme Court decisions of the 1920s.[107] Explicit legislative protection of those engaging in organizing activity, however, commenced as late as 1926, with the passage of the Railroad Labor Act (RLA), which, apart from requiring employers to bargain with unions, prohibited employers from discriminating against union members.[108] The RLA applied originally to interstate railroads and related undertakings but was later amended to include airlines engaged in interstate commerce. The Norris La Guardia Act (NLGA) of 1932, gave some federal sanction to the right of labor unions to organize and strike.[109] Implicitly, it also limited the ability of federal courts to enforce "yellow dog contracts," under which workers promised not to join a union or promised to discontinue union membership.[110] The National Industrial Recovery Act (NIRA) of 1933, the predecessor of the National Labor Relations Act, introduced the idea of codes of "fair competition," which fixed wages and hours in certain industries. Title I of the Act, which was declared unconstitutional in 1935, guaranteed the

---

[106] See, e.g., Adair v. United States, 208 U.S. 161 (1908). Paradoxically, American courts were very eager to protect workers whose discharge was caused by unions, say in the context of closed shop policies. Daniel R. Ernst, "Free Labor, the Consumer Interest and The Law of Industrial Disputes, 1885-1990," 36 *The American Journal of Legal History* 19, at 29 (1992), cites an alarmed Connecticut judge, who upon reviewing a closed job discharge, stated that such actions "were contrary to the genius of our people and to the fundamental principle of our government." Unless retrained by law, unions would be given the power to "unauthorized and irresponsible tribunals," which could ruin an independent worker, who "branded by the peculiarly offensive epithets adopted, must exist ostracized, socially and industrially, so far as his former associates are concerned. Freedom of will under such circumstances cannot be expected." Leonard W. Levy, *The Law of the Commonwealth and Chief Justice Shaw,* at 185 (1957) reports that between 1806 and 1842, the date of Shaw's "Hunt" decision, at least a dozen decisions involving union-led discharges resulted in the conviction of union leaders.

[107] Justices Brandeis and Holmes had opposed the abuse of temporary injunctions by employers in order to break strikes, see Duplex Printing Press v. Deering, 254 U.S. 443 (1921); and Coronado Coal Company v. United Mine Workers, 268 U.S. 295 (1925).

[108] The Railway Labor Act, 45 U.S.C. §§151-188, entailed elaborate dispute resolution mechanisms administered for the most part by the National Mediation Board (NMB). Provisions for extensive mandatory and voluntary arbitration procedures under the RLA were created in the interest of minimizing work stoppages in the transportation sector, which was believed to be vital to the national interest. Whilst in part modeled on the RLA, the dispute resolution mechanisms of the NLRA were less encompassing.

[109] Norris La Guardia Act, 29 U.S.C.A. 103 (1932).

[110] The Norris La Guardia Act effectively forbade federal court judges from issuing injunctions or granting damages in connection with labor disputes and forbade federal courts from enforcing anti-union contracts. The act sought to restore the protection given to unions by the Clayton Act of 1918, which the federal courts had removed.

right of employees to collective bargaining without interference or coercion—which included the dismissal of employees. [111]

The National Labor Relations Act (NLRA) of 1935, or Wagner Act, included some previously invalidated labor sections of the NRA, as well as a number of additions. Primarily concerned with restricting employer activities against union organizing and bargaining efforts, the NLRA prohibited employers from, firstly, "dominating or otherwise interfering with the formation of labor unions;" secondly, "interfering or restraining employees engaged in exercising their rights to organize and bargain collectively; and, thirdly, from "refusing to bargain collectively with unions representing a company's employees." In doing so, sections 7 and 8 of the NLRA effectively tied the legal protection of employees from retaliatory discharges to the right of employees to organize collectively. The Act stated to this effect that:[112]

> Sec. 7. Employees shall have the right to self-organization, to form, join, or assist labor organizations, to bargain collectively through representatives of their own choosing, and to engage in concerted activities, for the purpose of collective bargaining or other mutual aid or protection.
>
> Sec. 8. It shall be an unfair practice for an employer—
>
> 1) To interfere with, restrain, or coerce employees in the exercise of the rights guaranteed in section 7.
> 2) To dominate or interfere with the formation or administration of any labor organization or contribute financial or other support to it…
> 3) By discrimination in regard to hire or tenure of employment or any term or condition of employment to encourage or discourage membership in any labor organization…
> 4) To discharge or otherwise discriminate against an employee because he had filed charges or given testimony under this act.
> 5) To refuse to bargain collectively with the representatives of his employees…

Under the NLRA regime, employers were required "not to refuse to bargain collectively with the representatives of his employees" with regard to "rates of pay, wages and hours of

---

[111] The National Industrial Recovery Act, 40 U.S.C. 401 (1933) offered some protection to organized workers but was held unconstitutional by the Supreme Court, as were, in 1935, sections 7 and 8 of the National Labor Relations Act of 1935. The National Recovery Act was part of a bundle of reform bills that the President had sent to Congress in 1933, together with a request for authority to effect drastic economies in government. Most of the proposed reforms were vehemently opposed by the then-dominant legal establishment. Congressman James Beck, a distinguished constitutional scholar, for instance, commented: "I think of all the damnable heresies that have ever been suggested ... the doctrine of emergency is the worst ... It is the very doctrine that the German Chancellor is invoking today in the dying hours of the parliamentary body of the German republic, namely, that because of an emergency it should grant to the German Chancellor absolute power to pass any law, even though that law contradicts the constitution of the German republic. Chancellor Hitler is at least frank about it. We pay the constitution lip-service, but the result is the same," 77 *Congressional Record* 753, cited in Carl B. Swisher, *American Constitutional Development*, at 84 (1943).

[112] National Labor Relations Act, 49 Stat. 499 (1935), at section 7 and 8 (1-5). The provisions of the NLRA were upheld in NLRB v. Jones and Laughlin Steel Corporation, 301 U.S. 1, 57 S.Ct. 615 (1937). *De facto* enforcement of section 7 and 8 rules, however, had started in 1934, with the formation of the first Labor Relations Board, formed under NRA legislation. With the NLRB being primarily concerned with employer misconduct, Congress tried to "counterbalance" the NLRA with the Taft Hartley Act of 1947, which placed limitations on union conduct. The 1959 Landrum Griffin Act enacted legislation to deal with internal union affairs, with employee rights in union representation being the main issue.

employment, or other conditions of employment."[113] While the Act had made it clear that retaliatory dismissals of union members were illegal, it gave little guidance on the question of whether bargaining over "other conditions of employment" included issues relating to job security.[114] Moreover, despite the appearance of sweeping legislation, coverage under the NLRA's protective umbrella was narrow. Public sector employees at the federal, state, and local levels, agricultural workers, domestic workers, and supervisory employees were excluded.[115] Nonetheless, for those covered by the Act, statutory dismissal protection was available in connection with established categories of protected activity the courts had created. This included dismissals for strike action, union membership and related activities.

Indeed, at its outset, the NLRB rulings allowed significant numbers of dismissed employees to gain reinstatement. From the appointment of the Board in the Fall of 1935, until March 1939, the Board handled a total of 20,192 cases involving over 4.5 million workers. Of these cases, 19,018, or four-fifths, were closed. Of the total cases closed, about 52 percent were decided by agreements, while the remainder were dismissed, withdrawn or closed in some other way before coming to the Board. About two thousand cases were strike cases, involving 356 thousand workers, of which 75 percent were settled and in which 227 thousand workers had to be re-employed. An additional 15 thousand cases were decided in favor of workers alleging non-strike related discriminatory discharges and resulted in the reinstatement of the respective workers. Between the first January, 1938, and the first of April 1939, alone, the Board heard 1,675 cases alleging discriminatory discharges and ordered the reinstatement and/or compensation of 1,022 workers.[116]

---

[113] James B. Atleson, *Values and Assumptions of American Labor Law*, at 136 (1983), gives a detailed analysis of the NLRA's ambiguities with regard to the scope of mandatory bargaining and managerial prerogatives.

[114] See NLRA, *supra* note 112, at section 8(5) and section 9(a). Mark Barenberg, "The Political Economy of the Wagner Act: Power, Symbol and Workplace Cooperation," *Harvard Law Review*, 1381 (1993) provides an explanation for this lack of clear boundaries. According to Barenberg, the Wagner Act was profoundly cooperationist, not adversarial, as is conventionally assumed. As part of this cooperatist agenda, Wagner envisaged a political economy of high trust cooperation in which the boundaries of what could be negotiated could be set consensually by the parties involved.

[115] William B. Gould, *A Primer on American Labor Law*, at 37 (1986) suggests that there was no logical basis for the exclusion of these groups. Essentially, their exclusion from NLRA protection had resulted from their lack of political clout when the NLRA was enacted. An extension of coverage took place in 1974, when employees in non-profit health care institutions were included due to an extension of the definition of employer to non-profit enterprises. The 1994 Supreme Court decision in NLRB v. Health Care and Retirement Corp. of America 330 U.S. 485, again restricted NLRA coverage by declaring that nurses who directed less skilled employees were to be considered supervisors.

[116] These data are from "Report of the NLRB to the Senate Committee on Education and Labor" (April 26, 1939; Hearings. Pt. 3 at 478-84), which is reprinted in Julia E. Johnson, *The National Labor Relations Act; Should it Be Amended?* 136-151, at 138 and 153 (1940). It is worth remembering that prior to the establishment of NLRB jurisdiction, the courts only reluctantly enforced the contractual rights of employees emerging from collective bargaining agreements. Katherine van Wezel Stone, "The Post-War Paradigm in American Labor Law," 90 *The Yale Law Journal* 1509, at 1519 (1981) discusses the case of Hudson v. Cincinnati, N.O. and T.P. Ry., 152 Ky 711 (1913), where an employee was fired and tried to use the grievance procedure specified in his collective bargaining agreement in an appeal. When the supervisor refused to give Hudson a hearing, he sued on the contract for wages due. The court rejected his claim, arguing that the employee's name was not explicitly included in the agreement, that there was no evidence that the union had acted as his client, nor was there evidence that the plaintiff had ratified the agreement when he took the job. The court concluded that the collective bargaining agreement was no more than "a memorandum of rates of pay and regulation ... which acquires legal force because people make [individual] contracts in reference to it." The union's role was merely "to induce employers to establish usage in respect to wages and working conditions ... leaving it to its members each to determine for himself whether or not or for what length of time he will contract in reference to such usages."

In theory, there was a possibility that collective bargaining agreements would include job security guarantees of some form. Given existing cultural pre-dispositions amongst the judiciary and managers, however, the possibility of partial union control over personnel and investment decisions was remote. Judicial support for the right to manage had a strong pedigree, and its influence would not wane quickly. In the 1890s, some state courts had already felt the need to defend the right to manage. In the view of most courts, this right was as much a part of the free labor creed as was the right to work. "Free labor" required that both employers and individual workers were fully responsible for their decisions. Permitting workers to organize and successively influence managerial decisions was viewed as a danger to free economic competition. In *State v. Glidden*, an outraged Connecticut judge stated that once workers could influence managerial decision, no longer would the heads of industrial and commercial enterprises rise from the "ranks of the toilers, no longer could self-reliant ambitious men push to the fore."[117] Unable to manage as they saw fit, businessmen would stop risking their capital, time and experience. "At best, the nation's business would be conducted by paternalistic enterprises, at worst anarchy pure and simple ..." would prevail.

At the turn of the century, the aforementioned economists Frank Taussig had already predicted that union demands for job security would clash with managers' insistence on "the right to manage." His *Principles of Economics* stated to this effect that:[118]

> Private ownership carries with it the seeds of conflict—the inevitable clash between those who employ and who are employed. Disguise it as we may, smooth over to our utmost, adjust where we can, there the conflict is, ever liable to break out. ... The private employer ... regards his business as his own, its methods of management as subject to his own judgment. It is almost invariably urged by him and his spokesman that the effective working of the business machine depends above all on unfettered freedom in the selection and tenure of employees. So long as this attitude prevails, the workman will feel in turn that he must retain his weapon of defense, the strike, even though it entails injury to a wide circle of persons. ... Even if employers were to consent to restrictions on their power of discharge, contests would remain, strikes would brew. And on the other hand discharge is but one of the matters in which employers absolute rule is to be questioned. Discharge is conspicuous because it is the outstanding weapon.

As long as unions and their members had little formal protection through the law, management was able to assert its dominance with relative ease, if only by dismissing those who posed challenges. Once NLRA legislation protected concerted action, this situation had changed radically, and conflicts between unions and management over dismissal rights were pre-destined.

When President Truman called the second National Labor Management Conference in 1945, labor and management representatives found themselves unable to agree on the boundaries of collective bargaining. Disagreement had arisen particularly with regard to management's right to make workers redundant, close and/or relocate branches. The statement of the management representative at the conference expressed the employers dismay over this matter:[119]

---

[117] State v. Glidden (1887) 55 Conn. 46, 72 as cited in Ernst, *supra* note 106, at 31.

[118] See Taussig, *supra* note 99, at 285.

[119] See President's National Labor Management Conference, November 29, 1945, letter to Executive Committee, as cited in Joseph A. Raffaele, "The Changing Status of Management Prerogatives," 8 *The American Catholic*

Labor members of the committee on management's right to manage have been unwilling to agree on any listing of specific management functions. Management members of the committee conclude therefore that the labor members are convinced that the field of collective bargaining will in all probability continue to expand into the field of management.

The only possible end of such a philosophy would be joint management of enterprise. To this the management members naturally cannot agree. Management has functions that must not and cannot be compromised in the public interest. If labor disputes are to be minimized by the genuine acceptance by organized labor of the functions and responsibilities of men to direct manage the operation of an enterprise, labor must agree that certain specific functions and responsibilities of management are not subject to collective bargaining.

In theory, the evolving conflict about the appropriate limits of collective bargaining, and particularly about the rights of labor to contest management's redundancy and dismissal decisions, was resolved by reference to new management concepts such as the residual rights doctrine. In practice, a set of employer-friendly court decisions and the decline of unions in the US settled the issue, first, in rough terms, during the first decade of NLRA rule, and then, in greater detail, over the following three decades.

The notion of residual rights, which deserves a passing mention in this context, developed from the 1940s, onwards, to become a prominent feature of the management of US industrial relations in the 1960s and 1970s. The residual rights doctrine postulated that management rights were the result of an evolutionary process, whereby initially management possessed total freedom in ordering the affairs of the enterprise. This included freedoms with regard to whom to hire and dismiss and when to do so. Union demands and labor legislation encroached on this freedom. It followed that every time a manager made a contractual concession or every time a legal enactment restricted management options, the original rights of management were reduced. What remained then were the residual rights not specifically renounced by management or restricted by law.[120] If, for instance, management renounced the right to dismiss according to productivity or any other performance criterion and agreed to dismiss according to seniority, seniority replaced management's previous decision criteria. Meanwhile other issues, such as how many workers could be dismissed in a specific time period, remained within the exclusive sphere of managerial decision making.[121]

Adopting this view, many arbitration decisions applied a two-stage approach to questions about the appropriate bargaining remit of a union. If union representatives and management disagreed on whether an issue was a legitimate bargaining item, previous contractual

---

Sociological Review 170, at 177 (1947). Raffaele's article firther notes at 178 "The management members of this committee went further and stated those prerogatives which are not subject to collective bargaining. They include: 1. The determination of products or services to be rendered and the fixing of prices. 2. Business location. 3. Determination of layout and equipment. 4. Manufacturing and distribution techniques. 5. Materials to be used subject to health and safety standards. 6. Size and character of inventories. 7. Determination of financial policies including accounting reports to government and business. 8. Customer relations. 9. Determination of each producing or distributing unit. 10. Selection of employees to managerial positions. 11. Determination of job content. 12. Determination of the size of the work force. 13. Allocation and assignment of work. 14. Determination of policies affecting the selection of workers. 15. Establishment of quality standards and judgment of workmanship. 16. Maintenance of discipline and control. 17. The use of plant property. 18. Scheduling of operations and the number of shifts. 19. The determination of safety, health and property protection measures where legal responsibility of the employer is involved."

[120] Frank Elkouri and Edna Asper Elkouri, *How Arbitration Works*, at 412 (3rd edition, 1973) gives a detailed analysis of the residual rights doctrine.

[121] See, e.g. Edwin F. Beal, Edward D. Wickersham, and Philip K. Kienast, *The Practice of Collective Bargaining*, at 273-287 (5th edition, 1976).

agreements as well as legal requirements had to be investigated. If no explicit statement restricting management's rights in the respective matter could be found in these sources, the issue typically had to be considered as falling within management's remit. Since explicit renunciations of the rights to dismiss were typically rare, management usually maintained broad discretion over dismissals, which fell out with causes covered explicitly by just-cause rules.

Because existing practices and informal agreements had little legal bearing on conflicts over the interpretation of the NLRA, the residual rights doctrine was of little use to the courts in evaluating the legitimacy of union involvement in termination decisions. Here, an alternative, and in many ways even more restrictive approach, evolved over time. While the NLRB of the early years generally looked favorably upon workers whose discharge could in some way be linked to union activity, it also condoned a wide set of permissible grounds for dismissal. In this context, several NLRB decisions early on vindicated traditional assumptions about managerial prerogatives. Discharges were sustained by the NLRB in cases involving gross inefficiency of a worker, incompetence, change in equipment, "ruckus and horseplay," absenteeism, brawling, cursing of the boss, and the violation of company rules.[122] Most importantly, discharges in the absence of employee misconduct were generally thought to be permissible if there was no evidence for anti-union activity. This included discharges for lack of work, which were generally approved by the Board even in absence of union consultation, as long as anti-union bias could not be proven.

In its *Seagrave* decision of 1938, for instance, the Board set a precedent for the preservation of employment-at-will within collective bargaining.[123] Seagrave, an automotive equipment plant, had discharged an employee three weeks after he got his job. The foreman testified to the fact that the employee's work was satisfactory. The worker, a CIO member, had previously been arrested for disorderly conduct during a strike and alleged that he was fired because of this previous involvement, and, more specifically, because his foreman had received a blacklist showing his name. The spokesman of the company explained that the polisher was hired because of a temporary emergency arising from the receipt of a special order and that he was dismissed when the work on that order let up. The Board found no evidence for anti-union activity and declared the dismissal legal.

In the case of *Sheba Ann Frocks* (1938), similarly, thirty employees, who had been dropped from the payroll of the Sheba garment plant, complained to the Board alleging that their discharge was based on their CIO membership.[124] Company officials testified that the layoffs took place because of a lack of work at the end of the regular production season. The Board accepted this explanation because the company retained over half of its CIO employees and discharged non-union employees as well, although not proportionally. In its conclusion,

---

[122] Russell L. Greenman, *The Worker, the Foreman and the Wagner Act*, at 42-60 (1939), includes a chapter entitled "Discharge Sustained," which cites a number of early Board decisions including on inefficiency, Indianapolis Glove Co.--C-251, February 11, 1938, 5 NLRB. No. 34; on incompetence, Douglas Aircraft Co. Inc.--C-268-269, April 20, 1938, 6 NLRB. No. 108; on equipment change, Uxbridge Worsted Co. Inc.--C-131, April 21, 1938, 6 NLRB. No. 109; on ruckus and horseplay, American Radiator Co.--C-444, June 24, 1938, 7 NLRB No. 132.; and General Industries Co.--C-30, April 30, 1936, 1 NLRB. at 678; on absenteeism, Empire Furniture Co.--C-305 and R0-386, April 26, 1938: 6 NLRB. No. 124; on brawling, Harlan Fuel Co.--C-489, July 5, 1938, 8 NLRB. No. 3; on cursing the boss, T. W. Hepler--C-349, May 19, 1938, 7 NLRB. No. 34; on violation of rules, Cleveland Chair Co.--C-18, June 4, 1936, 1 NLRB. at p. 892.

[123] Greenman, ibid., at 42, discussing The Seagrave Corporation--C-189, January, 21 1938, 4 NLRB. 1093.

[124] Greenman, ibid., at 52, discussing Sheba Ann Frocks, Inc.--C-186, February 1, 1938, 5 NLRB. No. 5.

the Board stated that, in the case of a dismissal for legitimate business reasons such as slack work, no consultation with union members was required.

While NLRB decisions of the late 1930s, such as *Seagrave* and *Sheba*, delineated the space between dismissal protection and managerial prerogatives more or less by default, later court decisions attempted to define principles that that could be applied to a number of contexts. These efforts built on earlier case law which already showed a tendency toprotect managerial decision making on strategic issues from union intrusion; as was already notable in the Supreme Court's ruling on *NLRB v. Jones and Laughlin Steel*. In *Jones and Laughlin*, the landmark case better known for its acceptance of the NLRA.

In Jones, the Supreme Court had stressed that although the Act required bargaining, it did not "compel" agreement.[125] For the Supreme Court, in other words, the NLRA was legal because, and possibly only because "[t]he Act does not interfere with the normal exercise of the right of the employer to select employees or to discharge them.... [T]he Board is not entitled to make its authority a pretext for interference with the right of discharge when that right is exercised for other reasons than ... intimidation or coercion."[126] That, in defining normal rights, the Supreme Court emphasized the right to discharge workers did not bode well for those who expected the Act to significantly reduce arbitrary dismissals. With *Jones*, the court had indicated that out-with matters directly related to collective bargaining, employment-at-will was still very much in place, with restrictions only affecting those discharges that were explicitly declared illegal in the NLRA. More importantly, it had implied that would be difficult to create an agreement sanctioned and protected by the Act that would eliminate the right of employers to discharge workers for "legitimate" reasons.

In *NLRB v. Sands Manufacturing* (1938), a federal appeals court was even more explicit in affirming management's freedom to dismiss workers.[127] In *Sands*, a collective agreement between the company and MESA, a labor union, was broken by the union. The company apparently bargained collectively with MESA. After two months, the company signed an agreement with another union, some of whose members were employed in order to replace MESA members. The NLRB ordered reinstatement of the MESA employees and requested

---

[125] Gould, *supra* note 115, at 97, discusses this aspect of NLRB v. Jones and Laughlin Steel, 301 U.S. 1 (1937). Justice Holmes (writing for the majority) stressed the constitutionality of the NLRA by stating that "in the present application the statute goes no further than to safeguard the right of employees of self organization and to select representatives of their own choosing, for collective bargaining or other mutual protection without restraint or coercion by their employer. That is a fundamental right. Employees have as clear a right to organize and select their employees for lawful purposes as the respondent has to organize its business and to select its own officers and agents."

[126] NLRB v. Jones and Laughlin Corp., 301 U.S. 1, 45-46, 57 S.Ct. 615, 628, 81 L.Ed. 893 (1937). Harry Schulman, "Reason, Contract, and Law in Labor Relations," 68 *Harvard Law Review* 959, at 1007 (1955), illustrates that the Jones and Laughlin Steel court's narrow view of bargaining was accepted by many prominent arbitrators. Schulman, chief arbitrator for Ford and the UAW, argued that the NLRA conferred no substantial rights upon labor but merely presented a "bare legal framework" for facilitating the private ordering of labor relations by management and labor. Accordingly, "the questions of what the parties should bargain about and what they should leave to unilateral rather than joint determination could, of course, be left to the parties themselves. They could decide whether to bargain about pensions or the number of shifts in the same way that they decide whether to have a wage increase or how much of an increase. That would involve the possibility of a cessation of production because of stalemate on these issues; but such an interruption is an integral part of collective bargaining. The results might then differ from one enterprise to another; one might bargain about pensions, the other might not; one might place a matter under unilateral control, the other might make it a matter of joint determination. But such differences would be quite in accord with the postulate of autonomous determination through collective bargaining."

[127] NLRB v. The Sands Manufacturing Company, 96 F. 2nd 721, setting aside the NLRB's order for reinstatement, later affirmed in, 306 U.S. 332, 4 LRRM 530 (1939).

the circuit court to enforce its order. The 6th circuit set aside the order and dismissed the petition to enforce. With respect to the termination of the employer-employee relationship, the court stated that:[128]

> The statute [meaning the NLRA] does not interfere with the normal right of the employer to select or discharge his employees ... If employees violate their contract[s] they may be discharged for that reason and this does not constitute a discrimination in regard to tenure of employment nor an unfair labor practice, nor does it continue a discharge because the employees are members of a union. ... [T]he statute does not provide that the relationship held in status quo under Title 29, Section 152(3) [meaning the prohibition of dismissals during strikes] shall continue in absence of wrongful conduct on the part of the employer and of rightful conduct on the part of the employees. If such were its meaning, the right of the employer to select, and discharge his employees ... would be cut off.

The *Sands* decision was in many regards more radical than previous rulings. In *Sands*, the court had concluded that, provided the employer had engaged in bargaining, NLRA legislation had to be interpreted so as not to otherwise constrain the employers' rights to select and discharge employees. In other words, the court indicated that any action that would effectively restrict the right of employers to discharge after basic bargaining obligations were met, could be struck down.

While both the *Jones and Laughlin Steel* and the *Sands* cases redefined space for at-will discharges in relatively broad terms, the Supreme Court's 1942 *Montgomery Ward* decision attempted to provide a more comprehensive definition of management's rights, which gave managers broad control over discharge decisions.[129] In its *Montgomery Ward* decision, the 9th Circuit excluded from arbitrable grievances:[130]

> ... changes in business practice, the opening and closing of new units, the choice of personnel (subject, however to the seniority provision), the choice of merchandise to be sold, and other questions of a like nature not having to do directly and primarily with the day-to-day life of the employees and their relations with supervisors.

Although *Montgomery Ward* supported traditional concepts of managerial rights with respect to day-to-day arbitration, it left open a number of important questions with regard to dismissals arising as a consequence of longer term strategic decisions. This included questions relating to the dividing line between a rational business decision to relocate a plant and one involving, for example, the elimination of a unionized plant—an illegal anti-union activity. Moreover, the Court's decision to exclude changes in business practice from arbitrable grievances merely prohibited unions from insisting on arbitration in these matters. It hence relieved management from the legal duty to discuss these matters in good faith rather

---

[128] NLRB v. Sands, ibid., as cited in Ralph M. Goldstein, "The Obligations of Collective Bargaining," 18 *Boston University Law Review,* 750 (1938), reprinted in Johnson, *supra* note 116, at 34.

[129] NLRB v. Montgomery Ward and Co., 133 F.2d 676 (9th Cir. 1943).

[130] NLRB v. Montgomery Ward cited in James B. Atleson, "Wartime Labor Regulation, the Industrial Pluralists, and the Law of Collective Bargaining" in *Industrial Democracy in America: The Ambiguous Promise* 164 (Nelson N. Lichtenstein and Howell Harris, eds., 1993). In Montgomery Ward, the NLRB decided that the company had not bargained in good faith because it had been unwilling to discuss its business decisions. The appeals court decided that the NLRB's order should be set aside because a trial examiner failed to grant a fair hearing.

than prohibiting union representatives from bargaining about these issues when contracts were negotiated or rendering union involvement in these matters illegal or unenforceable.

The latter issue of bargaining about alleged management prerogatives was addressed first in 1952, in *NLRB v. American National Insurance Group*.[131] In *American National*, the Supreme Court held that management could enforce limits to bargaining on the basis of a management prerogative clause, under which the union was ousted from involvement in certain matters.

American National's management prerogative clause included issues of discipline and work schedules, that is, statutory rights with respect to mandatory bargaining. The court, nonetheless, rejected the Board's position that employers were obligated to establish ongoing bargaining during the terms of the collective agreement on issues subject to defined managerial prerogatives.

While in *American National* the company had attempted to impose broad limitations on bargaining rights, many companies insisted "only" on the type of management prerogatives listed in the *Montgomery* case, such as the freedom to decide on the closure of units. In the mid-1950s, Haber and Levison reported that over 80 percent of the contracts signed in the building industries contained one or another form of a managerial rights clause. Many of these clauses explicitly prohibited bargaining over issues of job security.[132] The management literature, meanwhile, welcomed *American National* because companies were now less likely to face NLRA proceedings if they refused to discuss issues of employment security. This was the case, not only where companies had gained past assurances that union representatives would respect managerial prerogatives, but also where such clauses could be "inferred" from existing bargaining agreements.[133]

Management rights in matters of dismissals and layoffs were "clarified" further in the 1958 Supreme Court decision on *NLRB v. Wooster Division of Borg-Warner Borg-Warner*, which is discussed in James Atleson's groundbreaking monograph *Values and Assumptions in American Labor Law* on which this narrative draws heavily. [134]

In *Borg-Warner*, the Court held that there were three subjects of bargaining: mandatory, non-mandatory, and illegal. The obligation to bargain, as specified in the NLRA, applied only to mandatory subjects.

---

[131] NLRB v. American National Insurance Co., 343 U.S. 395 (1952). The origins of management rights clauses during the World War II period are further discussed in Atleson (1993), ibid., at 166.

[132] See William Haber and Harold Levinson, *Labor Relations and Productivity in the Building Trades*, at 30 (1956).

[133] See, e.g., Leonard A. Keller, *The Management Function a Positive Approach to Labor Relation*, at 33 and 49 (1963). Some industrial relations experts of this period opposed the view that arbitrable issues should be further defined. Archibald Cox and John T. Dunlop, "Regulation of Collective Bargaining by the NLRB," 63 *Harvard Law Review* 389, at 394 (1950), for instance, argued that the original intent of the NLRA was concern "with organization for bargaining—not with the scope of ensuing negotiations nor with the procedures though which they are carried on." Cox and Dunlop, at 431, suggested that there is a "choice between pragmatic private accommodations and government rulings whose formulation, however carefully considered, must be somewhat theoretical, and whose application must be uniform, rigid, and doctrinaire. Experience with private adjustments demonstrates the value of collective bargaining in this area. Accordingly the NLRB should make it plain that it is not an unfair labor practice for an employer to bargain in good faith for an agreement assigning particular subjects of collective bargaining to management's exclusive control for the duration of the contract. ... Employers who went through the motions of bargaining with their minds sealed against the possibility of finding other solutions than their own would be subject to the charge of having failed to bargain in good faith. But the useful practice of defining the area of joint management-union responsibility by collective bargaining would be permitted to continue without further government intervention."

[134] See NLRB v. Wooster Division of Borg Warner Co., 356 U.S. 342 (1958) and the analysis of this and related cases provided by Atleson, *supra* note 113 at 115 and 133.

A non-mandatory subject was "permissive," meaning that it could be raised by either party. However, when a party insisted on a position regarding such an area to the point of impasse, it was acting illegally under the provisions of the Act.[135] Since the law had defined the mandatory subjects of bargaining relatively narrowly, *Borg-Warner* played an important role in the preservation of managerial prerogatives with regard to redundancies and dismissals. Under *Borg-Warner*, union demands for job security or employment guarantees could be blocked as long as they could not be reasonably classified as mandatory bargaining items.[136]

When determining what mandatory and non-mandatory bargaining subjects were, the NLRB and the courts of the 1950s and 1960s, continued to refer to the relevant NLRA section 9(a), which mandated bargaining for pay, wages, hours of employment, and other conditions of employment. Given this basis, any issue involving pay and hours was obviously a mandatory bargaining item, requiring both parties to bargain in good faith or face sanctions through NLRB proceedings. More problematic was the clause including "other conditions of employment." When issues like redundancies, mass layoffs and mass discharges were at stake, the courts and the Board usually interpreted "other conditions of employment" to mean that union involvement in decisions about which workers were to be laid off or made redundant was mandatory.

To this effect, union representatives were to be informed about planned manpower reductions. Union representatives were free to address issues related to discharges, make suggestions with regard to manpower relocation, or suggest alternative ways of cutting costs. If the company refused, unions, however, could not insist on a settlement of the issue. While strike action relating to these matters was not *per se* illegal, any protracted industrial action on non-mandatory manpower issues could run the risk of being considered an unfair labor practice by the NLRB or the courts.[137] This approach, needless to say, left unions with little power to influence a company's manpower decisions, even in industries where levels of organization were high. Since it was often difficult to link a redundancy decision to union avoidance or to invoke contractual clauses that limited the extent of subcontracting, one avenue available to unions was to offer concessions when the threat of discharge arose.[138]

---

[135] Borg Warner can, in line with Atleson's analysis [*supra* note 113, at 124], be interpreted as a significant blow against union involvement in termination decisions. In Borg Warner, the Supreme Court implied that employees could lose the protection of section 7 if they exert pressure upon the employer concerning an item that is thought not directly to touch the employment relationship, but rather to be a "management prerogative." William B. Gould, *Agenda for Reform: The Future of Employment Relationships and the Law*, at 170 (1996), takes a similarly critical view of the mandatory/permissive distinction, which Gould views as restricting the ability of unions to bargain over issues such as job security that are of vital importance to members.

[136] See Atleson, *supra* note 113, at 120, noting that the principle that there was no requirement to bargain over such decisions, but that union representatives had to be informed about the effects of a plant closing, was established in NLRB v. Darlington Manufacturing Co., 393 U.S. 1023 (1965).

[137] Gould, *supra* note 115, at 113 and 118.

[138] In United States Steelworkers v. Warrior and Gulf Navigation Co., 363 U.S. 574 (1960), better known for the courts deference to collective bargaining agreements, the U.S. Steelworkers union filed a grievance when the company subcontracted maintenance work. The company refused to arbitrate, relying on an ambiguous management rights clause. The court decided in favor of arbitration arguing that "doubts should be resolved in favor of coverage." See Roberto L. Corrada, "The Arbitral Imperative in Labor and Employment Law," 47 *Catholic University Law Review* 919, at 928 (1998), supporting the views of Atleson, *supra* note 113. Karl E. Klare, "Judicial Deradicalization of the Wagner Act and the Origins of Modern Legal Consciousness, 1937-1941," 62 *Minnesota Law Review* 265 (1978) also suggests that the judicial support for arbitration largely furthered the interests of management.

CONCESSION BARGAINING AND JOB SECURITY

In its *Borg-Warner* decision, the Supreme Court indicated that it thought a union to have violated its duty to bargain in good faith if it induced a strike in order to force employers to offer concessions in connection with an issue that was not a term or condition of employment. This decision, together with a host of successive case law, ultimately came to severely restrict the ability of unions to influence managerial decisions on redundancy, plant closures and relocation. During the late 1970s, and the first half of the 1980s, however, redundancies became a matter of major concern to unions particularly in the manufacturing sector. An estimate by the Bureau of Labor Statistics reported that "a total of 11.5 million workers 20 years of age and over lost jobs because of plant closings or employment cutbacks over the January 1979-January 1984 period," of whom 5.1 million had worked at least three years on their job; 2.1 million had worked in manufacturing, and slightly half had been union members.[139] Some industries were hit particularly hard. Thomas Kochan, Harry Katz and Robert McKersie reported that employment among the major auto producers and parts suppliers dropped from a December 1978 peak of 800,000 to about 490,000 in January 1983. In 1983, employment in the steel industry had dropped to 44 percent of peak 1979 levels.[140] While many of these redundancies could be attributed to a decline in profitability, it has been suggested that the redundancy craze of the time also entailed elements of a disinvestment strategy that was aimed at shedding "costly" union workers and moving production to the non-unionized South.[141]

Given the limited options available, the union leadership of key manufacturing unions started granting concessionary modifications to either existing or new contracts from the early 1980s, onwards. Such concessions were no novelty to US collective bargaining. What was novel, however, was that these concessions were granted within the "orderly" system of collective bargaining established under the NLRA. During the depression of the late 1920s and early 1930s, wage concessions had been widespread, causing the real weekly earnings of those employed in 1932, to fall to more than 20 percent below 1928 levels.[142] Since the Depression, however, instances of concession bargaining had been confined to specific industries undergoing structural change, such as the shoemaking industry in the 1950s, or unionized meatpacking in the 1950s and 1960s.[143] Throughout the early 1960s, however, the

---

[139] See Paul O. Flaim, and Ellen Sehgal, "Displaced Workers of 1979-83: How well have they Fared?" 108 *Monthly Labor Review* 3, at 3 and 5 (1985).

[140] See Thomas A. Kochan, Harry L. Katz and Robert B. McKersie, *The Transformation of American Industrial Relations,* at 115 (1986).

[141] See, .e.g., Barry Bluestone and Bennett Harrison, *The Deindustrialization of America: Plant Closings, Community Abandonment and the Dismantling of Basic Industry,* at 167(1982); and Joyce Kolko, *Restructuring the World Economy,* at 327 (1988).

[142] Peter Fearon, *War, Prosperity and Depression-The U.S. Economy 1917-45,* at 140 (1987) reports that although prices fell during the depression, real weekly earnings of production workers in manufacturing declined even more severely from $24.70 in 1928 to $21.32 in 1932.

[143] See George P. Shultz, and Charles A. Myers, "Union Wage Decisions and Employment," 40 *American Economic Review* 362, 366 (1950) on concession bargaining in the shoemaking industry; and Hervey A. Juris, "Union Crisis Wage Decisions," 8 *Industrial Relations* 247, at246 (1969) on the meatpacking industry. Hem C. Jain, "Recent Developments and Emerging Trends in Labour-Management Relations in the U.S.A. and Canada," 20 *Relations Industrielles/Industrial Relations* 540, at (1965) reports on an agreement reached in 1960, between the Pacific Maritime Association and the International Longshoremen's and Warehousemen's Union in which the union agreed to permit the introduction of labor-saving devices and methods on the docks in exchange for a series of measures "to protect them against the impact of the machine of their daily work and

NLRB as well as the national union leadership looked unfavorably upon bargaining concessions, which were often attributed to employer domination.

From the mid-1960s, onwards, nonetheless, some NLRB decisions lent implicit support to concession bargaining—prompted, in part, by the recognition that a number of companies had focused on ridding themselves of "costly" union labor. In its 1965 *Metlox Manufacturing* decision, the NLRB bolstered concession bargaining by supporting a union demand for disclosure of detailed financial information in connection with a company claim of inability to pay for a wage increase.[144]

Perhaps more far reaching was the court's award of damages to the union in *Local 461 v. Singer Co.,* which resulted from a failure of the company to honor its pledge to invest $2 million in exchange for wage and benefit concessions by the union.[145]

If the courts had no objection to concessionary modifications of existing contracts, employers certainly did not. What followed, in the early 1980s, was a bonanza of concession agreements in which union representatives, threatened by employment losses agreed to a host of wage, benefit, and work-rule concessions. Peter Capelli and Robert McKersie report that in the apparel, rubber, leather, metal, machinery, transportation equipment, and trucking sectors, between 30 percent and 50 percent of all unionized employees had to assent to some form of concession. In the first half of that year alone, 210 concession bargaining agreements had been reached. Of those 210 agreements, 98 percent were triggered by threats of layoffs or plant closings, while 90 percent of all plants involved had actually experienced layoffs. Despite this link between concession bargaining and employment termination, evidence for substantial and/or immediate effects of these agreements on job security has remained tenuous. Thus, Capelli and McKersie's 1985 study reported that between 1977 and 1981, twenty-two tire plants signed concession bargaining agreements—of which 16 plants successively closed, one was sold, and only five were still open in 1985.[146] Meanwhile, a *Business Week* poll of 1983, found that only two percent of the firms surveyed were willing to give unions explicit job guarantees in exchange for concessions, with a greater willingness being noted with regard to indirect measures such as keeping plants open for the time being or maintaining production levels for a certain period.[147]

The question of immediate effects aside, McKersie and Capelli noted that, in many cases, concession bargaining had expanded the range of issues over which the parties negotiated; and in so doing impacted positively on levels of union participation in management.

---

of their job security." Jain, ibid., at 546, also discusses the Kaiser plan in which steel workers agreed to a reduction in bonuses in exchange for job security guarantees.

[144] See Metlox Manufacturing Co., 153 NLRB 1388, 1395 (1965), enfd, 378 F.2d 728 (9th Cir. 1967), cert denied, 389 U.S. 1037, which is discussed in Robert E. Bloch, "The Disclosure of Profits in the Normal Course of Collective Bargaining: All Relevant Information Should Be on the Table," 2 *Labor Lawyer* 47, at 57 (1986)

[145] Local 461 v. Singer Co., 540 F. Supp. 442 (D.N.J. 1982) is discussed in Stephen D. Shawet, "Concession Bargaining: Legal and Practical Considerations in Light of Recent NLRB and Court Decisions," 12 *University of Baltimore Law Review* 233, at 240 (1982-1983).The court specifically found that, while the company was not obliged to keep the plant running under all circumstances, its failure to honor its promise to conduct this investment amounted to a break of the bargaining agreement.

[146] See Peter Capelli and Robert A. McKersie, "Labor and the Crisis in Collective Bargaining," in *Challenges and Choices Facing American Labor*, 227, at 228 and 237 (Thomas A. Kochan, ed., 1985) citing data for the years 1981 to 1982.

[147] See Capelli and McKersie, ibid. at 230. According the business survey reported by Capelli and McKersie, 42 percent of all employers stated that they would be willing to give temporary job guarantees. On the issue of union participation in management, see also Everett M. Kassalow, "Concession Bargaining: Towards new Roles for American Unions" 127 *International Labour Review* 573, at 573 (1988).

UNIONS VERSUS THE "CORE OF MANAGERIAL CONTROL"

According to James Atleson's groundbreaking work on the assumptions underpinning US labor law, the 1960s and 1970s saw a number of major court decisions that reinforced the legal right of management to decide on what Atleson so aptly described as "core issues of managerial control." [148] When closures and relocations of unionized plants occurred, this could raise questions, either about the need for unions to be consulted or even raise suspicions of such decision being based on anti-union animus, the latter being the case especially if a closure decision weakened or even destroyed the bargaining unit. Up until the mid-1960s, it was still somewhat unclear where the dividing line between the employers' duty to inform a union of a plant or branch closing and mandatory union involvement was to be drawn.

In its 1964 decision in *Fibreboard Paper Products v. NLRB*, the Supreme Court gave an, albeit incomplete, clarification on the question as to whether partial plant closings represented a mandatory bargaining item.[149] In *Fibreboard*, the company had subcontracted maintenance work, which resulted in the elimination of an entire bargaining unit. Deciding in favor of the union, the Supreme Court ordered the reinstatement of the maintenance workers and awarded substantial backpay to them. Although representing a defeat for the company involved, the *Fibreboard* decision posed severe limitations on the unions' ability to restrict layoffs. In deciding the case in favor of the unions, the Supreme Court applied three principles. First, whether the subject matter, a branch closing, was within the literal definition of conditions of employment; secondly, whether the negotiation of the subcontract would contribute to industrial peace in the company, and thirdly, whether the practice of the industry mandated negotiations about subcontracting. The last element—the nature of subcontracting—was of particular importance in the court's decision. Said Justice Potter Stewart in a special concurring opinion:[150]

> This kind of subcontracting falls short of such larger entrepreneurial questions as what shall be produced, how capital shall be invested in fixed assets or what basic scope the enterprise shall be. In my view, the Court's opinion in this case has nothing to do with whether any of those larger issues could under any circumstances be considered the subject of compulsory arbitration.

Atleson's notes that the Supreme court was keen to emphasize the special nature of Fibreboard's subcontracting by highlighting issues such as the fact that i) the respective subcontracting decision did not alter the company's basic operation, ii) the maintenance was still be performed in the plant, and iii) no capital investment was considered, as the existing employees were merely to be replaced with others. Only after those issues had been identified was the Court willing,to conclude that reinstatement was in order., In other words, the Court was only willing to restrict management's freedom to manage subject to a number of conditions and stipulations.

---

[148] See Atleson, *supra* note 113, at 124, which informs much of the analysis of this sections
[149] See Fibreboard Paper Products Co. v. NLRB, 379 U.S. 203 (1964). The Fibreboard decision held that subcontracting was a proper bargaining subject but then applied a number of restrictive conditions as to why this was the case.
[150] See Fibreboard, ibid., as cited in Russell Smith, Leroy Merifield, Theodore St. Antoine and Charles Craver, *Labor Relations Law: Cases and Materials*, at 623 (1984); and discussed in Atleson, *supra* note 113, at 126.

These stipulations, in turn, imposed significant restrictions on unions seeking to challenge or to stop discharges and plant closings. In theory at least, if, and possibly only if, in a redundancy decision, a company's operation remained unchanged and no investment was contemplated, then was a decision to replace union labor subject to mandatory arbitration. In his analysis of the *Fibreboard* decision, Atleson highlighted Justice Potter Stewart's desire to emphasize that not "every managerial decision which necessarily terminates an individual's employment is subject to the duty to bargain," and that some decisions that clearly affected "conditions of employment are excluded because of the nature of the managerial action." For Stewart, many managerial decisions did "affect job security yet cannot be subject to mandatory bargaining; many employer decisions may imperil, or terminate employment, yet are not within the scope of bargaining," including labor-saving investments, the liquidation of assets, or decisions to close business.[151]

According to Atleson, the *Fibreboard* decision established a trajectory for future decisions on plant closings that explicitly favored management interest. Thus, most post-*Fibreboard* appellate court decisions denied mandatory union involvement in managerial decisions leading to mass redundancies. In *NLRB v. Royal Plating and Polishing*, for instance, an employer, faced with economic difficulties and the prospect of ouster by redevelopment authorities, closed one of its two plants, terminated the employees there and sold the plant machinery and equipment.[152] The capital was then used to erect a new plant on a greenfield site.

The Board found failure to bargain, but the court of appeals reversed, reasoning that it was one to "recommit and reinvest funds in the business" and "involved a major change in the economic direction of the company."[153] Similarly, in the 1965 decision of *NLRB v. Adams Dairy*, the 8th circuit decided with reference to *Fibreboard* that the dispute focused upon "a change in the capital structure of Adams Dairy which resulted in a partial liquidation and a recoup of capital investment. To require Adams Dairy to bargain about its decision would significantly abridge its freedom to manage its own affairs."[154]

A potentially even more far-reaching affirmation of managerial prerogatives was given in the 1971 Supreme Court decision on *General Motors v. NLRB*.[155] In this case, GM had converted a self-owned and -operated retail outlet into an independently owned outlet to be operated by Trucks of Texas Incorporated. When Trucks informed the former GM employees that none of them would be retained, the union sought NLRB assistance. While the UAW contended that the transaction was akin to subcontracting, Justice Clark stated that the decision was fundamental to GM's business strategy and hence beyond the reach of mandatory consultation and bargaining requirements.

---

[151] Fibreboard, ibid., cited from Atleson, *supra* note 113, at 126.

[152] See NLRB v. Royal Plating and Polishing Co., 350 F.2d 191 (3d Cir. 1965) and Atleson, *supra* note 113, at 128.

[153] NLRB v. Royal Plating, ibid., as cited in Robert A. Gorman, *Basic Text on Labor Law, Unionization and Collective Bargaining*, at 518 (1976), and as discussed in Atleson, *supra* note 113, at 128. Although rejecting the need to bargain about the closure, the court held that the employer was obligated to bargain about the effects or impact of the closing, such as severance pay, seniority and pensions.

[154] See NLRB v. Adams Dairy Inc., 350 F.2d 108 (9th Cir. 1965) as cited in Atleson, *supra* note 113, at 128.

[155] See General Motors Co. v. NLRB, 191 NLRB 951 (1971), 470 F.2d 422 (D.C. Circuit 1972) as cited in Gorman, *supra* note 153, at 520, and discussed in Atleson, *supra* note 113, at 129. General Motors was preceded by the similar—and perhaps less dramatic—case of Morrison Cafeterias Consol. Inc. v. NLRB, 431 F.2d 254 (8th Cir. 1970). In Morrison, a chain of cafeterias closed down a cafeteria after a union election victory and dealt directly with the ousted employees on questions of transfer. The court found the shutdown not in violation of the NLRA, since "there was lacking an intention to chill out unionism at cafeterias other than the one closed."

Conceptually, the argument initiated in *General Motors* was brought to a close in the 1981 Supreme Court decision of *NLRB v. First National Maintenance,* which defined the line between non-arbitrable and arbitrable components of plant closings in a manner that informed most later decisions.[156] In *First National*, a dispute had arisen between the employer and a newly certified union because of the employer's decision to terminate a service agreement with a nursing home. The appellate court of the 2nd circuit decided in favor of the union. The Supreme Court rejected the appellate court's position arguing that the court's standard—a weighing of the potential benefits of union involvement with the potential detriments—was not sufficiently precise. Justice Harry Blackmun, writing for a majority of seven, argued strongly against union participation by suggesting that "the harm likely to be done to an employer's need to operate freely in deciding whether to shut down part of its business purely for economic reasons outweighs the incremental benefit that might be gained through the union's participation in making the decision."[157] The Court, moreover, noted that since it was unlikely that the union could make the company revise its decision, the delay would only harm management's interest in speed, flexibility, and secrecy. Accordingly, Blackmun concluded that the decision to partially close a company was not a subject of mandatory bargaining. Meanwhile, the effects of this decision, including relocation allowance, retraining or severance pay, were ironically deemed to be bargaining issues because they, unlike the loss of employment, affected working conditions.

PRESERVING MANAGERIAL POWER

Although interpretations of the political ideology underpinning the NLRA differ widely, there is some consensus that New Deal elites, on the whole, tended to view the unrestricted right of management to dismiss workers as contrary to the "orderly" extension of collective bargaining.[158] This recognition of a need to protect workers from arbitrary dismissals led, among other developments, to the creation of new labor rights, which partially restricted managerial discretion in hiring and firing decisions. How these rights were to be exercised, however, was not clearly stipulated by the Act. Perhaps unsurprisingly, in the late 1930s, some legal writers considered that further legislation defining job rights more extensively was to follow. In his 1937 Beacon lecture, the constitutional scholar Corwin, for instance, had mapped out his vision of legislatively protected positive labor rights:[159]

> In the Coppage case, as was mentioned earlier, the Court had held that an employer's right to "hire and fire" was an element of such liberty, and embraced the right to force an employee to choose between his job and his labor union. In the Wagner Act cases, the Court ruled, on the other hand, that the right of employees which the act protects "to form, join or assist labor organizations," and "to bargain collectively through representatives of their own choosing" is a fundamental right, "growing out of the fact that employees are helpless in

---

[156] See First National Maintenance Co. v. NLRB, 452 U.S. 666 (1981) as discussed in Atleson, *supra* note 113, at 134.

[157] See First National, ibid., as discussed in Smith, Merifield, St. Antoine and Craver, *supra* note 150, at 632.

[158] Mark Barenberg (1993), *supra* note 114, provides a detailed exposition of orthodox and non-orthodox interpretations of the Wagner Act.

[159] See Edward Corwin, "Standpoint in Constitutional Law" in *The Constitution of the United States: Given at Boston University 1928-1938,* 407, at 427 (1938).

dealing with an employer," and that "discrimination and coercion prevent the free exercise" of this fundamental right "is a proper subject for condemnation by competent legislative authority." From a purely *negative* concept, restrictive legislative power, liberty thus becomes a *positive* concept calling for legislative implementation and protection.

The expectation of an expansion of job rights remained unfulfilled during the War years, when the imperatives of War production took precedent over the assertion of labor rights. Later on, when, during the first two postwar decades, unions challenged termination decisions, US courts tackled the problems of interpreting the new rights created by the NLRA under conditions of "normal" industrial practice very much with a view towards preserving managerial rights.

In doing so, the courts effectively reaffirmed many of the traditional managerial prerogatives in matters of plant and branch closings. As a consequence, the idea of joint union-employer decision making, which some union leaders had ascribed to the NLRA in its early years gradually eroded, being replaced by a new mainstream ideology that restricted collective bargaining to matters of pay and hours.[160]

As Atleson notes, Justice Harry Blackmun's ruling on *First National Maintenance Corp. v. NLRB*, summarized a new orthodoxy that had come to replace expectations of extended bargaining rights. In this orthodoxy, there was no room for co-determination or even for a creeping extension of labor rights. Said Blackmun: [161]

> Congress stated ... that the scope of bargaining should be left, in the first instance, to the employers and trade unions, and in the second place, to those skilled in the field ... subject to the review by the courts. Nonetheless, Congress had no expectation that the elected union representative would become an *equal partner in the running of the business* in which the union members are employed. (emphasis added)

What was particularly problematic with Blackmun's analysis was that it did not explain how "inequality" could be reconciled with the notion that unions could act as as effective representatives of employee interests. If unions were to remain attractive to potential and actual members, they had to address the very real concerns that employees had over job security within the constraints the law had created. With legal doctrine on management rights having evolved since the inception of the NLRA to severely circumscribe the unions' ability to bargain for job security, the options available to unions had become severely restricted. One approach, which neither the courts nor employers appear to have clearly foreseen, was the pursuit of job security within the context of plant level bargaining. This issue is discussed in the next chapter under the somewhat oversimplified title of "Plant Level Dismissal Protection."

---

[160] Harry Schulman (1955), *supra* note 126, at 1024 discusses older non-judicial notions of "joint lawmaking" where substantive bargaining agendas were expected to emerge relatively autonomously from the day to day interaction of unions and firms.

[161] First National, supra note 156, cited from Smith, Merifield, St. Antoine and Craver, *supra* note 150, at 627-628; see also Atleson (1983), *supra* note 113, at 134.

Chapter 3

PLANT LEVEL DISMISSAL PROTECTION

> The problem to be solved, either as a matter of theory or as a matter of practical necessity, is at bottom always the same. How can the right of combined action be curtailed without depriving individual liberty of half its value; how can it be left unrestricted without destroying either the liberty of individual citizens, or the power of Government?
>
> Albert V. Dicey, *Lectures on the Relation between Law and Public Opinion in England during the Nineteenth Century*, at 468 (1919).

During the postwar Period, it became increasingly clear that the NLRA provided US trade unions with only limited means for protecting workers from collective redundancies. While it is difficult to evidence an unambiguous causal connection, it is perhaps reasonable to assume that ongoing job insecurity, especially amongst the more prosperous unionized blue collar workforce, encouraged local union officials to support alternative, plant-based measures aimed at protecting the jobs of their members; which may in many cases have been informed by practices of the pre-NLRA period such as spontaneous stoppages and sit-down strikes. unionism.

Adopting, again, a largely chronological structure, this chapter examines the evolution of these approaches and the problems that unions encountered in their implementation. Chronologically, there is a degree of overlap with the previous chapter, which arises from the fact that plant-level bargaining for job security flourished during the period from the mid-1940s to the late 1960s. Thematically, however, the focus of this chapter is on the frequently hidden conflicts over the control of dismissals that, being often part of a legal gray-zone, fell largely outside the direct remit of the courts.

These localized conflicts are relevant to one of the central tenets of this book, which proposes that, contrary to mainstream accounts of "business unionism" that commonly imply that US union leaders paid little attention to broader and/or long-term issues, unions did indeed prioritize the long-term job security of their members but did so in a manner that lacked in prowess and effectiveness. Accordingly, this chapter suggests that simplistic notions of business unionism must be weighed against evidence of unions engaging in a host of initiatives aimed at protecting jobs out with the courts or political lobbying.[162]

---

[162] William B. Gould, *Agenda for Reform*: The Future of Employment Relationships and the Law, at 45 (1996) makes a similar point by arguing that "whatever the strength or validity of this idea (meaning American Exceptionalism)—its responsibility for American Labor's contemporary state seems diminished by other factors as well as the point that Labor's decline is an international phenomenon—the fact is that American trade unionism arrived on the scene at a relatively late period. Whether this is attributable to the individualism

This weighting must also take into account the relative, albeit temporary, success of plant level measures, if only because these "low-level" challenges of managerial authority had the potential of giving unions a false sense of control that, in turn, may have discouraged a more open questioning of the *status quo* in legislative and political arenas. In other words, once we are willing to doubt well-stablished charges of business unionism, it becomes more difficult to attribute the failure of unions to impose more significant barriers to the dismissal of their members purely to the presumption of an inherent reluctance of US organized labor to address this issue but rather must consider more complex explanations, including the possibility that unions may have focused their efforts in this area on approaches that, over time, proved to be of declining effectiveness.

With hindsight, then, it may be all too obvious that plant-level bargaining for job security could only be effective as long as unions could count on high membership densities and relatively unsophisticated management practices. However, few of the parameters that adversely affected union strength were recognizable in the first two postwar decades. Once union coverage had declined, however, it was difficult to restart the political momentum—if there was a political will to do so—if only because the broad political climate had come to disregard organized labor as a principal object of policymaking.

WELFARE CAPITALISM AND JOB SECURITY

Following the establishment of a legal framework for union organizing activity in the 1940s, some members of the US union leadership maintained a surprisingly indeterminate attitude towards the protection of members' jobs.[163] In practice this menat that many unions paid lip service to the need to provide job security, without pursuing job guarantee measures with any rigor.

Moreover, once core issues regarding the format and remit of collective bargaining had been settled, the bulk of the US trade union movement appeared to show little interest in matters of individual employment rights, such as the right to pursue a wrongful discharge

---

bound up with the frontier, the Horatio Alger Myth or, as maintained by Forbath, the law itself, is problematical."

[163] The ambiguous attitude of U.S. trade unions towards job security was discussed early on by a number of observers. Thus, Frank Tannenbaum, "The Social Function of Trade Unionism," 62 *Political Science Quarterly* 161, at 167 (1947) noted that "To make the 'job' secure has been, and has remained, the largest item in trade-union policy: to make it secure, first, and to force it to yield a high pecuniary reward, second. That these ends may be incompatible, that a high wage and 'job security' may in any given case prove destructive of each other, is a bit of economic wisdom that is hard to learn." Similarly, Arthur M. Ross, "Labor Organizations and the Labor Movement in Advanced Industrial Society," 50 *Virginia Law Review* 1359, at 1382 (1964), suggested that U.S. unions paid lip service to the need to protect the job security of members, but were largely unable to set in motion significant measures to protect jobs: "It might be argued that the demand for job security against automation tends to push collective bargaining in some common direction. If we are to judge this proposition by the results, the evidence is certainly not convincing. To be sure, the Kaiser Long-Range Sharing Plan, the West Coast Longshore Mechanization and Modernization Agreement, and the Armour Automation Fund have enjoyed worldwide publicity in industrial-relations circles. These are notable experiments, but all three of them together cover only about 50,000 workers. The lavish attention showered on these plans indicates the unsatisfied hunger for something new and different, for some sign of dramatic 'movement,' in the field of collective bargaining. Seldom before have so many words been written and so many conferences been held concerning such limited undertaking."

claim outside the frameworks of "just cause"-based arbitration and seniority-based redundancy systems.[164]

Proposals for the restriction of dismissals, and the compensation of those dismissed on the plant level, had been discussed amongst union-friendly circles throughout the 1930s. At that time, some companies had already provided arrangements where workers would be guaranteed minimum levels of employment during recessionary periods.[165] Amongst the more elaborate proposals, Sumner Slichter advocated, in 1941, the creation of a national system of "dismissal wages."[166]

Slichter urged the Federal Government to encourage firms to establish reserves for the payment of dismissal wages by permitting corporations to count part of their contributions to these reserves as a credit on their federal income tax. Specifically, he suggested that the government provide a credit on corporate income tax of as much as 50 percent or more for contributions to such funds. Unions, meanwhile, would supervise the operation of these reserves, thus being able to articulate their member's preference with regard to their use.

Sumner Slichter and Albion Taylor, who had suggested a similar plan, both justified the establishment of such subsidies on the grounds that they would provide compensation for those workers who were victimized by "automation and labor-saving devices" and thus reduce union opposition to modernization. More specifically, Taylor argued that since technological change was subsidized by the patent system, it was only fair to subsidize those who bore the costs of these investments.[167] Taylor speculated that "laborers" would enjoy a greater sense of job security because the dismissal wage would provide an incentive to reduce layoffs. Taylor, moreover, noted that "the plan for preventing the displacement of men [sic] through a dismissal wage is commendable in that it provides a strong incentive to retain, transfer, and retrain workers." [168]

A more radical approach to protecting workers from dismissals was proposed in the early works of Commons and notably his 1905 book *Trade Unionism and Labor Problems*.[169] Here, Commons proposed that instead of paying into a fund, employers should be induced to retain employees under penalty of a tax. This tax would be fixed at a certain amount per day for each person dismissed and was to be operated for either a stipulated period of time or even until re-employment. Commons's proposals for penalizing individual companies that laid off workers were based on observations made in Europe during, and immediately after, World

---

[164] Ronald W. Schatz, "From Commons to Dunlop: Rethinking the Field and Theory of Industrial Relations" in *Industrial Democracy in America: The Ambiguous Promise* 87 (Nelson N. Lichtenstein and Howell Harris, eds., 1993), highlights the strong corporatist leanings of some union leaders and arbitrators, such as Dunlop, which implied a preference for collective, rather than individual, employment rights. Katherine Van Wezel Stone, "The Legacy of Industrial Pluralism: The Tension Between Individual Employment Rights and the New Deal Collective Bargaining System," 59 *University of Chicago Law Review* 575, at 576 (1992), similarly suggests that "judicial and scholarly thinking about collective bargaining in the postwar era" has been dominated by a particular conceptions of industrial pluralism "which resists the injection of statutory or judicially-created employment rights into the workplace, promoting instead a vision of the workplace as a self-sufficient realm."

[165] See Albion G. Taylor, *Labor Problems and Labor Law*, at 234 (1940).

[166] See Sumner Slichter, "Lines of Action, Adaption, and Control," 22 *American Economic Review*, 41, at 45 (1932).

[167] See Albion G. Taylor, "Technological Change and Unemployment," *American Economic Review*, March Supplement, 60, at 60 (1932).

[168] See Taylor, *supra* note 165, at 236.

[169] See William F. Willoughby, "Public employment offices in the United States and Germany," 602, at 616, in *Trade Unionism and Labor Problems* (John R. Commons, ed., 1905).

War I. Thus, Commons and Andrews document instances where legislation was enacted in some European localities, compelling the employment of ex-soldiers and banning the dismissal of employees in certain plants.[170]

Interestingly, in 1915, the Illinois and Pennsylvania legislatures had indeed passed acts to regularize employment. At this time, restrictions on terminations for large plants were considered, but few concrete measures were undertaken primarily due to growing US involvement in the First World War. Similarly, New York's 1921 Act in Relation to Labor—ostensibly written to accommodate organized labor's new political role—declared the regularization of employment as the express public policy goal of the state. Section 530 stated to this effect that "as a guide to the interpretation and application of this article, the public policy of this state is declared as follows: Economic insecurity due to unemployment is a serious menace to the health, welfare, and morale of the people of this state." [171] In its sections on implementation, however, this policy mandate was merely interpreted to authorize the Commissioner of Labor to investigate the causes of job insecurity. Section 531 of the act explained:[172]

> One of the purposes of this article is to promote the regularization of employment in enterprises, industries, localities, and the state ... the commissioner may employ experts and may carry on and publish the results of any investigations and research which he deems relevant ... Also, to this end, the commissioner shall undertake investigations of technological developments in industry in order to obtain information necessary for evaluating the effects of such developments on the geographical, industrial, and occupational employment patterns of the state. The commissioner shall also undertake investigations of occupational training needs of workers unemployed because of technological developments...

However, it appears that the commissioner could not draw on resources to introduce measures that would indeed "regularize" employment, which suggest that the act seems to have limited the state's intervention to an investigation of the problems associated with job loss.

The labor acts of other states also appear to have lacked detailed provisions for achieving the goal of regular employment. Thus, the labor acts of the states of California and Wyoming, both passed in the period between the early to late 1920s, expressed a desire for a regularization of employment without imposing a duty on states with regard to protecting employees from job loss.[173] Overall, research into this period of state lawmaking suggests that despite the passage of of more than 130 different labor regulations, few concrete measures were undertaken to combat mass layoffs and unemployment.[174]

While the US state governments hesitated to implement concrete measures to protect workers who were dismissed or laid off, some large manufacturing companies had put a

---

[170] See John R. Commons and John B. Andrews, *Principles of Labor Legislation*, at 42 (1936).

[171] See New York State, Consolidated Laws, An Act in Relation to Labor Constituting Chapter 3 of the Consolidated Laws, Labor Law, sec 531, 1921.

[172] New York State Laws, ibid., at section 531.

[173] Wording relating to employment regularization can be found, among others, in the California Labor Code; Wyoming's Title 27, Labor and Employment; and Utah's amended Labor statute, Labor Code of the State of Utah, Title 34, Labor in General, Chap. 20, Employment Relations and Collective Bargaining, section 34-20-1, which stated that the state should ensure a "regular income for the employee."

[174] See Rebecca Holmes, "The Impact of State Labor Regulations on Manufacturing Input Demand During the Progressive Era, Dissertation Summary," 65 *Journal of Economic History* 531, at 531 (2005).

number of such schemes into place from the mid-1930s, onwards. The history of US welfare capitalism, accordingly, contains several examples of mostly unionized companies giving some form of employment guarantee or setting aside funds in order to support temporarily dismissed workers.

Albion Taylor's 1940 book on *Labor Problems* reports that during the mid-thirties, several large manufacturing companies and associations had established dismissal funds and/or given employment guarantees.[175] These included the Dennison Manufacturing Co, Procter and Gamble, and General Electric Co. The largest among these plans was that of the National Electrical Manufacturers' Association. This plan, like that of some smaller companies, essentially prohibited the permanent layoff of male full-time employees and guaranteed employment for a specified number of weeks per year. Some companies, including Procter and Gamble of Cincinnati, Fels and Co. of Philadelphia, both soap manufacturers, and the canner Conserve Co. of Indianapolis, experimented with full-time employment guarantees; apparently aimed at attracting scarce skilled workers and reducing turnover. The William Wrigley Jr. Company, meanwhile, instituted a plan of private employment assurance, which provided that workers temporarily laid off were to receive from 60 percent to 80 percent of their wages for periods varying from 16 to 28 weeks, depending on their length of service. In 1940, this plan, which included a guarantee not to lay off workers permanently, covered over 2,000 workers. The B.F. Goodrich company tried to reduce dismissals of employees during downturns by providing a voluntary early retirement plan for 21,000 workers.

Given that these measures had been instituted in a period when the collective strength of unions had declined, some union leaders may well have expected that post-World War II job security agreements could be gained relatively easily. In 1945, over 14 million Americans, about 35 percent of the workforce, belonged to labor unions, following 12 years of continuous union growth. The American Federation of Labor and the recently founded Congress of Industrial Organizations had succeeded in creating a substantial presence among manufacturing, mining, and construction workers in the Northeast and the Midwest.[176] Undoubtedly, this membership translated into political leverage with regard to national affairs;in line with the fact that the war and postwar years had brought clear advantages to unions, primarily in terms of a massive increase in union membership. The prospects for union-friendly legislation looked bright, especially when compared to previous periods of union decline and the state support for management which characterized much of the period from 1920 to and 1933.

Labor unions had also gained from their inclusion in the New Deal coalition, and this position was strengthened further during wartime when the emphasis on output led federal authorities to encourage worker representation. Wartime expansion of employment, particularly in heavy industry, and the spread of union security arrangements had sustained membership growth that coupled with automatic deductions of union dues from pay-packets had augmented the unions' financial resources.

Despite this increase in strength, many union leaders were reluctant to press individual companies for employment guarantees. This, in turn, led to criticism from external observers and some academics, who felt that trade unions should take a broader approach to the

---

[175] See Taylor, *supra* note 165, at 232.
[176] See Michael French, *U.S. Economic History since 1945,* at 91 (1997).

advancement of the interests of their members. Among the early critics of "New Deal unionism," the economist Broadus Mitchell argued in 1937, that:[177]

> American Unions have been more intent upon protecting wages than upon advancing them; they have been defensive rather than offensive in their tactics. They have cherished little idea of social change in behalf of the worker; they have been content to bargain within and accepted wage range. Particularly in the [recent] past they have clung to the "make work policy" or the "lump of work theory." That is they have believed that there is only so much work to be done and that it must be made to last by restriction of output of the worker, by going slow on the job.

Mitchell's criticism, however, appears to ignore some of the efforts made by large unions to obtain mixed systems of employment guarantees and dismissal funds from major companies. In 1945, for instance, United Automobile Worker (UAW) representatives, knowing that GM had made huge profits that due to government wage controls could not be used for wage increases, demanded that GM create a fund for workers who could not be provided with a 48-hour work week. The fund was to purchase war bonds that after the war would be used to supplement the income of workers who were put on short-time work or permanently laid off. General Motors refused to discuss the UAW plan and submitted the issue to arbitration.

The arbitration board agreed with GM that the union's demand was "essentially a profit sharing plan and is beyond the powers ... to adjudicate." The UAW made further attempts to pursue such plans and eventually, in the 1960s, forced some UAW firms to established supplementary unemployment funds.[178]

Beyond these funds, employment guarantees were generally not forthcoming; and where special policies in relation to job security were introduced, these were often limited in funding and scope. Other unions, such as the International Ladies Garment Workers Union, meanwhile, succeeded in requiring employers to contribute relatively small sums to union health and recreation funds.[179]

Perhaps because of the isolated nature of these agreements, mainstream labor history has queried why the financial and numerical strength of unions in the first two postwar decades

---

[177] See Broadus Mitchell, *General Economics,* at 442 (1936).

[178] See General Motors Co., *War Labor Reports* 22, 484 (1945) as discussed in James B. Atleson, "Wartime Labor Regulation, the Industrial Pluralists, and the Law of Collective Bargaining" in *Industrial Democracy in America: The Ambiguous Promise* 164, at 165 (Howell Harris and Nelson N. Lichtenstein eds., 1993).

[179] Aaron Levenstein, *Labor Today and Tomorrow,* at 103 (1946), gives a detailed account of these funds. Levenstein describes how up until the passage of the *Social Security Act,* unions provided most of the unemployment insurance to their members either directly or via collective bargaining agreements with certain industries. Since 1923, for instance, the clothing trade in Chicago was covered by an agreement that paid idle workers 40 percent of their wages after the first two weeks of idleness. Since the inception of the plan in 1926, 30,000 members received approximately $3,000,000 in benefits. In 1928, similar regulations were concluded for the entire men's clothing industry. In 1926, a clause was added to the Chicago arrangements that provided for a "discharge wage" of up to $500 if a worker was made permanently redundant because of technological improvements. In some cases, union insurance funds accumulated substantial amounts of capital. The Brotherhood of Locomotive Engineers, for instance, carried approximately $200 million during the mid-1920s, and paid out approximately $2.5 million each year. The Firemen's union carried about $150 million during the same period. In 1921, the national crafts union of the AFL paid out approximately $5.5 million in insurance benefits. Prior to 1929, however, only about 250,000 individuals out of a wage-earning population of about 26 million were covered by such arrangements.

did not translate into a greater impact of unions on employment regulation, with some of the claim of US exceptionalism resting on this phenomenon.[180]

In this context, it has been argued that union leaders had come to recognize that an expansion of the legal protection of workers would reduce the attractiveness of union membership, as unions monopolized these services.[181] Such claims are obviously hard to verify, since few union leaders of the time openly expressed indifference and opposition to employment regulation. What is more, there is ample support for the alternative hypothesis that rather than ignoring the need to protect workers from job loss, unions adapted their job protection strategies to an environment that favored non-legislative and local approaches.

JOB SECURITY IN THE POSTWAR PLANT

As a bargaining imperative, the job security of union members was already high on the agenda of most unions during both the war and the immediate postwar years; as was the issue of securing re-employment for returning veterans. At that time, unions feared that massive job losses, and possibly a new depression, would follow the dismembering of the war economy.

Nonetheless, in the forties, many union leaders were afraid to question the managerial prerogative with regard to manpower decisions and discharge rights. Accordingly, James Atleson cites a 1940 publication by CIO trade union officials that stated that:[182]

> To relieve the boss or the management from proper responsibility for making success of the enterprise is about the last thing any group of employees—organized or unorganized—would consider workable or desirable. The Unions are on record in numerous instances as recognizing in the last analysis that management has to manage, if any concern is to be a success financially or in any other way.

While, at least on paper, such statements appear to support the image of business unionism, the above-cited subservient acknowledgement of the right to manage was hardly matched by the record of the time. Unofficial sources record that when the UAW tackled Chrysler and then GM in the 1930s, union members defended their right to remain in plants in sit-down strikes, claiming that their jobs were a property right in the same way as employers owned their factory. Following an estimated record of 192,000 workers engaging in sit-downs in March 1937, these practices had become a common response to unwelcome managerial

---

[180] Larry G. Gerber, "Shifting Perspectives on American Exceptionalism: Recent Literature on American Labor Relations and Labor Politics," 31 *Journal of American Studies* 253, at 260 and 270 (1997), argues that "while it is a misreading of the pre-war period to view American workers and working-class politics as exceptional, or to paint too stark a contrast between the American and British labor movements, [even] revisionists acknowledge that at some point prior to World War I, a distinctive American pattern of development did begin to emerge," which ultimately let to a path where the American labor movement failed "to support an independent labour party or to become committed to a socialist vision for America."

[181] William B. Gould, "Stemming the Wrongful Discharge Tide: A Case for Arbitration," 13 *Employee Relations Law Journal* 404, at 417 (1988), argues that unions were reluctant to support just-cause legislation for non-union workers, because the provision of arbitration at the unionized workplace provided "a principal selling point for unions involved in organizational campaigns where the attempt is to reach workers concerned with job security." Gould suggests that "the union's fear has been that the availability of such procedures would erode its ability to attract new members."

[182] See Philip Murray and Morris L. Cooke, *Organized Labor and Production*, at 84 (1940), as cited in James B. Atleson, *Labor and the Wartime State: Labor Relations and Law during World War II*, at 99 (1998).

decisions, albeit that this was usually on a much smaller scale. Aleine Austin's 1949 *Labor History* cites a union song that epitomizes the sit-down as the workers' infallible prescription for all complaints and particularly for the discharge or disciplining of union members. Based on a tune composed by Maurice Sugar in the late 1930s, this song, which is said to have been widely popular in the Midwest, reads:[183]

> When they tie the can to a union man,
> Sit down! Sit down!
> When they give him the sack they'll take him back,
> Sit down! Sit down!
> When the speed-up comes, just twiddle your thumbs,
> Sit down! Sit down!
> When the boss won't talk don't take a walk,
> Sit down! Sit down!

Apart from relatively crude tactics involving wild cat strikes and sit-downs, unions bolstered the employment security of their members through various creative applications of their collective bargaining rights. One strategy, the tactic of featherbedding, involved the formal expansion of employment beyond the targets set by management through the use and negotiation of work rules and job classifications.[184]

According to figures from the Association of American Railroad Carriers, cited in a 1960 article in *Fortune Magazine*, the carriers were paying approximately 200,000 employees in engine and train services approximately $500 million more "than they should."[185] This amount roughly equaled the wage bill for an additional 60,000 railroad employees. Amongst those employed against the will of managers were about 35,000 to 40,000 railroad firemen, costing approximately $200 million, who had, according to management spokespersons, become obsolete due to diesel conversions. The same article noted that some $80 million was wasted through excess crew laws, interpretative rulings, and collective bargaining agreements that compelled carriers to employ more people than necessary.

Whether these claims were exaggerated or not, they suggest that although labor legislation, the NLRB, and the courts had made job security guarantees for union members difficult some of this had been achieved via plant and industry-specific bargaining agreements. Examining the link between featherbedding and limited formal provision of job security for union members in 1961, the industrial relations specialist William Gomberg characterized the policies involved in featherbedding as "an assertion of property rights." In

---

[183] See Aleine Austin, *The Labor Story; A Popular History of American Labor 1786-1949,* at 203 (1949). Austin suggests that these strikes were carried out with almost military precision. Accordingly, sit-down strikers made sure that the plant was properly barricaded and ensured that food and sanitation was provided. In larger and more prolonged sit-down strikes, moreover, strike committees formed self-governing bodies, which ensured that doors and gates were picketed and rules such as bans on alcohol and tobacco followed.

[184] Albert Rees, *The Economics of Trade Unions,* at 133 (1973), describes featherbedding as one of many forms of indirect bargaining over employment. George E. Johnson, "Work Rules Featherbedding, and Pareto-optimal Union-Management Bargaining," 8 *Journal of Labor Economics,* 237 (1990) suggests that that this type of bargaining over employment continues to represent a particular characteristic of the U.S. industrial relations system, with some U.S. collective bargaining agreements specifying the number of persons assigned to a machine and/or requiring negotiation about the use of new machinery. .

[185] See Gilbert Burck, "The Great Featherbedding Fight" in *Readings in Labor Economics* 424, at 427 (Gordon F. Bloom, Herbert R. Northrup and Richard L. Rowan, eds., 1963), which is an abbreviated reprint of Gilbert Burck, "The Great Featherbedding Fight" 63 *Fortune Magazine* 151, March (1960).

an article published in the *Annals of the American Academy of Political Science*, Gomberg specifically argued that in absence of job guarantees local collective bargaining provided unions with an opportunity to assert "group control" over the production process. Gomberg stressed the importance of such work rules by arguing that:[186]

> Many of the work rules define an emerging property right of the worker in his job. For example, a jurisdictional claim of a yard worker that he and he alone can handle a train in the yard and the corresponding claim of a road worker that he and he alone can handle a train on a road, stem from a property right of each craft in the particular job area ...
>
> It would be silly and pointless to deny that work in many cases could be performed more cheaply if these property rights and the penalties for their violation did not exist. In a democracy, other values than those of productivity receive equivalent attention from the community.

This benign view of job control unionism as a legitimate assertion of worker's rights, meanwhile, was perhaps predictably rejected by the political establishment of the time.
Starting in the immediate postwar period, Congress passed several pieces of legislation that were explicitly aimed at curbing union control over employment decisions. These early statutory attempts to reduce union control over jobs typically combined measures to limit "excess" employment with aggressive legislation against so-called "labor racketeering."
Amongst the first attacks on union control over manpower decisions was the Lea Act of 1946, which was targeted at a specific group of employees. This Act, also known as the Anti-Petrillo Act, in dubious honor of the then head of the Federation of Musicians, was passed as an amendment to the Federal Communication Act.[187]

Aimed at the featherbedding practices of the Federation, it declared illegal any action of unions to compel radio firms to, firstly, employ unnecessary men; secondly, pay for musicians' services not actually rendered; and, thirdly, refrain from educational broadcasting or the broadcasting of foreign programs.[188]

The provisions of the Lea Act were supposed to be implemented in a series of high-profile prosecutions. However, despite hopes that these actions would provide a decisive strike against the policies of the Musicians union, as well as other unions engaged in similar practices, the outcome of the successive legal confrontation proved disappointing to the Act's sponsors. In *United States v. Petrillo*, the Supreme Court reversed a decision of a District Court, which had held the Lea Act unconstitutional. The District Court had argued that "the definition of the numbers of workers who were necessary was so vague a criterion that to

---

[186] See William Gomberg, "Featherbedding: An Assertion of Property Rights," 333 *The Annals of the American Academy of Political and Social Science* 119, at 120 (1961).

[187] The Lea Act is also known as section 506 of the Federal Communications Act; 47 U.S.CA para. 506. Actions against featherbedding were also maintained under another criminal statute, the Copeland (Anti-Racketeering) Act, 48 STAT. 979 (1934), as amended; whereby 18 U.S.C. para.para 420a-420e (1946), as consolidated, 18 U.S.C. para 1951 (Supp. 1952) is also sometimes referred to as Hobbs, or as Hobbs-Copeland Act [see below]. These acts "provided that robbery or extortion accompanied by force or violence or threats of force or violence was a felony if it affected inter-state commerce, but expressly exempted demands for wage payments in a bona fide employment relationship;" See Anonymous Note "Featherbedding and Taft-Hartley," 52 *Columbia Law Review* 1020, at 1023 (1952).

[188] The Lea Act specifically forbade "the use of force, violence, or duress to compel the employment in the communications industry of superfluous workers. The maximum penalties are $1,000 fine and one year in prison, or both;" See Peter M. Brown and Richard S. Peer, "Anti-Racketeering Act: Labor and Management Weapon against Labor Racketeering," 32 *New York University Law Review* 965, 975 (1957).

define ... a criminal act ... constituted a breach of the Fifth Amendment."[189] Despite its
defense of the Act in principle, the Supreme Court's reasoning was indicative of the problems
any attempt to involve judiciary in second-guessing manpower decisions was like to create:[190]

> One holding of the District Court was that, as contended here, the statute is repugnant to
> the due process clause of the Fifth Amendment because its words, "number of employees
> needed by such licensee," are so vague, indefinite and uncertain that "persons of ordinary
> intelligence cannot, in advance, tell whether a certain action or course of action would be
> within its prohibition. . . ." ... And the motion to dismiss on the ground of vagueness and
> indefiniteness squarely raises the question of whether the section invoked in the indictment is
> void in toto, barring all further actions under it, in this, and every other case.
>
> We could not sustain this provision of the Act if we agreed with the contention that
> persons of ordinary intelligence would be unable to know when their compulsive actions
> would force a person against his will to hire employees he did not need. But we do not agree.
> Of course, as respondent points out, there are many factors that might be considered in
> determining how many employees are needed on a job. But the same thing may be said about
> most questions which must be submitted to a fact-finding tribunal in order to enforce statutes.
> Certainly, an employer's statements as to the number of employees "needed" is not conclusive
> as to that question. It, like the alleged willfulness of a defendant, must be decided in the light
> of all the evidence.
>
> Clearer and more precise language might have been framed by Congress to express what
> it meant by "number of employees needed." But none occurs to us, nor has any better
> language been suggested, effectively to carry out what appears to have been the Congressional
> purpose. The argument really seems to be that it is impossible for a jury or court ever to
> determine how many employees a business needs, and that therefore no statutory language
> could meet the problem Congress had in mind. If this argument should be accepted, the result
> would be that no legislature could make it an offense for a person to compel another to hire
> employees, no matter how unnecessary they were and however desirable a legislature might
> consider suppression of the practice to be.
>
> The Constitution presents no such insuperable obstacle to legislation. We think that the
> language Congress used provides an adequate warning as to what conduct falls under its ban,
> and marks boundaries sufficiently distinct for judges and juries fairly to administer the law in
> accordance with the will of Congress. That there may be marginal cases in which it is difficult
> to determine the side of the line on which a particular fact situation falls is no sufficient reason
> to hold the language too ambiguous to define a criminal offense. It would strain the
> requirement for certainty in criminal law standards too near the breaking point to say that it
> was impossible judicially to determine whether a person knew when he was willfully
> attempting to compel another to hire unneeded employees.

Conceptually, the *Petrillo* decision reflected an intriguing dilemma. In trying to protect
employers from union attempts to increase employment and prevent terminations in the
broadcasting industry, the court faced the two options of either accepting the employers'
accusations or of getting actively involved in the assessment of staffing decisions. If the court

---

[189] See Gomberg, *supra* note 186, at 125, discussing United States v. Petrillo, 332 U.S. 1 (1947). In Petrillo, the
Supreme Court upheld the Lea Act against constitutional charges of vagueness, as well as against an equal
protection challenge for the allegedly irrational exclusion of employees in the broadcast industry other than
musicians. Mr. Petrillo was nevertheless acquitted for lack of knowledge that the extra musicians for whom he
sought employment were not needed.

[190] See United States v. Petrillo, 332 U.S. 1, at 6 (1947).

accepted employer claims on overstaffing point blank, it would give employers a powerful weapon against unions, possibly one that would allow management to undo much of the progress of the past years. Unions would have faced the threat of criminal charges from any employers who had grounds to allege that the enterprise had been forced to employ an excessive number of workers. This was clearly unacceptable, and, since the courts could not, without major difficulty, assess adequate staff levels independently, the enforcement of this Act was ultimately extremely difficult.[191]

Despite a lack of legal enforcement and its limited applicability to the broadcasting industry, contemporary commentators expected the Lea Act to have an immediate effect on union leaders, who now had to reckon with a Congress willing to eliminate the "fruits" of the harsher forms of collective bargaining that some unions had adopted. Not untypical for the time, the section on the Lea Act in Raymond Bye and William Hewett's 1947 textbook *Applied Economics* concluded its chapter on labor relations with the following statement:[192]

> The constitutionality of the Lea Act was upheld by the Supreme Court in 1947... Some specific applications of the law may subsequently be declared unconstitutional, but the broad principle has been validated. Further legislation against "featherbedding" is likely to be forthcoming.

Another, no more successful, legislative attempt to reduce union influence on employment and termination decisions, the Hobbs Anti Racketeering Law, was passed at the end of the same year.[193] The Hobbs Law, an amendment to the 1934 Federal Anti-Racketeering Act, provided for the punishment of union members who interfered by means of robbery, extortion, or other violent means—defined as those causing fear of injury to the victim—with interstate commerce. While broad in its scope, the law was primarily aimed at the alleged practices of the Teamster trucking union and more specifically by the failure to gain convictions in *United States v. Local 807*.[194]

---

[191] Charles H. Tower, "Law and Labor Relations in the Broadcasting Industry," 23 *Law and Contemporary Problems* 62, at 99 (1958) notes that the Petrillo case was the only federal action under the Lea act. The series of unsuccessful cases that led to the *de facto* suspension of the Act included: In Gremio de Prensa, Radio, Teatro y Television de Puerto Rico v. Voice of Puerto Rico, Inc., 121 F. Supp. 63 (D.P.R. 1954) "the conduct complained of was found to be permitted by contract." In Lang-Worth Feature Programs, Inc. v. Manning, 27 NLRMM 2511 (N.Y. Sup. Ct. 1951) "an action by a transcription company against AFTRA [American Federation of Television and Radio Artists] alleging, "a violation of the Lea Act in connection with AFTRA efforts to compel the company to sign the transcription code," collapsed when the court found AFTRA's demand for reuse payments did not violate the law. Lastly, in Opera on Tour, Inc. v. Weber, 285 N.Y. 348, 355, 357, 34 N.E. 2d 349, 351, 353 (1941), cert. denied, 314 U.S. 615 (1941), the court ruled that "For a union to insist that machinery be discarded in order that manual labor may take its place and thus secure additional opportunity of employment is not a lawful labor objective." 7 L.R.R.M. 2511 1951, in which the New York supreme court struck down an attempt to apply the Lea Act.

[192] See Raymond T. Bye and William W. Hewett, *Applied Economics: The Application of Economic Principles to the Problems of Economic Control*, at 219 (1947).

[193] The Hobbs Act, 18 U.S.C. para.para 420a-420e (1946), as consolidated 18 U.S.C. § 1951 (1952), was an amendment to the 1934 Copeland Anti-Racketeering Act, which carried a penalty of up to twenty years' imprisonment and a $10,000 fine—rather than the maximum penalties, which are $1,000 fine and one year in prison, or both—of the Lea act. See Brown and Peer, *supra* note 188, at 975.

[194] Gomberg, *supra* note 186, at 124, notes that in United States v. Local 807, 315 U.S. 521 (1942), farmers had complained that in delivering produce to New York City, they had to pay fees, equivalent to a day's pay for a union driver, for the privilege. The unions, in denying responsibility for any violent acts, suggested that, in the past, the International Brotherhood of Teamsters had required any truck carrying produce to take on an additional driver when entering New York City. The new truck driver would then take the truck to its destination, unload it, and return it to its origin; which obviously left the original truck driver with little or

In enforcing the Lea Act, the courts had encountered difficulties in defining, for instance, what "necessary labor" was. The Hobbs Law posed a different dilemma in that, except in the most blatant cases of racketeering, the sophisticated featherbedding practices of many unions hardly took recourse to the violent actions enjoined by them. Effectively then, the Hobbs Law also did little to curb union featherbedding activities, primarily because of difficulties in establishing the evidence necessary to gain convictions.

Commenting on *United States v. General Laborers Union*, a case in which an injunction was placed on a union that forced contractors to take on additional construction workers, Gomberg concluded that: [195]

> It can readily be seen that the Hobbs-Copeland Racketeering Act becomes applicable to work rules situations where a union uses illegal means—means that would be outlawed in the pursuit of any objective at all in the pursuit of its objective. Had the union confined itself to the strike sanction without the use of threatening language or implied violent acts, the court would probably not have interfered with the union's operation. To all intents and purposes, the Hobbs-Copeland Act offers little interference in collective bargaining over work rules or alleged feather bedding.

The third major legislative piece aimed at reducing union inference with manning decisions was section 8(b)(6) of the Taft Hartley Act. In section 8(b)(6), the Taft Hartley amendment to the NLRA declared it an unfair labor practice for a union "... to cause or attempt to cause an employer to pay or deliver or agree to pay or deliver any money or other things of value, in the nature of an exaction for services which are not performed or not to be performed."[196]

Facing similar problems as those in the cases arising out of the Lea Act, the 1953 Supreme Court rulings in *Newspaper Publishers Association v. NLRB and NLRB v. Gamble Enterprise* fatally undermined the applicability of sections 8(b)(6) of the Taft Hartley Act to the fighting against featherbedding.

In *American Newspaper*, the publisher had taken action against the International Typographical Union, which insisted on resetting all of the material it received as molds or mats from other newspapers, who had already set up advertising material. By mutual agreement, this so-called "bogus" work was set in odd hours and days when no other work was available.

Investigating the Newspaper Publisher Associations' claim that this practice constituted an unfair labor practice under the Taft Hartley amendments, Justice Harold Burton, writing

---

nothing to do. The Supreme Court overruled the convictions gained under this law against the New York teamsters, on the grounds that the offer to perform the work did not constitute a "terrorist act."

[195] See Gomberg, *supra* note 186, at 124, discussing United States v. General Laborers Union, 246 F.2d 155 (1957), in which a conviction had been gained under the Hobbs Act on account of evidence that the union had used "threats of violence to persuade a contractor to use unwanted or unused laborers." Brown and Peer, *supra* note 188, at 966 observe that "whereas only a few scattered cases of labor racketeering were filed by the Department of Justice under the Hobbs Act up until 1952 ... from January 1, 1953 to December 31, 1956, seventy-eight indictments have been obtained involving one hundred seventy defendants and producing eighty-nine convictions, and new cases are being referred to the department at a rate of about forty per month."

[196] See Anonymous Note, *supra* note 187, at 1025, which notes that "Violation of para. 8 (b)(6) of the Taft-Hartley Act subjects the violator to a cease and desist order of the Board, para 10(c), or possibly to a temporary injunction before the Board, hearing, para. 10(j). However, private parties cannot get injunctions against unfair labor practices. ... In addition to the possibility of being enjoined, the featherbedder may also be required to repay what has been exacted."

for the majority, took a much broader view of collective bargaining than many member of Congress may have anticipated:[197]

> The Act now limits its condemnation to instances where a labor organization or its agents exact pay from an employer in return for services not performed or not to be performed. Thus, where work is done by an employee, with the employer's consent, a labor organization's demand that the employee be compensated for time spent in doing the disputed work does not become an unfair labor practice. The transaction simply does not fall within the kind of featherbedding defined in the statute.... Section 8(b)(6) leaves to collective bargaining the determination of what, if any, work, including bona fide "made work," shall be included as compensable services and what rate of compensation shall be paid for it.

Again writing for the majority, Justice Burton was equally explicit in refusing to enforce the Act in the *Gamble* case. In *Gamble*, the Musician's union had demanded that whenever a "name band" was employed, a local band had to stand by to play for intermissions. Here, Burton argued that:[198]

> Payments for standing by or for the substantial equivalent of standing by are not payments for services performed, but when an employer receives a *bona fide* offer of competent services, it remains for the employer through free and fair negotiation to determine whether such an offer shall be accepted and what compensation should be paid for the work done.

While the courts had resolved the dilemma of judging managerial prerogatives in relation to the "Lea cases" by handing down an essentially ambiguous judgment, they returned the ball to the field of collective bargaining in dealing with section 8(b)(6) of the Taft Hartley Act. In both instances, the courts were reluctant to engage in technical judgments on manpower needs.

Unwilling, or unable, to investigate the factual basis of disputed management claims on appropriate staffing levels and work practices, the courts responded to the challenges posed by section 8(b)(6) with retreat.

By implication, this suggested that because management claims on necessary manpower were on their own not credible evidence of union misconduct, such actions could not be readily enforced and, therefore, would have to be dealt with within the realms of the collective bargaining system. This, in turn, encouraged some legal commentators to question whether, at least for the time being, legislative intervention was at all warranted in this area, as is exemplified by this conclusion to a 1953 law review article:[199]

---

[197] See American Newspaper Publishing Association v. NLRB, 345 U.S. 100 (1953), cited in Benjamin Aaron, "Governmental Restraints on Featherbedding," 5 *Stanford Law Review* 680, at 709 (1953); and also Gomberg, *supra* note 186, at 127.

[198] See NLRB v. Gamble Enterprises Inc., 345 U.S. 117 (1953), cited in Gomberg, *supra* note 186, at 127.

[199] See Aaron, *supra* note 197, at 721. Notwithstanding Aaron's proposition that the limited harm caused by featherbedding would not justify the massive legislative intervention that may be required in preventing it, there seems to be marked tendency for the topic to have reappeared in periods of economic downturns. Thus, and Anonymous Note, "Drafting Problems and the Regulation of Featherbedding - An Imagined Dilemma," 73 *Yale Law Journal*, 812, at 849 (1964) suggests a position that is diametrically opposed to Aaron's analysis in stating that: "The costs of regulation, both in relation to immediate and precedential effects on the bargaining process, previously believed prohibitive, have been shown to be within reason. It is on the subject of the gain to be derived that a regulatory decision must turn, and a legislator's decision to opt for regulation

The review in this article of the experience with various statutory restraints on featherbedding indicates the difficulty of legislating against objectives rather than against the means by which they are achieved. The dangers inherent in such an approach seem substantially to outweigh the potential benefits, if any. No attempt to draft the statutory prohibition in such a way as to exclude acceptable objectives without rendering the provision nugatory has been successful so far, and there can now be discerned a regrettable tendency to adopt broad and inclusive language which would prohibit demands for anything regarded by the employer as useless or unnecessary. A move in this directions seems unwarranted for two reasons: first, because it is fundamentally inconsistent with our national labor policy of collective bargaining, and second, because the problem of featherbedding is not so serious a threat to the economy as to require governmental control.

Ironically, the Supreme Court had now come to defend the integrity of the very collective bargaining system whose creation it had so staunchly opposed up until the mid 1930s.

In doing so, it implicitly bestowed a level of legality on a gray-zone of bargaining over job security that the unions had gradually been able to establish over a number of years. Discussions about crew size, job classifications, work rules and similar issues, which as "conditions of employment" were mandatory bargaining items, had become a partial substitute for the bargaining for job security, which court decisions such as *Fibreboard* and *First National* had forestalled.

Initially, there was little the employers or the courts could do to constrain the new job control unionism. For employers to act against could create difficulties because such measures potentially violated the duty to bargain in good faith and to refrain from unfair labor practices. For the courts, meanwhile, the imposition of legal restrictions on such practices had proven difficult, both because of a lack of expertise in manpower matters and because of a "natural" unwillingness to interfere with managerial decision making. Unable to achieve recognition of union demands for job security in key labor cases, and excluded from formal manpower decisions, unions had thus been able to create some measure of job security by controlling the production process on the plant level. In this sense, at least during the first two postwar decades, the US union structure appeared to be better suited to affect job security on the micro-, or meso-, level of plant bargaining than it had been in gaining such protection through legislative initiatives.

With the evidence suggesting that job control unionism was widespread, it is not impossible to argue that the very success of these measures at the plant level—rather than an ideological commitment to business unionism—may have distracted unions from engaging in more lasting efforts to efforts to restrict terminations. Indeed, the sheer pervasiveness of job control unionism seems to suggest that plant-level measures to increase job security were as much part and parcel of the US culture of collective bargaining as were more direct forms of political lobbying.

Accordingly survey of collective bargaining agreements have continued to confirm the presence of "featherbedding-type" arrangements. As one example of this, tThe industrial relations expert Stephen Allen, noted that a 1979 survey of agreements covering almost half the union work force in the building trades "… found that almost 20 percent of their sample contracts contained crew-size restrictions. … Assuming that management would utilize 10

---

must be based on a favorable outlook as to the viability of the economy, as to the ability of the economy to limit unemployment with or without governmental aid, and as to the ability of the government to salvage significant portions of the waste of men without jobs."

percent fewer workers for 10 percent of the tasks assigned to these crafts … crew-size provisions result in an annual excess cost of $42 million"[200] While estimates, past and present, regarding the extent and significance of featherbedding in US industry appear to diverge widely, it is clear that job control unionism has remained a recurrent theme and defining characteristic of US industrial relations, leading to that topic becoming a recurrent public policy concern during periods of economic downturns.[201]

ARBITRATION

While featherbedding in its various incarnations represented a proactive attempt at preventing terminations by controlling workloads, unions of the early postwar decades also engaged in a host of retroactive measures to protect members who were threatened with dismissal or had already been dismissed. These retroactive measures were primarily implemented through the grievance arbitration process and involved the prevention and delay of the dismissal of individual workers or groups of workers.

During World War II, and the immediate postwar years, managerial authority over disciplinary matters appears to have been comprehensive. Thus, although the War Labor Relations Board held that disciplinary matters were subject to arbitration, it generally supported the notion that management had the authority to take prompt action against employees, including suspending or removing an employee, pending investigation. Accordingly, a 1945 paper by Jesse Freidin and Lloyd Ulman, two influential members of the War Labor Relations Board, was able to state that "arrangements have never been directed whereby the unions' approval must be sought before discipline can be meted out."[202]

In the 1950s most labor agreements contained a lengthy list of grounds for discharge, which included the violation of company rules; failures to meet work standards;

---

[200] See Stephen G. Allen, "Union Work Rules and Efficiency in the Building Trades," 4 *Journal of Labor Economics*, 212 at 217 (1986); citing *Business Roundtable, Constraints Imposed by Collective Bargaining Agreements. Construction Industry Cost Effectiveness Project Report C-4*. New York: Business Roundtable, September 1982.

[201] Mindy Schwartz, "American Federation of Musicians: An Unearned Encore for Featherbedding," 47 *Wayne Law Review* 1339, at 1355 (2001), for example, examines ongoing practices of featherbedding in the U.S. music industry, which includes the employment of "walkers," or unneeded local musicians hired in cities when a Broadway-type show performs on tour; the term "walker" having originated from the fact that that the musicians never play a note but simply "walk in" to collect their paychecks.

[202] See Jesse Freidin and Lloyd Ulman, "Arbitration and the War Labor Board" 58 *Harvard Law Review* 309, at 355 (1945), where the authors note that "Rejecting the view that final determination of what is a just cause for discharge is exclusively a management prerogative, the Board has nevertheless strongly supported management's authority to take prompt disciplinary action, including ordering an employee from the job, suspending him pending investigation or a hearing of his case, and discharge, subject to the right to have the discharge heard as a grievance. Arrangements have never been directed whereby the union's approval must be secured before discipline can be meted out." Freidin and Ulman further cite two cases in support of their view. In Brewster Aeronautical Co., N. W. L. B. No. III-3372-D, 12 WLR 40 (Oct.29, 1943) an "arrangement of that kind … was changed by the parties in conferences in which a Board representative participated, so as to restore to management its initial power to discipline." In Norge Machine Products Division of Borg-Warner Corporation, N. W. L. B. No. III-5665-D, I5 WLR 652 (April 27, 1944), forty-one employees walked off the job because the company refused to fire three employees because of their high productivity. The Board confirmed the right of management to discipline these workers and "directed that any of the forty-one employees might apply for reinstatement, and that management should decide whether or not he would be reemployed, and whether with or without seniority on the basis of his individual responsibility for the stoppage."

incompetence; the violation of the collective bargaining contract, including the instigation or participation in a strike or slowdown in violation of the agreement; excessive absenteeism; intoxication; dishonesty; insubordination; wage garnishments; and fighting on company property.[203]

By the 1960s, such formal grievance procedures for the implementation of just-cause dismissals had become widespread, even in the South and in Southern non-unionized plants; and a 1962 survey of southern companies reported that 54 percent of all non-union firms had formal grievance procedures, while 97 percent of union plants provided for such arrangements. [204] Most collective bargaining contracts, moreover, contained the general statement that an employee could be discharged only for just-cause. In addition, bargaining agreements commonly contained clauses formally specifying the number, duties, and rights of job stewards.

Many unions, meanwhile, felt that it was one of their principal tasks to ensure adequate representation at the level of shop floor relations. This representation ultimately rested on the strength of the individual union. In some industries, where unions possessed this strength, the use of these committees in regulating the labor relations of a plant was extensive. A 1962 article in *Industrial Relations* cites the case of a company of over 2,000 employees, which paid approximately $300,000 in wages each year to stewards for the handling of grievances; these stewards processed approximately 1,500 grievances every year, being paid almost $275 for each written grievance.[205]

In day-to-day practice, the critical interpretation of just-cause was based on industrial practice and court decisions, with unions pushing for an increased control over initially very broad notions of just-cause. Arthur Sloan and Fred Witney's *Labor Relations*, a popular textbook in this field, noted in its 1972 edition that the largest percentage of arbitration cases in manufacturing companies involved discharges. Sloan and Witney suggested that this was due to the fact that the unions' acceptance of permissible causes had gradually diminished.[206]

In the fifties and sixties, most unions had insisted that rather than listing one or more specific grounds for discharge, collective bargaining agreements should distinguish between

---

[203] See, e.g., Arthur A. Sloane and Fred Whitney, *Labor Relations*, at 420 (1972), which exemplifies the type of lists of just causes for dismissals that could still be found in most industrial relation textbooks of the 1970s and 1980s.

[204] See H. Ellsworth Steele and Homer Fisher, Jr, "A Study of the Effects of Unionism in Southern Plants" 87 *Monthly Labor Review* 258, at 264 (1964). Philip Selznick, "The Moral Commonwealth: Social Theory and the Promise of Community," at 306 (1992), notes how grievance and arbitration agreements achieved a quasi-governmental status during the heydays of collective bargaining in the Supreme Court ruling on Steelworkers v. Warrior and Golf, 363 U.S. 574 (1960) which stated that "the collective bargaining agreement states the rights and duties of the parties. It is more than a contract; it is a generalized code to govern a myriad of cases, which the draftsmen cannot fully anticipate ... The collective agreement covers the whole employment relationship. It calls into being a new common law, the common law of a particular industry or of a particular plant."

[205] See George Strauss, "The Shifting Power Balance in the Plant," 1 *Industrial Relations* 65, at 87 (1962). Stephen B. Goldberg, "Mediation of Grievances under a Collective Bargaining Contract: An Alternative to Arbitration," 77 *Northwestern University Law Review* 270, at 274 (1982), cites reports suggesting that the arbitrator's daily fee had increased from a range of $150 to $225 in 1972, to an average daily fee of $275 by 1980, while the average arbitrator's charge per case, exclusive of all other costs of arbitration, were approximately $1,000; See *33rd Annual Report*, Federal Mediation and Conciliation Services, at 37 (1981). Goldberg further notes that "Costs in excess of $2,000 for arbitrating a single grievance are not uncommon. Delay also presents a serious problem. According to the most recent report of the Federal Mediation and Conciliation Service (FMCS), an average of 163 days-over five months-elapsed from the conclusion of the internal steps of the grievance procedure to the issuance of the arbitrator's award."

[206] See Sloane and Witney, *supra* note 203, at 420.

causes for immediate discharge and employee offenses, which would require only a warning. A large number of bargaining agreements then specified, usually on the demand of union representatives, elaborate procedures for the discharge of union members or those covered by a collective bargaining agreement.

Frequently, unions ensured that a lesser form of discipline be agreed upon, even though the employer had grounds for discharge. Labor agreements typically provided that a discharge case had priority over all other grievances. In addition, many agreements waived the first steps in the grievance procedure and started a discharge case at the top of the procedural ladder, thus ensuring that high-level union representatives would be involved in the proceedings.

The effectiveness of these policies was obvious: a 1959 analysis of published arbitration awards showed that the penalty imposed by management was lowered in 20 percent of all disciplinary and in 36 percent of all discharge cases.[207] Similarly several quantitative studies were able to confirm the job-security enhancing effects of these practices.

In 1980, the labor economist Richard Freeman, for instance, published an analysis using data from the Panel Study of Income Dynamics and the National Longitudinal Survey of Young Men, which showed that trade unionism was "associated with significantly greater job tenure and conversely with significantly lower probabilities of separation."[208] Freeman's study implicitly attributed the reduction in the number of dismissals to grievance systems, or more broadly the "industrial jurisprudence mode of operation," rather than monopoly effects of unions, as previous studies had done.

Analyzing the gradual expansion of grievance systems, Philip Selznick's 1969 monograph *Law, Society and Industrial Justice* concluded that the elaboration of formal rules, which had taken place from 1945, onwards, had created expectations regarding the consistency and fairness of managerial action.[209] For Selznick, the increased formalization of industrial relations had created a commitment to industrial justice that was shared by organized labor and management. Workers now expected that management would not act in a discriminatory and arbitrary manner.

Discipline would still be exercised, but the rules according to which it would be meted out would follow predictable standards; or as Selznick suggested, because the rule was double edged, limiting the rule maker and the potential offender, the formalization of American industrial relations had become a major source of self-restraint on for both unions and management. This did not mean that personnel policies no longer grew out of the self-interest

---

[207] See Orme W. Phelps, *Discharge and Discipline in the Unionized Firm,* at 122 (1959).

[208] See Richard B. Freeman, "The Effect of Unions on Worker Attachment to Firms," *National Bureau of Economic Research Working Paper* No 400, at 39 (1980), also published as Richard B. Freeman, "The Effect of Unions on Worker Attachment to Firms," 1 *Journal of Labor Research* 29 (1980). Freeman's working paper [at 34] reports that 98.8 percent of all major collective bargaining agreements included grievance clauses, and 96.1 percent included arbitration clauses.

[209] See Philip Selznick, *Law, Society and Industrial Justice*, at 84 and 86 (1969). Selznick's argument about the link of rule-based company governance and "managerial self-restraint," is based on a comparison with traditional models of pre-war non-unionized plants, and Sleznick cites several surveys that provided evidence for the growth in the adoption of formal personnel policies. These include William R. Spriegel, and Alfred G. Dale, "Personnel Practices in Industry," *Personnel Study* No 8 (1954), which reports that in a 1947 survey of 325 firms, 46 percent had written personnel policies, whereas a 1952 sample of 628 firms identified 67 percent of all forms as having such policies; and Bureau of National Affairs, "Disciplinary Practices and Policies," *Personnel Policies Forum Survey* No 42 (1957), in which 160 personnel managers of a stratified sample of companies reported that in 1957, three out of four companies had written personnel rules.

of management, but it meant that where efficiency dictated it managers were willing temper their own authority.[210]

The remit of discharge arbitration, however, typically extended only to individual workers or small groups of workers who were accused of some form of misconduct. It rarely covered discharges for economic reasons or permanent layoffs. For these types of terminations, an additional set of rules, embodied in the seniority system, came into play. Seniority rules with regard to promotion, layoffs, and rehire represented the core of most written personnel policies on redundancies.

According to Selznick, almost all collective bargaining contacts he surveyed around 1965, included a seniority provision, which he assumed to have been fairly readily granted, especially in connection with the regulation of layoffs.

The management literature of the immediate postwar years had indeed actively encouraged the adoption of the seniority standard on two grounds. Firstly, conceding to the seniority rule was deemed rational because of the absence of other adequate rules. Applying seniority to temporary or permanent terminations, said Selznick, provided for "objective criteria that [c]ould ... be applied easily, [and] systematically and with beneficial effects on employee morale." Secondly, the seniority rule was assumed to have beneficial effects on employee morale. Seniority, as an "impersonal standard," was expected to "minimize discrimination and favoritism in matters affecting a worker's job" and hence provided a key component in the maintenance of "sound labor-management relations."[211]

During the 1960s and 1970s, a heavy reliance on temporary layoffs in unionized plants went hand in hand with the application of seniority rules in the selection of workers. In 1979, the economist James Medoff concluded, on the basis of data from 1958 to 1971, that labor adjustment in US manufacturing took a "substantially different form under unionism than in nonunion settings."[212]

According to an econometric analysis by James Medoff, union firms relied more heavily on temporary layoffs than on wage cuts, reductions in hours, and discharges; as compared to similar nonunion firms. Medoff further observed that laid-off union members typically returned to their previous jobs after only a short spell of unemployment. He concluded that because of the subsidies provided through the unemployment insurance system union firms were able to provide greater protection from permanent termination than nonunion firms did.

This benign view of layoffs, however, was closely associated with the period before 1980. From the early 1980s, onwards, layoffs increasingly became the route to permanent job loss. In 1982, for instance, 6.2 million workers were on layoff, of which 4.1 million—over 66 percent—resulted in permanent job loss.

---

[210] Selznick's optimistic view of modern personnel practices was typical of several industrial relations scholars of the 1960s. Thus, Clark Kerr, John T. Dunlop, Frederick Harbison, and Charles Myers, *Industrialism and Industrial Man: The Problems of Labor and Management in Economic Growth,* at 216 (1960) similarly suggested that there had been a global transformation of capitalism whereby "The elite regards the class of industrial workers as fellow citizens. The web of rules is largely established jointly by management and workers in direct negotiations within a framework of procedural rules established by government with participation by workers' organizations and management."

[211] See Selznick, *supra* note 209, at 88, where Selznick surveys a number of studies including John J. Speed, and James J. Bambrick, "Seniority System in Non-Unionized Companies," *Studies in Personnel Policy* No 110 (1950).

[212] See James L. Medoff, "Layoffs and Alternatives under Trade Unions in U.S. Manufacturing," 69 *American Economic Review* 380, at 394 (1979).

In 1989, of about 570 thousand workers experiencing layoffs in excess 30 days, 360 thousand had lost their jobs by 1990. Interestingly, the number of those on layoff for over 30 days in manufacturing—about 270 thousand—was smaller than the number of jobs lost in manufacturing during the same period (about 330 thousand).[213]

Today, we would view seniority and layoff policies perhaps more critically than Selznick and other writers of the 1960s and 1970s did. For management, the adoption of the seniority rule was not primarily about providing a sense of security to employees but rather presented a means of facilitating reductions in wage costs in the absence of militant union responses. Terminations were redistributed through seniority rules, but they were not necessarily reduced by them.

By formalizing the procedure through which workers whose employment was to be terminated were chosen, seniority arrangements allowed management to distract workers from the actual job insecurity they experienced. Likewise, decisions to permanently lay off workers, which continued to be part of the managerial prerogative, were obfuscated and given a quasi-legal standing through the adoption of the abstract, formal standard of seniority.. As long as the number of permanent layoffs stayed relatively small, any criticism of these actions could be countered by employers and union representatives as showing a lack of solidarity or an element of disrespect for established customs and practices. In addition, assurances about future recalls could act as a means for tempering opposition to termination decisions.

The system of industrial justice that Selznick and some of his contemporary commentators saw as making inroads into a more democratic form of workplace governance, arguably, did not center on the creation and implementation of a stable set of employment rights. Rather, it was about creating convenient and palatable means for pursuing managerial agendas, given the constraints imposed in some industrial sectors by then seemingly powerful unions.

Many of the cases reported in industrial relations textbooks and casebases, perhaps unsurprisingly, convey a picture where "industrial justice" was often little more than a misnomer for bargaining for job security.[214] While management tinkered with the application of "just" discharge causes, unions creatively used the grievance system to forestall "bogus" discharges as well as dismissals for previously acknowledged causes. This, in part, provided unions with a chance to bolster dismissal protection beyond what the actual letter of the agreement would have permitted. Labor relations textbooks and case collections are rife with incidents in which disciplinary proceedings, including discharges, were held off through employee grievances. Thus grievances about safety and health issues were cited to justify the

---

[213] The 1982 layoff and job loss estimates are from Paul Osterman, and Thomas A. Kochan, "Employment Security and Employment Policy," in *New Developments in the Labor Market* 155, at 157 (Katherine Abraham and Robert B. McKersie eds., 1990). The 1989 estimates were derived from the BLS survey, *Mass Layoffs*, various years. The high rate of job loss associated with layoffs in 1989 was due to a wave of corporate restructuring, buyouts and mergers, as well as, in the case of manufacturing, cuts in the defense industry. In this specific context, it made little sense for firms to put workers on layoff with promises of recall. The high rate of job loss relative to layoffs during the 1980s had been due to a wave of bankruptcies, partial and full plant closings, which ultimately led to massive job loss. Medoff's analysis, relying on data up until 1971, does not capture these developments.

[214] Morris Stone, "Why Arbitrators Reinstate Discharges Employees," 92 *Monthly Labor Review* 47, at 47 (1969), presents a survey that identified "Mitigating circumstances," "Inconsistent enforcement of rules," Poor applicability of published schedules of penalties "(Making the punishment fit the crime)," Lack of evidence, Procedural errors, Substantive errors and "The limited reach of discipline" as the main causes that allowed arbitrators to reinstate discharged workers.

violation of company rules, failure to meet standards, insubordination or even wild cat strikes. Company production standards and manning were criticized by union representatives in direct response to management complaints about the low productivity or incompetence of a worker. Automation and the introduction of new machinery similarly were used to justify slowdowns, and, in some cases, absenteeism.

The nature of the arbitration process itself allowed for contentious "reinterpretations" of arbitrable issues. Once a case had gone to arbitration, the arbitrators were typically concerned with the quality of proof that management or union representatives provided, and hence tended to be critical of employer claims if they were countered by union statements about inadequate working conditions.[215] Union representatives were further helped by what industrial relations lawyers have referred to as the "cardinal rule" of the arbitration process: namely, the rule that a discharge "must stand or fall upon the reason given at the time of the discharge."[216]

That grievances occurred before, or while, management undertook disciplinary measures or proposed terminations for economic reasons does not derogate the legitimacy of such grievances. Since it is unreasonable to expect workers to perform faultlessly if working conditions are inadequate, the boundary between a "legitimate grievance" and a "makeshift grievance" is often a fuzzy one. In this sense, "creative" uses of the grievance system illustrate the limits of fact finding within such systems rather than providing evidence for "unethical" conduct by either party. On the whole, there is probably little point in examining whether unions or employers did in the past abuse the grievance system. What is more important is to recognize that the grievance mechanisms established in the first postwar decades provided an important instrument for unions in their day to day fight dismissals and their effort to assert employees' rights to a secure job. [217]

---

[215] Selznick, *supra* note 209, at 92. Selznick partly concedes this point by stating that "there are fundamental limits upon its [meaning the firm's] capacity to make decisions in the spirit of legality: (1) The enterprise is not mainly in the business of dispensing fairness. Its primary obligation, as seen by responsible leaders is to ensure survival and growth by getting the job done... (2) Bureaucratic authority is not easily checked and challenged from below ... For most employees there is no adequate opportunity to check the rules themselves in the course of presenting grievances." Edwin F. Beal, Edward D. Wickersham, and Philip K. Keinast's *The Practice of Collective Bargaining,* at 507 (1976), notes that both courts and arbitrators affirmed highly questionable grounds for dismissal. In the Cutter Laboratories case of 1955, the arbitrator refused to uphold a discharge of a lab worker on the grounds of Communism. In this case, the California supreme court overruled, saying that the employee "as a Communist was not at any time or in any of her activities truly serving an American labor union ... she was but doing the bidding and serving the cause of her foreign master who tolerates no deviation and no debate" [23 LA 715 (1955)]. According to another arbitrator, the *New York Times* was justified in discharging an employee who admitted that he had been a member of the Communist party because he worked in a "sensitive" position—the rewrite desk.

[216] See Alan Carlson and Bruce Phillip, "Due Process Considerations in Grievance Arbitration Proceedings," 2 *Hastings Constitutional Law Quarterly* 519, at 532 (1974), suggesting that the dictum that "The discharge . ... must stand or fall on the reason given at the time of the discharge" dates back to West Virginia Pulp and Paper Co., 10 Lab. Arb. 117, 118 (1947) (Guthrie, Arbitrator); and the dictum that "The company may not properly be permitted to state only some of the charges against the employee and then later defend its discharge action upon the basis of additional charges to which the employee . . . had not an opportunity to reply" traces its origins to Bethlehem Steel Co., 29 Lab. Arb. 635 (1957) (Steward, Arbitrator).

[217] There is some disagreement about the economic effects of just-cause standards. Whereas the older literature typically considered just-cause regulations as an obstacle to the efficient operation of firms and labor markets, some recent analyses have adopted a different view. Thus David I. Levine's, "Just-Cause Policies when Unemployment is a Worker Discipline Device," 79 *American Economic Review* 902, at 902 (1989), suggests that "moving toward just-cause (that is, increasing the evidence required for a dismissal) can increase efficiency." This is the case because "private calculation of the costs of a dismissal policy ignores the

For the late 1960s, in particular, when the first major automation wave swept through US industry, there is ample anecdotal evidence that localized bargaining became a source of, albeit temporary, job security. The following case illustrates the point. During the sixties, some companies had negotiated maximum attrition clauses—a nonmandatory bargaining item—with certain small occupation groups. One such agreement between Southern Pacific Railroad and the Order of Railroad Telegraphers placed an upper limit of two percent on the number of jobs that could be abolished for any reason in a given year, not including attrition by natural causes such as retirement or voluntary quits. Surveying this and other agreements in 1963, Derek Bok and Max Kossoris observed that:[218]

> If they [meaning the employers] are bound to follow attrition by agreement, temptation may arise to hasten departure of employees by imposing onerous working conditions or otherwise make the job less attractive. Further controversy may result if the agreement does not answer such questions as to whether employee must agree to transfer or to accept more demanding positions and assignment in order to remain on the payroll.

This agreement, perhaps more than many other examples, illustrates the blurring between different types of dismissals and instruments for their regulation. For many union representatives, the availability of grievance was important—not because employers wanted to rid the company of one or several troublesome workers, but rather because it also enabled them to fight management decisions to dismiss workers that were based on economic purely considerations. In this, as in other cases where no attrition quotas were imposed, localized bargaining and grievances provided at least a means of delaying discharges.

THE REASSERTION OF MANAGERIAL RIGHTS

While initially relying on the in-house grievance process, unions during the seventies brought an increasing number of cases before the NLRB. From 1965 to 1980, the number of cases in which the NLRB offered reinstatement to workers roughly doubled with approximately twice the number of workers, about 10,000, being reinstated in 1980.[219] Over the same period, employer charges against unions and from 1967, onwards, employee against union charges also increased at a similar proportion. This increase in the litigiousness of all parties reflected, among other things, the less tolerant attitude that management had adopted towards "union interference" in "management matters," as well as the generally greater inclination toward the restructuring of company operations.

By the early 1970s, more aggressive and more sophisticated management tactics appear to have led to an increased reliance by unions on the NLRB. According to Strauss, the management of many large companies had started adjusting to the challenge of union interference by adopting new strategies. One of these strategies—relevant with regard to the right to discharge—was to deny concessions between contract negotiations and to make disputed issues part of the bargaining process. Many managers saw the elimination of

---

externality ... [that] the hiring rate increases. The increased hiring rate reduces the expected duration of unemployment for other firms."

[218] This is cited from Sloane and Whitney, *supra* note 204, at 430 (1972).

[219] Robert J. Flanagan, *Labor Relations and the Litigation Explosion*, at 29 (1986).

flexibility in arbitration, and the movement away from a problem-solving attitude, as a key prerequisite to the reconquest of managerial prerogatives. In his 1962 article, Strauss quotes one personnel manager as saying:[220]

> [Before my time] the union made all its gains through "creeping"—establishing all the precedents they could. Now, we make the contract creep for us. If nothing prevents us from changing a condition in our favor we will change it ... Now I have a feeling of health. I am captain of the ship ... [Six months after I took over] the union chairman blew his stack. He felt things had been taken away from him day by day.

The picture that emerges from a review of the industrial relations literature on management control of the late sixties and seventies is that union inroads on managerial prerogatives were being gradually rolled back through a number of measures. Strauss himself cites a 1959 news report that encapsulated much of the spirit of the period:[221]

> It is the employers who are on the march this year, taking the offensive after a quarter of a century of what they consider undue subservience to "monopolistic" unions...the feeling of many leaders of the main production industries is that they have ridden the wage-price tandem to the last stop is reinforced by a belief that investments in friendly union relations have not paid off in heightened plant efficiency...The aim of the corporate rebellion is to restore management's initiative at the bargaining table and in the plant. This determination to climb back into the driver's seat was emphasized by the industry in the pre-truce negotiations in steel. "You have been pushing us around for eighteen years and we're going to stop it," was the blunt way one of them put it ...

As a consequence of these attitudes, the use of job control or the grievance system as a tool of restricting the termination of union members became gradually more difficult to apply. For unions, difficulties arose from two sources: the increased sophistication of personnel management policies and, perhaps more importantly, a decline in union densities in key industries.[222] Since plant-level bargaining had become a major feature of ensuring the job security of individual workers, the combined effects of both developments had a dramatic impact on the job security prospects of union members and the US workforce as a whole.

In the first three postwar decades, unions had, by and large, sustained the spectacular gains they made since the 1930s, although the earlier momentum had diminished. In the early 1980s, however, absolute numbers of union members had started to fall rapidly. Total union membership had risen unsteadily, from 14.3 million at the end of the war to 16.8 million in 1955, and 19.3 million in 1970, with the fastest growth occurring during the economic upswings of the early 1950s and the late 1960s.[223] As a proportion of the total labor force,

---

[220] Strauss, *supra* note 205, at 86.

[221] Strauss, ibid., citing "Labor: A New Era of Bad Feelings" *New York Times Magazine* 8, July 51959). Selnick, *supra* note 209, at 115, also commented critically on the manipulative nature a new generation of personnel policies by stating that "the individual is not seen as a goal achieving creature. Rather he is considered an inert 'element' that does not act unless acted upon and manipulated by means of human relations 'skills.' The aim of human relations is to produce contented workers much as the dairy farms seeks contented cows. Thus the social science of the factory research is not a science of man, but a cow-sociology."

[222] See Michael Goldfield, *The Decline of Organized Labor in the United States*, at 57 (1987); and Thomas A. Kochan, Harry C. Katz, and Robert B. McKersie, *The Transformation of American Industrial Relations*, at 21 (1986).

[223] Bureau of the Census, *Statistical Abstract of the United States*, 393 [no 621], 435 [no 687] (1993).

union membership peaked at 25.5 percent in 1953, remained fairly stable throughout the 1960s, but declined to around 20 percent in the late 1970s. As a percentage of non-agricultural employment, the highest postwar union density occurred in 1945, at approximately 35.5 percent; in 1955, the proportion was 33.2 percent, declining to approximately 27.4 percent in 1970. By 1990, union members represented only 16.1 percent of the non-farm labor force, which was about equal to the level of the mid-thirties.[224]

Within the overall trend, there were contrasting tendencies within different sectors. The economic historian Michael French estimated that in 1945 the highest union densities were in construction, mining and transport, primarily the railroads. From 1945, onwards, union densities declined consistently in the construction and mining industries, with rates falling in the latter sector from 83 percent in 1947, to 36 percent in the mid-sixties, and to 15 percent in the mid-eighties.

The most spectacular growth during the thirties had occurred in manufacturing, where union densities peaked in 1953. Over the next two decades, union densities in manufacturing followed a fluctuating but downward course, dropping rapidly during the 1980s, when the manufacturing sector became the main source of the absolute fall in union membership. According to French's estimates, union densities in manufacturing fell from approximately 40 percent in 1947, to 32 percent in 1980, and 25 percent in 1985.[225]

Union densities in the transport sector followed a similar course. The centers of union expansion of the thirties hence accounted for most of the unions' decline. The principal growth sector of the unions after the war, meanwhile, was the public sector where, according to Melvin Reder, union densities rose from under 12 percent to 39.6 percent between 1947 and 1975. Job security in the public sector tended to be relatively high, with the exception of a brief period in the early eighties when federal and local budget cuts led to a wave of layoffs.[226]

In the manufacturing sector, in contrast, employment losses had been dramatic. From the late fifties onwards, productivity gains reduced the number of blue-collar industrial workers, particularly in the old heavy industries, which tended to strike against union strongholds. This process accelerated when declining US exports and a crisis in consumer demand triggered massive layoffs in the late 1970s and early 1980s. The steelworkers union, for instance, lost over half of its members in the decade up to 1980.

Fast-growing sectors, such as the electronics industry, meanwhile, were characterized by low levels of union organization. Here, firms like IBM operated extensive corporate welfare systems virtually without union representation. Meanwhile, union advances in the service sector were very slow. In 1947, unions accounted for nine percent of service workers, three decades, later barely 14 percent of full-time workers in the service sector were union members.[227]

By tying efforts to stabilize job security, and more generally the enforcement of individual employment rights to plant level bargaining, US unions had ultimately, and perhaps unknowingly, played a dangerous game. Since employment protection had become,

---

[224] See Mary E. Fredrikson and Timothy P. Lynch, "Labor: The Great Depression to the 1990s," in *Encyclopedia of American Social History*, Vol. II, at 1488 (1990).

[225] French, *supra* note 176, at 93.

[226] Melvin W. Reder, "The Rise and Fall of Unions: The Public Sector and the Private," 2 *The Journal of Economic Perspectives* 89, at 106 (1988).

[227] French, *supra* note 176, at 93.

at least to some degree, a matter of bargaining rather than a matter of regulation and law, a decline in unionization had devastating consequences for individual employment rights. At the very time when union strength was most needed to secure member's jobs, the unions' powerbases in key industries had virtually collapsed.

UNIONS AND INDIVIDUAL EMPLOYMENT RIGHTS

Apart from economic implications, the unions' attempt to secure job stability through plant-level bargaining had extracted a substantial political price. In order for grievances to be a means of furthering the union agendas, workers had to be unified in their demands. Requiring employees to act with one voice, however, sometimes meant that individual demands were to be sacrificed in favor of union control over discontent.

The labor historian Patrick Renshaw suggests that during the first postwar decade, unions had increasingly seized control over discontent. This meant that increasing focus was placed on those elements of worker complaints that could be monetarized. While locals continued to strike over plant-specific matters, such as work content and staffing levels, these issues were increasingly subordinated to the bargaining agenda. These developments were not without cost to the unions in terms of the way they were perceived by ordinary members. Accordingly Renshaw cites the case of a worker who upon being asked what changes major unions had undergone between the 1930s and 1950s, stated that:[228]

> When I was a kid, if somebody asked me to define a grievance, I'd say it was something we don't like. Today a grievance is something not in accordance with standards of arbitration. We're even told what the hell to be dissatisfied with these days.

Just how antagonistic the relationship between individual employment rights and grievance arbitration could be became dramatically obvious in a set of court cases starting in the late sixties. In these cases, the courts tried to establish individual grievance rights against union representatives; usually prompted by allegations by an individual worker, or several workers, that unions had not represented them fairly in a discharge case.

Typical of the litigation arising from the plant-based dismissal protection established by unions and employers in the early 1960s, was the case of *Union News Co. v. Hildreth*.[229] *Union News* involved the blatantly unjust discharge of a lunch counter employee who had worked for the company for over ten years. Ms. Gladys Hildreth, together with five other workers, was "temporarily" laid off by the company, who alleged that money had disappeared from the counter. Upon replacement of the five employees with temporary workers, no cash disappeared. One month later, the replacement workers were made permanent and the five workers on layoff, including Ms. Hildreth, were dismissed. Ms. Hildreth met with union officials in order to convince them that her discharge was unjust, but the union representative decided not to process her discharge. Subsequent to her discharge, an office girl, who had counted the money received at the counter, was found to be embezzling those funds and was

---

[228] Patrick Renshaw, *American Labor and Consensus Capitalism, 1935-1990*, at 143 (1991), citing an interview from Studs Terkel's *Hard Times*, at 357 (1971).

[229] Union News Co. v. Hildreth, 295 F. 2d 658 (6th Cir. 1962).

discharged for it. Ms. Hildreth was awarded damages in a jury trial, but this decision was reversed by an appeals court decision. The court stated that:[230]

> By virtue of the union's authority as exclusive bargaining representative the union and the company can mutually conclude, as a part of the bargaining process, that the circumstances shown by the evidence provided just-cause for the layoff and discharge of the plaintiff ... Unless such bilateral decisions, made in good faith, and after unhurried consideration be sustained in court, the bargaining process is a mirage, without the efficacy contemplated by the philosophy of the law which makes its use compulsory.
>
> ...We consider that the union was acting in the collective interest of those who by law and contract the union was charged with protecting. Under the philosophy of collective responsibility an employer who bargains in good faith should be entitled to rely upon the promises and agreement of the union's representatives with whom he must deal ... The collective bargaining process should be carried on between parties who can mutually respect and rely upon the authority of each other.

The Supreme Court denied *certiorari* to review a decision brought by the appeals court, arising from the same group discharge as the *Hildreth* case, in *Simmons v. Union News Co.*[231] Justice Hugo Black, with Justice Warren concurring, wrote an opinion dissenting from this denial of the *certiorari*. Using uncommonly strong language, Black argued that the court had permitted a new type of, what we would now call, biased in-group injustice to arise from the grievance system. He said:[232]

> This case points up with great emphasis the kind of injustice that can occur to an individual employee when the employer and the union have such power over the employee's claim for breach of contract. Here no one has claimed from the beginning to the end of the Hildreth lawsuit or this lawsuit [meaning the Simmons suit] that either of these individuals was guilty of any kind of misconduct justifying their discharge ... There is no evidence that the respondent has ever been dissatisfied with their work before the company became disappointed with its lunch counter about a year prior to discharges. Yet both were discharged for "just-cause," as determined not by a court but by an agreement of the company and the union ... There has been a sacrifice of the rights of a group of employees based on the belief that some of them might possibly have been guilty of misconduct ... I cannot believe that those who passed the act [meaning the NLRA] intended to give the union the right to negotiate away alleged breaches of contract.

In Black's view, a union's misuse of arbitration rights had deprived an employee from the remedies against unjust dismissal that the unionized workplace was supposed to provide. But there was no easy solution. Remedies for unjust dismissal *per se* were only available in unionized workplaces. The enforcement of the enhanced just-cause rights of employees therefore ultimately rested on the fair and proper conduct of plant level union representatives, who in this case had failed to follow expected standards of justice. The court's initial ruling on *Hildreth* and *Simmons* represented an unsatisfactory situation. Workers who were formally granted just-cause rights could be dismissed if unions and management agreed on the

---

[230] Union News, as cited in Archibald Cox, Derek Curtis Bok and Robert A. Gorman, *Labor Law: Cases and Materials*, at 1008 (1986).

[231] Simmons v. Union News Co., 382 U.S. 86 (1965).

[232] Simmons, as cited in Cox, Bok and Gorman, *supra* note 230, at 1009.

termination, and once such an agreement had been reached, workers had very little recourse to fight such a decision at the plant level.

Following *Hildreth* and *Simmons*, the 1967 Supreme Court's decision in *Vaca v. Sipes* re-affirmed the right of unionized workers to sue employers for breach of contract, irrespective of whether the union supported the claim.[233] In *Vaca*, Benjamin Owens, a union member, alleged that he had been discharged for his employment at Swift and Co., a Kansas City Meatpacking Plant, in violation of the collective bargaining agreement then in force between Swift and the Union. Owens also alleged that the union had "arbitrarily, capriciously and without just or reasonable reason or cause" refused to take his grievance with Swift to arbitration under the fifth step of the bargaining agreement's grievance procedures. Owens, a long-term high blood pressure patient, entered a hospital on sick leave from Swift. After a long period of rest during which his blood pressure was reduced, Benjamin Owens was certified to be fit to resume his work at the meat packing plant. Swift's company doctor examined Owens upon his return and concluded that Swift was unfit for work. After securing a second opinion from an outside physician, Owens returned to the plant and resumed work on January 1960. Two days later, when the doctor discovered that Owens had returned, he was discharged on the grounds of bad health. Owens' challenge to the discharge was pursued by his union representatives at a lower level. The union then refused to pursue the matter at a higher level, where local and regional union representatives would have been involved. No reasons for this refusal were given by the union.

While perhaps less spectacular than the *Hildreth* case, *Vaca* illustrated the tension between individual and collective interests and highlighted the dangers of the union-employer centered system of dismissal protection. It pointed to the possibility of employers and union leaders acting indifferently, or even conspiring against, workers who had little standing in a plant.

The Supreme Court's solution to this problem was at best tangled and at worst indecisive. While the *Vaca* Court failed to establish any wrongdoing by the union with regard to its duty of fair representation, and attributed all damages to the employer, the case, at least in principle, pointed the way to a potential liability of unions in such cases. Writing for the majority, Justice Byron White argued that, while collective arbitration placed an obligation on the employer to seek adjudication through the grievance process, the grievance apparatus could not establish final and exclusive adjudication. Said White:[234]

> [I]f the wrongfully discharged employee himself resorts to the courts before grievance procedures have been fully exhausted, the employer may well defend on the ground that the exclusive remedies provided in the contract have not been exhausted ... For this reason it is settled that the employee must at least attempt to exhaust exclusive grievance and arbitration procedures established by the bargaining agreement ... However because these contractual remedies have been devised and are often controlled by the union and the employer, they may well prove unsatisfactory or unworkable for the individual grievant.
>
> ...We think that [one] situation when the employee may seek judicial enforcement of his contractual rights arises, as is true here, if the union has sole power under the contract to invoke the higher stages of the grievance procedure, and if, as is alleged here the employee-

---

[233] Vaca v. Sipes, 386 U.S. 171 (1967).
[234] Vaca, as cited in Cox, Bok and Gorman, *supra* note 230, at 1009.

plaintiff has been prevented from exhausting his contractual remedies by the union's refusal to process the grievance ...

To leave the employee remediless in such circumstances would, in our opinion, be of great injustice. We cannot believe that Congress in conferring upon employers and unions the power to establish exclusive grievance procedures, intended to confer upon unions such unlimited discretion to deprive injured employees of all remedies for breach of contract.

In dealing with employee claims of violation of the duty of fair representation, the Court faced a serious dilemma, which resembled in some ways the problems thrown up by the question of staffing levels in the "Lea cases." On the one hand, the Court was reluctant to second-guess arbitrators. On the other hand, the Court was aware of the possibility that without the right to break an arbitration deadlock, the individual employment rights of unionized workers could fall short of those intended by the original legislators of the NLRA. The solution, in this instance, was thought to be found in a two-stage process in which the employee first had to exhaust contractual remedies. Then, provided the employee could prove that the union breached its duty of fair representation, a direct action could be brought against the employer for breach of contractual rights.

Justice White believed that neither the complete access to litigation against employers nor the requirement that unions process all grievances at all levels would be practically feasible. He stated with regard to the latter approach:[235]

If the individual employee could compel arbitration of his grievance regardless of its merit, the settlement machinery provided by the contract would be substantially undermined, thus destroying the employers' confidence in the unions' authority and returning the individual to the vagaries of independent and unsystematic negotiation. Moreover under such a rule, a significantly greater number of grievances would proceed.

Observing a fundamental tension between the preservation of individual employment rights, and the functioning of the established grievance system, the court had eventually put its weight in favor of the arbitration system.[236] This emphasis on the integrity of the existing arbitration system and the consensus between employer and unions, rather than individual employment rights, however, came to place an implicit burden on unions. The requirement that the employee first exhaust remedies and that there was proof that the union had breached its duty of fair representation, before judicial enforcement of contractual rights could be sought, had the potential of negatively affecting the employment rights of individual workers.[237]

If, for instance, an employee, working in a non-unionized workplace, or one governed by a non-certified employer association, was dismissed in violation of a prior contractual

---

[235] Vaca as cited in Cox, Bok and Gorman, *supra* note 230, at 1000.

[236] Justice Black's strongly worded dissent with the majority took particular issue with this point. He stated: "I simply fail to see how the union's legitimate role as statutory agent is undermined by requiring it to prosecute all serious grievances to a conclusion or by allowing the injured employee to sue his employer after he has given the union a chance to act on his behalf" 386 U.S. at 209. The contrasting view was expressed by several industrial relations scholars, including David E. Feller's, "A General Theory of the Collective Bargaining Agreement," 61 *California Law Review* 663, at 705(1973).

[237] This point is stressed in William B. Gould, *A Primer on American Labor Law*, at 154 (1986), where Gould argues that, compared to the Steelworkers Trilogy, "even more formal are the barriers that exist by virtue of the Court's decision in Vaca v. Sipes."

agreement, the employee could sue the employer for breach of contract without having to resort to arbitration. More importantly, if the employee in a unionized workplace was unable to prove that the union breached its duty of fair representation, not only would the action against the union be dismissed but also would the contract action against the employer not be determined, regardless of its merits.[238]

Justice Hugo Black, in particular, was concerned with the problems such an approach created for employees. He stated in a dissenting opinion:[239]

> [This] decision ... converts what would otherwise be a simple breach of contract into a three-ring donnybrook. It puts an intolerable burden on employees with meritorious grievances and means that the worker will frequently be left with no remedy. Today's decision while giving the employee an ephemeral right to sue ... creates insurmountable obstacles to block his far more valuable right to sue his employer for breach of the collective bargaining agreement.

If the presence of a plant level bargaining and arbitration apparatus prevented individual employees from pursuing claims against employers, a much broader issue was at stake. This issue centered on the question as to whether the collective bargaining process actually empowered individual workers or whether it had come to limit individual rights with regard to the critical issue of employment termination.

Ultimately the requirement of *Vaca* that employees exhaust the grievances processes did much to delay the spread of employment rights litigation as well as the evolution of individual employment rights *per se*. Most cases following *Vaca* upheld compulsory arbitration against rivaling claims. As recently as 1991, the Supreme Court affirmed the basis of the *Vaca* doctrine against claims arising from the Age Discrimination in Employment Act of 1967.[240]

Although some union leaders welcomed the court's willingness to preserve the integrity of the bargaining process, the *Vaca* doctrine carried significant indirect costs for the unions. Among others, *Vaca* laid the ground for decisions that held unions liable for the unjust discharge of employees. Less tangibly, *Vaca* also had the potential of positioning workers against their unions.

One direct effect of the implementation of the *Vaca* doctrine was that unions became directly responsible for damages in cases where employees could prove unfair representation. Several years after *Vaca*, in *Bowen v. US Postal Service* (1983), the Supreme Court

---

[238] Clyde Summers, "Trade Unions and Their Members," in *Civil Liberties in Conflict*, 65, at 78 (Larry Gostin, ed., 1988), suggests that the Vaca decision may have had adverse effects on minority rights on account of the fact that, in the face of an exclusive bargaining agent, a minority employee is not entitled to force an employer to negotiate with them individually or with their civil rights representative over questions of discrimination.

[239] Vaca as cited in Cox, Bok and Gorman, *supra* note 230, at 1007.

[240] In Gilmer v. Interstate/Johnson Lane Co., 500 U.S. 20 (1991), a stockbroker, was terminated by NYSE at age 62, claiming, *inter alia,* violation of Age Discrimination in Employment Act rules. NYSE rule 347 provides for arbitration in termination cases. The court decided that ADEA remedies were not immediately available to Gilmer, because his claim was subject to compulsory arbitration: "Since the Federal Arbitration Act manifests liberal policy in favoring arbitration ... and since neither the text nor the history of ADEA explicitly precludes arbitration, Gilmer is bound by agreement to arbitrate unless he can show an inherent conflict between arbitration and the ADEA's underlying purposes." Justice Stevens, with whom Justice Marshall joined, cited an earlier Burger decision in their dissent. "For Federal Courts to defer to arbitral decisions reached by the same combination of forces that had long perpetuated invidious discrimination would have made the foxes guardians the chickens."

established that the union was liable to a discharged employee where failure to take the grievance to arbitration had increased the employer's liability to the employee.[241] Because of the considerable period of time between potential reinstatement and trial, the practical effect of Bowen was to impose most of the damage liability arising in such an unjust discharge on the union. Mr. Bowen had been discharged following an altercation with another employee. His union, the American Postal Workers Union, declined to take his grievance to arbitration. Bowen sued the Postal Service and the union in a federal district court, seeking damages and injunctive relief. The District court entered judgment against the Postal Service for $22,954 and against the union for $30,000. The court of appeals concurred with the trial court regarding the total amount ($52,954) but held that the union should not be responsible for damages, as ultimately the injury to the worker had been caused by the employer's actions. The Supreme Court reversed the judgment of the appeals court and allocated the trial court's damages against both the Postal Service and the union.

Aware of the problem that the damage to the employee resulted in the first instance from the employer's misconduct—namely his wrongful discharge of the employee—Justice Lewis Powell established an alternative conception of the unionized worker's employment contract. In his view, shared duties were imposed on the employer and union. Starting with a review of the union's position, Powell established the joint liability of employer and union:[242]

> The union feels itself as liable only for Bowen's litigation expenses resulting from its breach of duty ... The union contends that its unrelated breach of the duty of fair representation does not make it liable for any part of the discharged employee's damages; its default merely lifts the bar to the employee's suit ... against the employee.
>
> The difficulty with this argument is that it treats the relationship between the employer and employee as if it were a simple contract of hire governed by traditional common law principles. This reading of Vaca fails to recognize that a collective bargaining agreement is much more than traditional common law employment, terminable at-will. Rather it is an agreement creating relationships and interests under the federal common law of labor policy.

For Powell, this joint liability implied that damages had to be paid by the union. This was the case for two reasons—firstly, because otherwise employers would be made responsible for the union's breach of duty and secondly, because it would prevent the employee from recovering full damages. Said Powell:[243]

> The fault that justifies dropping the bar on the employee's suit for damages also requires the union to bear some responsibility for increases in the employee's damages resulting from its breach. To hold otherwise would make the employer alone liable for the consequences of the Union's breach of duty. Even though the employer and the union have caused the damage suffered by the employee, the union is responsible for the increase in damages, and, as between the two wrongdoers, should bear its portion of the damages ...
>
> Although each party participates in the grievance procedure, the union plays a pivotal role in the process since it assumes the responsibility of determining whether to press ahead employees' claims. The employer for its part, must rely on the union's decision not to pursue an employee's grievances ...

---

[241] Bowen v. U.S. Postal Service, 459 U.S. 212, (1983).
[242] Bowen, as cited in Cox, Bok and Gorman, *supra* note 230, at 1020.
[243] Bowen as cited in Cox, Bok and Gorman, *supra* note 230, 1020 and 1021.

Taking Powell's decision at face value, the employment contract of the unionized employee did not merely establish a contractual relationship between employer and employee in which the workers could seek protection through the union, rather it also established a contractual relationship between the employee on the one side and the employer and the union on the other side. Legally, both the employer and the union had obligations towards the employee. Employer obligations arose from the general requirement to observe fair labor practices and the specific requirements of the labor contract that she or he subscribed to, whereas unions had a duty to represent employees fairly in all matters including discharge related grievances. Powell's decision formalized what previous decisions, including *Vaca*, had already implied—namely that the employee was effectively a contractual party of both the employer and the union. This dual contractual relationship implicitly restricted the rights of the employee vis a vis the employer. Since responsibility for employment rights fell on the employer and the union, the employee was required to exhaust union procedures before legal action regarding a breach of the contract could be undertaken.

Apart from putting a potentially substantial financial liability on the unions, the practice of plant level regulation, as it had evolved by the eighties, placed a high responsibility on unions, which was predestined to lead to tension between union representatives and individual workers. In the late 1960s, and throughout the 1970s, charges by workers against unions accelerated and began to constitute a main element in the general growth of litigation under the NLRA. This acceleration corresponded roughly with Supreme Court decisions that expanded the concepts of fair representation.[244]

By 1970, *Vaca*-type employee charges against unions had become numerous, with more charges against unions being raised by employees than by employers in most years. Whereas in 1970, a roughly equal number of charges of unfair labor practices were filed by workers against unions (approximately 3,200), unions faced more than 6,300 charges from employees in 1975, and only 4,250 from employers. Although the number of charges filed against unions by workers declined in the late seventies, almost 7,800 charges were filed by workers, while less than 5,000 charges were filed by employers. Over the decade from 1970, onward, the ratio of worker to employer charges against unions increased from 1:1 in 1970, to 1.5:1 in 1975, to 1.6:1 in 1980.

While the NLRA regime had severely limited the ability of unions to bargain for the job security of their members, it had paradoxically imposed crucial responsibilities with regard to individual employment rights on the union. When a wave of terminations hit US industry in the late 1970s and early 1980s, this setup provided all the elements of a vicious cycle, where the limited impact of unions on terminations reduced the attractiveness of unions to their members, while loss of support from workers in turn further reduced the effectiveness of union action.

Politically, the plant-level component of post-NLRA dismissal regime remains one of the most difficult aspects of US workplace governance to evaluate. One the one hand, the presence of a host of plant-level initiatives to restrict, control, and prevent dismissals refutes the notion of postwar "business unionism," i.e., the belief that US unions were characterized by a short-sighted singular focus on wage gains of union members. On the other hand, it is difficult to characterize the plant-level route to dismissal protection as a success or even as a necessity. In the first two or three postwar decades, when open challenges to managerial

---

[244] Flanagan, *supra* note 219, at 29.

authority were difficult, plant-level initiatives were one of the pathways open to unions who sought to provide some semblance of job security to their members. During the automation drives of the 1960s and 1970s, when the courts increasingly came to the defense of managerial authority, plant-level initiatives did perhaps contribute to the job security of those covered by collective bargaining agreements. Yet, while initially successful, these strategies proved costly in the long run.

Plant-level job security was predicated on a broad coverage of the workforce by unions. When union densities plummeted, not only did coverage by plant level job security measures decline, but so also did the legislative and political influence of unions. Had unions pushed for legislative measures of dismissal protection in the 1960s, or even the late 1970s, such initiatives might well have seen at least limited success. Once union coverage had declined and the political landscape had shifted to the right, it was too late for such initiatives.

What is more, the enforcement of job security through collective bargaining also was implicitly predicated on a diminution of individual employment rights: firstly, in the narrow sense, through the restriction of the individual's right to assert her or his claims directly against the employer's breach of contract; and secondly, in the wider sense, through the neglect of individual employment rights by the unions. As early as 1970, Bok and Dunlop, otherwise staunch supporters of a union-centred system of workplace governance, noted that:[245]

> The majoritan view recognizes that a union will, because of ineptitude, laziness, or even petty personal reasons, sometimes abuse its power and refuse to process grievances. But rather than permit the individual to have a court resolve his [sic] contract claim, majoritarians urge that he merely be allowed to sue the union for failure to handle his grievance in a fair and impartial manner...
>
> Experience in other areas of labor law indicates that few employees will press their claims when they run the risk of having to pay substantial litigation costs. And those who do bring action are likely to do so only where they have a strong interest at stake. Thus, the overwhelming number of individual court cases in the past have involved situations where the aggrieved has been discharged from employment. It is in these cases that inept or discriminatory treatment cause the greatest harm and injustice to the employee...
>
> All things, therefore, access to the grievance process—at least in discipline and discharge cases—seems an appropriate area in which to give greater freedom to the individual without undue risk to the legitimate concerns of the majority.

Taking a broader perspective, James Atleson's 1993 analysis tellingly noted that the workplace contractualism, which represented the principal element of job protection for unionized workers, had, apart from limiting access to industrial justice, failed workers in a number of ways. Said Atleson:[246]

---

[245] See Derek C. Bok and John T. Dunlop, *Labor and the American Community,* at 104 (1970).

[246] See Atleson, *supra* note 178, at 171. See also Katherine van Wetzel Stone, "The Post-War Paradigm in American Labor Law," 90 *Yale Law Journal* 1509, at 1511 (1981), suggesting that the "industrial pluralism view of industrial relations" that dominated postwar U.S. labor relations was "based upon a false assumption: the assumption that management and employees have equal power." As a false but powerful description of industrial relations "industrial pluralism obscure[d] the real issues and problems posed by the exercise of power in the workplace..." Stone further argues that with "increased government intervention in employment relations, industrial pluralism is proving an ill suited tool for the problems that arise" and proposes that "the internal contradictions within the model" are now "coming to light."

... despite the gains the practices and law of arbitration also have negative effects on industrial democracy. First, arbitration focuses on the written agreement as the exclusive source of employee rights. The argument is the result of economic struggle and, thus, represents the balance or imbalance of economic power. Indeed the reliance on contractualism means that rights are based upon the very kinds of economic imbalance that the Wagner Act sought to ameliorate. Moreover, the relative power of the parties itself is badly affected by the interpretations of the NLRA, often not favorable to union interests, especially in periods when unions are perceived to be weak. Second, arbitration removes the conflict, and its resolution, from the workplace and its workers. Just as important, arbitration and centralized bargaining alter the kinds of issues that are thought to be important.

For individual workers in the unionized workplace and for those working in plants that were covered by union contracts, dismissal protection had not been won. Some job protection could nevertheless be provided, either through the active and comprehensive enforcement of just-cause clauses (during periods of "normal business"), or concerted policies such as concession bargaining agreements (during downturns). But it was not a matter of rights. In the non-unionized workplace meanwhile, no procedures for grievance or bargaining were specified—unless by voluntary agreement—and individual employment rights were limited to statutory provisions and the exemptions granted so far by state courts (on the latter see the consecutive chapter). As a whole, dismissal protection in the US had neither evolved within common or statutory law nor in the arena of collective bargaining.

When in 1970, the prominent industrial relation scholars Derek Bok and John Dunlop summarized the "successes" of unions with regard to the legal positioning of workers, they tellingly stressed psychological factors rather than actual power gains. Said Bok and Dunlop:[247]

> Even if unions do not have strong direct impact...their presence helps to gain general acceptance for the rates of pay and working conditions that prevail, even in unorganized plants. In the last analysis, no one can be sure of the wages and other terms that would exist if workers were wholly unorganized. Under these circumstances the existence of unions, the opportunity to join such organizations ... all of these things help persuade the workers that the conditions under which he labors are tolerably fair. Without unions this assurance could not be given and workers might easily demand government regulation as the only practical alternative. Our experience ... suggests that this alternative would exact a heavy price in red tape and in a loss of flexibility for our firms and labor markets.

Whatever might be thought about Bok and Dunlop's analysis, it is remarkable that the authors of *Labor and the American Community* saw the avoidance of civil strife and regulation as one of the chief accomplishments of the postwar US industrial relations system. If one of the main results of unionization was the avoidance of employment regulation, and dismissal legislation in particular, things had indeed gone formidably wrong for US workers.

---

[247] See Bok and Dunlop, *supra* note 245, at 464.

Chapter 4

UNJUST DISMISSAL LITIGATION

> This is not a contract of employment. An individual may be terminated by the employer for any reason. Any written statements or promises to the contrary are hereby expressly disavowed and should not be relied upon by any prospective or existing employee. The contents of this handbook are subject to change at any time at the discretion of the employer.
>
> Joseph Lawson, *How to Develop an Employee Handbook,* at 357 (2ⁿᵈ edition, 1998)

Today there is wide agreement that levels of employment protection in the US lag behind those of most Western European countries, as well as Canada, Australia or New Zealand.[248] This mainstream view of US dismissal regulation is based primarily on the combination of an incomplete system of common law discharge protection with a highly selective framework of statutory regulation, both of which were the subject of analysis in the previous chapters. Although most collective bargaining agreements include clauses that prohibit the discharge of employees except for "good cause," no effective source of employment protection is available for the majority of US workers.[249] This is due to three factors. Firstly, the coverage of the workforce through union contracts is low with estimates suggesting that fewer than 20 percent of the non-farm workforce are now included in collective bargaining agreements.[250] Secondly, current industrial relations law still allows union representatives to limit access to the grievance apparatus of a companies. Thirdly, even where employees are supported by a union in their claim, the courts are unlikely to provide redress where a company can link discharges to economic considerations.

One response to this situation has been the growth in individual unjust dismissal litigation. This litigation has expanded in the past three decades, primarily as a consequence of state court decisions which have ceased to support the doctrine of employment at-will and

---

[248] William B. Gould, "Stemming the Wrongful Discharge Tide: A Case for Arbitration," 13 *Employee Relations Law Journal* 404, especially at 420 (1987). Gould emphasizes the more advanced nature of European discharge legislation and criticizes Chicago-School economists, who assumed that higher unemployment rates in Europe during the 1980s and 1990s were attributable to European dismissal and plant closing laws. Rather than advocating the adoption of European type legislation in the U.S., Gould proposes a system of compulsory arbitration based on Canadian examples.

[249] See, e.g., Jay E. Grenig, "The Dismissal of Employees in the United States" 130 *International Labor Review* 569, at 569 (1991).

[250] Susan Mendelsohn, "Wrongful Termination and its Effects on the Employment Relationship in the United States," *OECD Labor Market and Social Policy Occasional Papers* No 3, at 2 (1990).

have allowed dismissed employees to sue employers for breach of contract, the violation of their constitutional rights, and/or employer actions that counter public policy goals.

Although it is questionable that this litigation has contributed in a significant manner to the protection of "average employees" from "average dismissals," or enhanced the job security of US workers, it has evidently encouraged a more critical attitude towards managerial rights, which is potentially reshaping future expectations with regard to justice at the workplace.[251]

The evolution of at-will exemptions itself can be attributed to the confluence of several factors, operating both on the supply and demand side.[252] Looking at the supply side, progressive state courts started questioning the acceptability of the at-will doctrine in various contexts since the late 1970s or early 1980s.[253] Their leadership has provided a strong impetus for federal and state courts elsewhere in the United States to depart from a rigid adherence to the at-will standard. The pioneering judgments of these progressive courts seem to have arisen in the context of developments in other areas such as the rise of consumer, environmental and civil rights movements—all of which were influential in querying a dogmatic application of the at-will doctrine. In terms of their internal logic, meanwhile, many of the early judicial deviations from the at-will standards were characterized both a heightened awareness of public policy issues in combination with a recognition that the dogmatic application of existing legal doctrine could lead to socially undesirable outcomes. For instance, once a judiciary acknowledged that improving consumer protection was an important public policy goal, it also had to face the question of whether it was still permissible to allow employers to dismiss workers whose discharge could be linked to complaints about unsafe practices or products. Likewise, if environmental protection was to be taken seriously by companies, they could not be permitted to freely dismiss workers who refused to engage in illegal activities that caused environmental harm. Despite these links

---

[251] See, e.g., Anne Marie Lofaso, "Talking is Worthwhile: The Role of Employee Voice in Protecting, Enhancing, and Encouraging Individual Rights to Job Security in a Collective System," *14 Employee Rights and Employment Policy Journal* 101, at 115 (2010), discussing the evolving role of notice requirements and the Worker Adjustment and Retraining Notification Act.

[252] In terms of social expectations, the rise of unjust dismissal litigation and the associated doctrines can also be related to theories of post-contractual jurisprudence. Jethro K. Lieberman, *The Litigious Society* (1981) distinguishes between two form of jurisprudence, a contractual and a fiduciary legal system. According to Lieberman, the former dominated pre-war jurisprudence, while the latter system evolved after WWII. The contractual model assigns rights and duties contractually. As such, rights are explicit and specific, and a judge is expected to adjudicate individual disputes on the basis of clear and unambiguous rules. The unadulterated at-will right of the employer can be seen as belonging to the contractual system. In the at-will regime, individuals only have rights that evolve from explicit contractual specifications. Under the fiduciary model, in contrast, rights are based on trust and confidence among the parties. Because these relate to potentially ill-defined standards of trust, they must be inferred from the fiduciary relationship between litigants or between the state and its citizens. Exemptions based on public policy criteria or notions of implied contract and good faith to some degree exemplify fiduciary elements. According to J. Robert Prichard, "A Systematic Approach to Comparative Law: The Effect of Cost, Fee, and Financing Rules on the Development of Substantive Law," 17 *Journal of Legal Studies*, 451 (1988), the expansion of private employment litigation in the U.S. can be attributed primarily to cost factors rather than cultural preferences. In the UK, for instance, where private employment litigation remained the exception, rather than the rule, the size of awards is limited, and the use of contingent fees is uncommon. Further to this, the availability of legal aid in the UK, which is accessible in meritorious and substantive cases to lower income persons, involves a pre-selection of cases and encourages officials (including judges) to reject novel cases that may lead to costly future legal aid claims.

[253] Lewis Maltby, "The Decline of Employment At Will-A Quantitative Analysis," 41 *Labor Law Journal*, 51, at 53 (1990). Maltby discusses the lead role of the California courts and suggests that the narrower construction of exceptions to the at-will doctrine granted in other states are likely to result in a greater number of workers being victimized in other states.

between progressive policymaking and the decline of at-will employment, the evolution of unjust dismissal litigation cannot exclusively be associated with so-called "progressive" or "leftist" policy agendas. Rather, it is possible to identify some elements within the political right who also supported these legal changes, primarily because of a preference for individual litigation over regulation and collective action, and/or because of a recognition that the *status quo* was not conducive to the emerging law and order agendas.[254]

Looking at demand factors, meanwhile, there is reason to believe that the continuing decline of union coverage, increased job insecurity amongst managerial employees, as well as a general rise in litigiousness at the workplace and elsewhere, all contributed to an increased demand for unjust dismissal litigation, in line with, or in excess of, the expansion of other types of employment litigation.[255]

In examining the evolution of unjust dismissal litigation as an alternative to statutory regulation or plant-level and union-centered approaches to protection, this chapter moves from a largely historical analysis of the evolution of unjust dismissal litigation to an assessment of the limits of private litigation as a means of employment protection. In examining these issues, this chapter highlights the incompatibility of contemporary conceptions of individual rights with doctrines of the employment relationship that have historically shaped the US common law of employment, as well as some of the statutory framework of the post-NLRA industrial relations system. This chapter concludes its examination of current practices in this area by suggesting that the existing system of exemptions to the at-will rule represents only an insufficient remedy for the existing lack of a comprehensive system for the regulation of dismissals.

THE "EROSION" OF AT-WILL EMPLOYMENT

The first notable exemption to the at-will right of employers to dismiss workers was granted by a predominantly republican California State Court in 1959, in connection with a worker who was employed by a Teamster union local.[256] Specifically the case of *Petermann v. International Brotherhood of Teamsters* involved the dismissal of an employee who refused to commit perjury on behalf of his employer. Facing a situation where the court would have been forced to uphold a dismissal that was grounded in the refusal of an employee to commit a criminal act, a unanimous decision was made by the court to break with the employment at-will rule.

At its core, this break with the at-will rule centered on the argument that even though in the absence of contractual limitations an employer enjoyed broad discretion to discharge, as a

---

[254] Leo Troy, "The Rise and Fall of American Trade Unions: The Labor Movement from FDR to RR," in *Unions in Transition* 75, at 82 (Seymour M. Lipset ed., 1986), questions claims that U.S. workers desire greater collective representation, but acknowledges their interest in individual employment rights.

[255] See, e.g., Kenneth T. Lopatka, "The Emerging Law of Wrongful Discharge - A Quadrennial Assessment of the Labor Law Issue of the 80s," 40 *Business Lawyer* 1, at 5 (1984), noting that "Today's employees are perceived to be more dependent on their corporate employers for economic survival, while in the nonunion situation, they suffer from a marked inferiority of bargaining power, which debilitates them from protecting themselves against unfair terminations. Moreover, the proponents of change perceive an inequity in job security between unionized and nonunionized employees and argue that employers' widespread acceptance of collectively bargained restrictions on their discharge rights should pave the way for redressing, via the common law, these inequalities and inequities."

[256] Petermann v. International Bhd. of Teamsters Local 396, 174 Cal. App. 2d 184, 189, 344 P.2d 25, 28 (1959).

matter of "public policy and sound morality" this specific employer's conduct could not be condoned.[257] Specifically, the court argued that this dismissal was objectionable because it was not in the interests of the state to allow an employer to fire at-will if such a dismissal contravened the state's own penal code. The court explained that:[258]

> The commission of perjury is unlawful [Pen. Code, 118] ... It would [therefore] be obnoxious to the interests of the state and contrary to public policy and sound morality to allow an employer to discharge any employee, whether the employment be for a designated or unspecified duration to commit perjury, an act specifically enjoined by statute ... The public policy of this state as reflected in the penal code section referred to above would be seriously impaired if it were held that one could be discharged by reason of his refusal to commit perjury. To hold that one's continued employment could be made contingent upon his commission of a felonious act at the insistence of his employer would be to encourage criminal conduct upon the part of both the employee and the employer and serve to contaminate the honest administration of public affairs.

With its relatively broad wording, the *Petermann* decision already hinted at the possibility that, even in the absence of an explicit statutory provision prohibiting the discharge of a worker who refused to conduct a criminal act, fundamental principles of public policy could require an exemption from the at-will doctrine. Indeed, in later years, the notion of a public policy interest, as established in *Petermann*, proved general enough to allow future courts to expand exemptions from the at-will doctrine in two directions: firstly, to those instances in which the plaintiff was not actually forced to commit an illegal act but merely objected to others doing so and secondly, to instances in which the relevant issue was not actually deemed criminal by law but merely stood in violation of professional or other codes of conduct. Up until the mid-1970s, California courts and courts in other states, nonetheless, made little of the potential innovation encapsulated in the *Petermann* ruling. This situation changed in the late 1970s, when the state courts of several states started questioning the blind application of the at-will doctrine in several contexts.

One of the most significant extensions of the *Petermann* doctrine was given in the oft-cited 1980 case of *Tameny v. Atlantic Richfield Co.*[259] The *Tameny* court was confronted with an employee who had acted as a wholesaler for Arco and who had objected to the price fixing practices of that company. Although the practices of the wholesaler were not *per se* criminal, the plaintiff-employee was granted tort remedies and received punitive and compensatory damages.

Hired by Arco in 1960, as a relief clerk, Tameny had received regular advancements, merit increases, and commendatory evaluations in his initial years with the company. In 1966, he was promoted to the position of retail sales representative, which he held until he was discharged in 1975. His duties as a retail sales representative included, among other matters, the management of relations between Arco and the various "independent" service station dealers in his assigned territory. During the early 1970s, Arco's district manager pressured Tameny to "threaten and cajole" the so-called independent service station dealers in his territory to cut their gasoline prices at, or below, a designated level specified by Arco. When

---

[257] Peterman, ibid., at 188, 174 Cal. App. 2d.
[258] Peterman, ibid., at 188 and 189, 174 Cal. App. 2d.
[259] Tameny v. Atlantic Richfield Co., 27 Cal. 3d 167, 610 P.2d 1330, 164 Cal. Rptr. 839 (1980).

Tameny refused to yield to his employer's pressure, his supervisor told him that his discharge was imminent, and soon thereafter Tameny was fired. Although Arco indicated in its personnel files that Tameny was discharged for "incompetence" and "unsatisfactory performance," no supporting evidence for such unfavorable performance record could be found, and Tameny successfully argued that the sole reason for his discharge was his refusal to commit the illegal acts required by his supervisor.

In 1975, Tameny sought recovery from Arco, contending *inter alia*, that Arco's conduct was tortuous. A Los Angeles county trial court ruled that remedy was available to Tameny only in contract and not in tort. This decision was reversed by a higher Californian court, which argued that "an employer engaging in such conduct violates a basic duty imposed by law upon all employers, and thus an employee who has suffered damages as a result of such a discharge may maintain a tort action for wrongful discharge against the employer."[260] With no precedent of tort action involving a wrongful discharge claim available, the California court referred to the nineteenth century case of *Sloane v. California Railroad Co.*, in which a California court had construed an action in tort growing out of a contractual breach.[261] This led the *Tameny* court to conclude "if the cause of action arises from a breach of promise set forth in the contract, the action is *ex contractu*, but, if it arises from a breach of duty growing out of the contract it is *ex delicto*."[262] Extending this principle of a dutyholder to the employer, the court concluded that employers had a contractual duty not to dismiss an employee for a refusal to conduct illegal actions. Failure to act on this duty by the employer entitled the employee to seek tort remedy. An employee's action for wrongful discharge, therefore, was typically *ex delicto* and subjected the employer to tort-liability. The court noted that:[263]

> ... as the *Petermann* case indicates, an employer's obligation to refrain from discharging an employee who refuses to commit a criminal act does not depend upon any express or implied "promises set forth in the employment contract" (*Eads v. Marks*, 39 Cal. 2d at p. 811), but rather reflects a duty imposed by law upon all employers in order to implement the fundamental public policies embodied in the state's penal statutes. As such, a wrongful discharge suit exhibits the classic elements of a tort cause of action.

Arguing that the employment contract of the "at-will" employee included the employer's duty in tort not to discharge in violation of public policy, the court concluded:[264]

> We hold that an employer's authority over its employee does not include the right to demand that the employee commit a criminal act to further its interests, and the employer may not coerce compliance with such unlawful directions by discharging an employee who refuses to follow such an order. An employer engaging in such conduct violates a basic duty imposed by law upon all employers, and thus an employee who has suffered damages as a result of such discharge may maintain a tort action for wrongful discharge against the employer.

---

[260] Tameny, ibid., at 178, 174 Cal. 3d.
[261] Tameny, ibid., at 175, 174 Cal. 3d. discussing Sloane v. Southern Cal.R.Co., 111 Cal. 668, 44 P.320 (1896).
[262] Tameny, ibid., at 175, 174 Cal. 3d.
[263] Tameny, ibid., at 175, 174 Cal. 3d.
[264] Tameny, ibid., at 178, 174 Cal. 3d.

The ruling that an unjust discharge violating public policy warranted action in tort was of crucial importance to the evolution of unjust dismissal litigation for two reasons. Firstly, it established the notion that the legality of a dismissal had to be assessed against a potentially broadening set of obligations that an employer owed to the state. Secondly, it created a precedent that suggested that dismissals failing to meet such obligations could be treated as torts, thus providing a potential economic incentive for an expansion of dismissal litigation. In other words, by allowing for punitive damages together with payment of back wages or reinstatement, the courts had created the potential for significant monetary rewards wich could encourage legal professionals and potential litigants to pursue these types of actions.

By the early 1980s, *Tameny* and similar judgments then had set the parameters for a future expansion of wrongful discharge litigation. However, at that time, the application of emerging at-will exemptions was limited by the requirement that the dismissal resulted from the refusal of an employee to commit a criminal act and the potential additional qualification that there was *prima facie* evidence of a permanent employment relationship.

The first important step in the expansion of wrongful discharge litigation beyond this was the decision to treat public policy claims in all employment relationships as an action in tort. This rule was established first in the 1986 case of *Koehrer v. Superior Court*, where a California Appeals Court ruled that the tortious nature of a dismissal violating public policy was unrelated to the characteristics of the employment relationship.[265] The *Koehrer* court stated with regard to this:[266]

> As Tameny explained, the theoretical reasons for labeling a discharge wrongful in such cases [meaning cases involving public policy claims] is not based on the terms and conditions of the contract, but rather arises out of duty implied in law on the part of the employer to conduct his affairs in compliance with public policy ... [T]here is no logical basis to distinguish cases of wrongful termination for reasons violative of fundamental principles of public policy between situations in which the employee is an at-will employee and [those] in which the employee has a contract for a specified term. The tort is independent of the terms of employment.

Following *Koehrer*, the state courts of California and other states allowed for an increasing number of actions to be framed under the public policy exemption. By the mid-1980s, at which time several states had granted similar exemptions from at-will employment, these included, firstly, discharges for refusing to engage in prohibited activities;[267] secondly, discharges for complying with a legal obligation, such as jury service or a grand jury subpoena;[268] thirdly, discharges for engaging in an activity that was either encouraged or protected, such as the filing of a worker compensation claim;[269] and, lastly, discharges for

---

[265] Koehrer v. Superior Court, 181 Cal. App. 3d 1155, 226 Cal. Rptr. 820 (1986).

[266] Koehrer, ibid., at 1116, 181 Cal. App. 3d.

[267] See, e.g., Sabine Pilot Serv., Inc. v. Hauck, 687 SW2d 733 (Tex. 1985), which involved the termination of an employee who refused to pump bilges at a place that was prohibited by federal law.

[268] See, e.g., Palmateer v. International Harvester Co., 85 Ill. 2d 124, 421 NE 2d 876 (1981), which, like Petermann, involved the wrongful termination of an employee who refused to perjure himself on behalf of his employer; and Wiskotoni v. Michigan Nat'l Bank-West, 716 F.2d 378 (6th Cir. 1983), which involved the wrongful discharge of an employee who correctly submitted subpoenaed material to a grand jury.

[269] See, e.g., Novosel v. Nationwide Ins. Co., 721 F.2d 894 (3d Cir. 1983), which involved the wrongful termination of an employee who exercised his first amendment rights in objecting to lobbying for employee-based state legislation; and Kelsey v. Motorola, Inc., 74 Ill. 2d 172, 384 NE2d 353 (1978), which involved the wrongful discharge of an employee who sought workers compensation.

whistleblowing, i.e., the notification of a government authority or the media of an employers' wrongdoing.[270] Underlying this expansion of the public policy doctrine was the reasoning that if certain types of conduct were declared illegal by a legislature, the at-will right of employers could not be allowed to undermine this.

Initially, most courts interpreted the public policy doctrine to imply that claims had to be based on the violation of a clearly stated public policy mandate. Under this rule, the courts had little difficulty in identifying a claim for wrongful discharge. Had an employer terminated an employee for refusing to engage in an act prohibited by statute, then, and only then, did such a claim arise. Many issues, however, could not be traced to a statute but, nonetheless, related to more general broadly accepted public policy principles. Such general public policy principles were particularly prominent in such areas as consumer protection and patient rights, where legal formalization of rules of conduct was in a state of flux.

One of the first broad public policy exemptions going beyond the requirement of a clearly defined statute was handed down, again, by a California court in the case of *Dabbs v. Cardiopulmonary Management Services*. *Dabbs* involved the dismissal of a therapist who had refused to work on account of patient safety concerns and was terminated as a result.[271] The plaintiff alleged that she had stopped working because she was the only experienced therapist on duty, when customarily there were three experienced therapists to serve the patients on her shift. The court concluded that her termination was due to her refusal to work under conditions that would jeopardize the "health, safety, and physical well-being of the patients," and accepted that her actions were in protest of conditions that were in "violation of fundamental public policy consideration."[272] Asking the question "how may public policy be determined?" the court then explicitly rejected the notion that public policy could only be found in statutes or regulations as opposed to sources of "more general public policy:"[273]

> [W]e need not look to the *Respiratory Care Practice Act* alone. We find support for our decision in general societal concerns for the quality of patient care. This policy militates against allowing an employer to discriminate against or discharge an employee for voicing dissatisfaction with procedures he or she reasonably believes might endanger the health, safety, and welfare of the patients for which the employee is responsible.

With its *Dabbs* decision, the court indicated that public policy exemptions could rely on a broad discretionary interpretation of public policy. This discretion in interpreting what constitued a public policy, in turn, gave potential litigants and their legal representatives greater leeway for challenging dismissals on general principles or ethical grounds in areas (where statutory violation could not necessarily be documented). As a consequence of *Dabbs* and related rulings, unjust dismissal suits based on the public policy exemption initially counted amongst the most prominent cause of action claimed in the context of dismissal litigation.

---

[270] See, e.g., Sheets v. Teddy's Frosted Foods, 427 A.2d 385 (Conn. 1980) involving the improper discharge of an employee who reported the company for not complying with the state's food and drug act; McQuary v. Bel Air Convalescent Home, Inc., 69 Ore. App. 107, 684 P.2d 21, rev. den., 298 Ore. 37, 688 P.2d 845 (1984) involving the wrongful dismissal of an employee who reported violations of the Oregon nursing home patient's bill of rights; and Watassek v. Michigan Dep't of Mental Health, 143 Mich. App. 556, 372 NW2d 617 (1985) involving the discharge of an employee who reported incidents of patient abuse.

[271] Dabbs v. Cardiopulmonary Management Servs., 188 Cal. App. 3d 1437, 243 Cal. Rptr. 129 (1987).

[272] Dabbs, ibid., at 1444 and 1445, 188 Cal. App. 3d.

[273] Dabbs, ibid., at 1444, 188 Cal. App. 3d.

A second route of departure from the at-will rule evolved from the gradual legal recognition by several courts that the conditions associated with individual employment contracts had moved beyond the traditional "hire and fire" employment relationship. During the 1970s, some courts were confronted by litigants who provided evidence that their employment contracts included implied promises of permanency that, under certain conditions, were enforceable in law. In acknowledging the validity of these claims, several state courts introduced two additional types of at-will exemptions, though not necessarily as actions in tort. Under the first of these exemptions—the implied contract exemption—oral and written assurances of termination only for good cause, or some other specified standard, were interpreted as enforceable contracts. Starting in 1972, with *Drzwiecki v. H. R. Block*, California courts found dismissals wrongful because of assurances constituting an implied contract.[274] Following several less significant cases, guidance on an implied contract breach was given in *Pugh v. See's Candies Inc.*, in 1981.[275] In *Pugh*, a California Appeals Court ruled that:[276]

> The presumption that an employment contract is intended to be terminable at will is subject, like any presumption, to contrary evidence … In determining whether there exists an implied-in-fact promise for some form of continued employment courts … [c]an consider … a variety of factors … . These have included, for example, the personnel policies or practices of the employer, the employer longevity of service, actions or communications by the employer reflecting assurances of continued employment and the practices of the industry in which the employee is engaged. …[P]ersonnel policies or practices of the employer, the employees longevity of service, actions or communications by the employer reflecting assurances of continued employment, and the practices of industry in which the employee is engaged (citations omitted) can give rise to an enforceable contract.

This notion of an implied contract exemption, like that of the earlier public policy exemption, was again broadened in a succession of court rulings. In its 1984 ruling on *Rulon Miller v. IBM*, for instance, a California Court of Appeals found in favor of a plaintiff who had been dismissed on the basis of a code of conduct policy that the court found to lack clarity.[277] Similar cases generally construed the presence of personnel policies and handbooks as evidence for promises of permanency.

The third type of at-will exemptions related to the claim of breach of the covenant of good faith and fair dealing. One of the earliest cases recognizing that claim, *Cleary v. American Airlines Inc.* of 1980, held that the discharge, without just-cause, of an employee with a satisfactory record of long-term employment was a breach of the implied covenant and gave rise to action in tort.[278]

The claim of unjust dismissal in *Cleary* was based on company policy statements that had expressed, albeit somewhat vaguely, that an employee would not be dismissed without cause. This, and similar assurances, the court saw as representing an implied contract, the violation of which could represent an unjust dismissal.

---

[274] Drzewiecki v. H. and R. Block, Inc., 24 Cal. App. 3d 695, 101 Cal. Rptr. 169 (1972).

[275] Pugh v. See's Candies, Inc., 116 Cal. App. 3d 311, 171 Cal. Rptr. 917 (1981).

[276] Pugh, ibid., at 324 and 327, 116 Cal. App. 3d.

[277] Rulon-Miller v. IBM, 162 Cal. App. 3d 241, 208 Cal. Rptr. 524 (1984).

[278] Cleary v. American Airlines, Inc., 111 Cal. App. 3d 443, 168 Cal. Rptr. 722 (2d Dist. 1980).

A further clarification of this doctrine was given in the California cases of *Khanna* in 1985, and *Huber* in 1988.[279] In these cases, the respective courts ruled that employees who had been dismissed without good-cause had available unjust dismissal remedies even in the absence of a specified grievance procedure. Whereas, in *Cleary*, the contract had specified an employment dispute resolution procedure, the *Khanna* and *Huber* courts found that such procedures were not a pre-requisite for a claim of good faith and fair dealing. Specifically the *Khanna* court argued that dispute resolution procedures:[280]

> ... are not the *sine qua non* to establishing a breach of the covenant of good faith and fair dealing implied in every employment contract ... To the contrary, a breach ... is established whenever the employer engages in bad faith action extraneous to the contract.
>
> ... a breach of the implied covenant of good faith and fair dealing in employment contracts is established whenever the employer engages in "bad faith action ... combined with the obligator's intent to frustrate the [employees] enjoyment of contract rights." [citations omitted]. The facts in Cleary establish only one manner among many by which the employer might violate this covenant.

In *Huber*, a federal appeals court decided that bad faith could also be inferred merely from evidence that an employers' discontent with an employee was unfounded—or in other words, that the employer lacked good-cause for termination. Huber had factually contested the employer's reason for the discharge, leading the court to note that because Huber:[281]

> presented affidavit evidence reciting easily verifiable facts contradicting each of [the employer's] stated reasons for termination, Huber has raised genuine issues of material fact as to the existence of a prima facie case of breach of the covenant of good faith and fair dealing.

Huber, of course, cannot be misread to imply that any termination of a non-union employee lacking just cause can be challenged in court; the ruling is in fact much narrower. Huber's action ultimately rested on the factual questionability of his employer's accounts of his past performance rather than the failure of the employer to give a just cause for the dismissal.[282] The rights conferred upon employees in *Huber* therefore are not comparable to those of a unionized employee working under a just-cause standard. The remedies available to an employee who successfully asserts the wrongfulness of a dismissal in a *Huber* type case, however, can paradoxically exceed those of a unionized employee. Thus, while the standard arbitral remedy under collective bargaining for a wrongful discharge is reinstatement plus backpay for lost wages and benefits, non-union employees can, in theory, recover substantial damages for their wrongful dismissal, especially if they are highly paid and/or their dismissal attracts tort remedies.

In contrast to arbitral remedies, moreover, litigation-based remedies are constrained geographically and practically. Geographically speaking, only the public policy doctrine is accepted by an overwhelming majority of states. Both the implied contract and good faith and

---

[279] Khanna v. Microdata Corp., 170 Cal. App. 3d 250, 215 Cal. Rptr. 860 (1985) (upholding a jury award for bad faith termination after employee filed suit to recover commissions); and Huber v. Standard Insurance Co., 841 F.2d 980 (9th Cir. 1988).

[280] Khanna, ibid., at 262, 170 Cal. App. 3d.

[281] Huber, ibid., at 987, 841 F.2d.

[282] See Richard Moon, "Attack/Counter Attack: The Continuing Evolution of Wrongful Discharge Claims," in *Labor Law Developments 1990* Chapter 7 (Southwestern Legal Foundation, ed., 1991) for a detailed discussion of Huber and related cases.

fair dealing doctrines, meanwhile, are available in fewer than half of the states. Practically speaking, a host of additional limitations arise, as we shall see, for wrongfully dismissed plaintiffs both on account of the affordability of litigation and the uncertainties associated with jury verdicts.

THE STATE AND UNJUST DISMISSAL LITIGATION

By the late 1980s, several state legislatures alleged that the departure of state and federal courts from the at-will standard was having significant adverse resource implications on businesses enterprises and the court system. Subsequent attempts to limit the effects of unjust dismissal litigation generally centered on two agendas. Firstly, some state legislatures explored proposals aimed at protecting business interests from "arbitrarily high" jury awards. Secondly, some legislatures discussed bills that were aimed at protecting the courts from the undue strains that the new litigation was assumed to be creating. Roughly at the same time, several state courts handed down rulings that were expected to halt the expansion of dismissal litigation.

In its 1988 ruling on *Foley v. Interactive Data Co.*, the California supreme court took steps to limit access to unjust dismissal remedies.[283] In *Foley*, the court affirmed all three exemptions from employment-at-will (i.e., the public policy, implied contract, and good faith exemptions) and then gave guidance as to what constituted a proper claim and proper remedies. Amongst other issues, the court concluded that a merely private purpose, which served only the interests of the employer and employee and not the public at large, was inadequate to state a claim for breach of public policy.[284] With regard to implied contract claims, the court concluded that it would continue to recognize existing doctrines but noted that it would treat these actions as a contract claim consistent with traditional contract law analysis rather than as actions in tort.[285] Specifically, the court declined to analogize the implied contract in the employment setting to the implied covenant in insurance contracts that gave rise to tort claims. This reasoning was based on the understanding that employers did not perform a quasi-public function comparable to that of insurers, as a previous court decision had argued. Whereas the threat of tort action was necessary to protect the public from the inherent tension between the insurers and the insured, the employment relationship did not require a tort context, as it involved processes of "mutual accommodation."[286]

---

[283] Foley v. Interactive Data Corp., 47 Cal. 3d 654, 765 P.2d 373, 254 Cal. Rptr. 211 (1988).

[284] Foley, ibid., at 670, 47 Cal. 3d.

[285] Foley, ibid., at 681, 47 Cal. 3d. Initially, it was thought that California courts would strictly enforce a rule whereby successful implied contract claims could only recover damages for economic loss and not punitive damages or damages for emotional distress. Due to plaintiffs alleging multiple courses of action and dividing lines between the three exemptions being less than clear, this rule seems to have become less relevant over time.

[286] See Foley, ibid., 684 and 689, 47 Cal. 3d. According to the Foley court, previous judgments on the implied covenant assigned the employment contract a status similar to an insurance contract. In doing so, it forced employers to perform quasi- "public responsibilities," which required them to act fairly under the threat of tort action. Feeling that too much of a burden is imposed on the employer under this doctrine, the Foley court adopted a distinctly neoclassical economics-based interpretation of the employment contract. In this interpretation, conditions of employment are not subject to a rigid interpretation of the contract, meant to protect the employee primarily, but rather to processes of flexible negotiation. The employment contract as is merely provides a framework to this process of negotiation. When action against the employer arises, this

Since *Foley*, California case law has been less than clear with regard to the role of juries in determining and assessing wrongful discharge claims. Thus, in the 1998 cases of *Cotran v Rollins Hudig Hall International* and *Silva v. Lucky Stores*, the courts overturned jury verdicts on account of the fact that the employer had "reasonably believed" that the alleged misconduct took place and that it otherwise acted "fairly;" indicating that it was not the jury's role to second-guess employers.[287] In the 1999 case of *Carrisales v. Department of Corrections*, in contrast, the Appeals Court ruled that an employer could be held liable for wrongful discharge in a harassment case, even though he had put a sexual harassment policy in place and provided for training in this respect.[288]

In his 1990 review of *Foley*, the practicing labor lawyer Richard Moon concluded that despite the narrowing of the public policy exemption and the elimination of action in tort on other matters, *Foley* was unlikely to have a major impact on current litigation practices.[289] Moon suggested that the implied contract, as well as good faith and fair dealing cases, might become somewhat less lucrative in California. This, Moon argued, would, however, merely encourage attorneys to represent higher paid employees with projected future losses of at least $150,000. If the number of employees seeking court action continued to increase, this restriction would have little effect on aggregate case numbers. More importantly, Moon suggested that California's temporary retreat from a further expansion of dismissal litigation could in fact be a boon to plaintiffs' lawyers in other states. He predicted that the court's exacting analysis in *Foley* would be used as a weapon to expand public policy and implied contract claims in other jurisdictions, where such issues were as yet unresolved.

Contrary to premature predictions of a "death" of unjust dismissal litigation, current evidence would suggest that Moon's prediction of *Foley* having only a very limited impact was by and large correct.[290] Thus, in the decade following Foley, a further five states have adopted the public policy exemption, ten states the implied contract exemption and four states the implied covenant of good faith and fair dealing.[291]

Notwithstanding the California courts largely unsuccessful efforts to curb unjust dismissal litigation, several state legislatures have attempted to regulate unjust dismissals

---

should therefore merely serve to restore the integrity of the contract, rather than penalizing one or the other party.

[287] See Cotran v. Rollins Hudig Hall Int'l, Inc., 17 Cal.4th 93; 69 Cal.Rptr.2d 900 (1998) and Silva v. Lucky Stores, Inc., 65 Cal. App. 4th 256 (1998).

[288] Carrisales v. Department of Corrections, 21 Cal. 4th 1132, 988 P.2d 1083, 90 Cal. Rptr. 2d 804 (1999).

[289] Moon, *supra* note 282, at 7-2 and 7-9.

[290] Following Foley, California court and courts of other states continued to award million dollar damages, with judgments closely mirroring pre-Foley rationales. See, e.g., Walia v. Aetna, Inc., 113 Cal. Rptr. 2d 737, 746 (Cal. Ct. App. 2001), reviewed by, 41 P.2d 548 in which the California Appeals court affirmed all elements of a verdict that had awarded $54,312 in compensatory damages, $125,000 in emotional distress damages and $1,080,000 million in punitive damages. Walia involved a law school graduate who was dismissed on account of her refusal to sign a non-competition provision. Referring to the California Business and Professions Code §16600, which notes that the "the interests of the employee in his own mobility and betterment are deemed paramount to the business interests of the employer," the Appeals Court affirmed the wrongful discharge exemption on public policy grounds. This followed the earlier judgment of D'Sa v. Playhut, Inc., 85 Cal.App.4th 927 (2000), which applied the public policy exemption to non-compete provisions even though the employer's actions had not been criminal and there was no clear precedent of narrow anti-compete provisions giving rise to a public policy claim.

[291] These figures are based on a comparison of 1990 and 2000 data as reported in Alan .B. Krueger, "The Evolution of Unjust Dismissal legislation in the United States" 44 *Industrial and Labour Relations Review* 644 (1991) and David Autor, John J. Donohue III, and Stewart J. Schwab, "The Costs of Wrongful Discharge Laws," *National Bureau of Economic Research Working Paper No. 9425*, at 34: Legal Appendix (2001).

through statutory means. Driven by concerns over the high cost of wrongful discharge suits, bills were introduced in the California and Michigan legislatures in 1984 and 1982, respectively, which provided general protection against unjust discharge. Under these bills, dismissals were to be assessed on the basis of a just-cause standard, with the amount recoverable by an employee being limited by law. In neither of these states—both pioneers of wrongful discharge legislation—did these or similar bills come to pass.[292]

The first state to pass a dismissal statute was Montana, which introduced its Wrongful Discharge from Employment Act in 1987.[293] The passage of the act was prompted by special circumstances.[294] Between 1981 and 1986, an unusually large number of unjust dismissal suits, 182 in all, were filed in Billings, Montana. This flood of lawsuits was related to downsizing efforts in Montana's health and tourism industry. In a 1986 case, the Montana Supreme Court awarded its highest punitive damages ever, with $1.3 million going to an employee. Some months later, the state court held that liability for wrongful discharge was not a "covered occurrence" under a general liability policy. Following complaints by employers, legislative committees heard testimony that liability insurance to cover wrongful discharge could not be easily purchased by Montana employers. Employer representatives, moreover, claimed that they could face bankruptcy by reason of the expense of defending such litigation. When the State Supreme Court widened its interpretation of wrongful discharge to require that employers must investigate claims on which dismissals are based, the legislature feared that a further wave of costly litigation would face local companies and accelerated the drafting and passage of its Wrongful Discharge Act.

The Montana act defines wrongful dismissals relatively narrowly as: a) instances where the dismissal was in retaliation for an employee's refusal to violate public policy of reporting such a violation; b) instances where the employee had completed her probationary period, and there was no good cause for firing her; and c) cases where there was an express written personnel policy that did not permit such a dismissal. For all three types of violations, the statute limits damages to four year's lost wages and required the employee to exhaust internal company appeals procedures. As part of this act, all common law claims were successively preempted.

Due to its comparatively narrow definition of wrongful discharges—employees who cannot rely on an express statue in their public policy claim or merely exercise a legal right were excluded unless protected by federal statue—and its limit on damages, employer representatives initially welcomed the introduction of the act; a view that appears to have changed over time on account of a relatively large number of employees being paid compensation under the act.[295]

---

[292] In 2002, Arizona had introduced a limited bill protecting employees whose employers had violated public policy; Arkansas had an interim bill comparable to that of Montana pending; Delaware had a wrongful discharge bill before Senate; Missouri had introduced a limited bill protecting employees whose employers had violated public policy; New York had a wrongful discharge bill before state house; and Texas had a bill pending that was to give statutory protection to workers employed for ten years whose employer had violated public policy. See <http://www.laborlawtalk.com/forumdisplay.php?f=6> accessed during various years,

[293] Montana Code Annex §§39-2-903 to 39-2-915 (1993).

[294] Janice Jackson and William T. Schantz, "A New Frontier in Wrongful Discharge" *Personnel Journal* 101, 102 January (1990).

[295] In Andrews v. Plum Creek Mfg., 2001 MT 94, 305 Mont. 194, 27 P.3d 426, the court found in favor of a newly hired clerical employee who was transferred to a production job in the company's mill on account of a mismatch of invoices and deposit slips. The court ruled that the employer had not provided the training

In 1989, the constitutionality of the act was challenged in *Meech v. Hillhaven West*. The Montana Supreme Court upheld the constitutionality of the act and all its components, even though the act eliminated damages for wrongful discharge for pain, suffering, and emotional distress.[296] This ruling led some observers to expect that similar legislation would be passed in other states. Influenced by the Montana policy, the National Conference of Commissioners on State Laws, an association of high-ranking civil servants, drafted its Model Uniform Termination Act.[297] The creation of the Model Act was ostensibly driven by the goal of creating uniformity in terms of employees' substantive rights and remedies across states. More likely, work on the Act commenced because conference members had voiced concerns over the high caseload of state courts, which could partially be attributed to increases in wrongful dismissal litigation. Less generous than the Montana statute, the Uniform Termination Act was subject to severe criticism early on.[298]

William Mauk, a plaintiff's attorney, reported that even employer associations were critical of the act, primarily on account of fears of new red-tape being created. Support for the act, interestingly, came primarily from the National Association's employee representatives, which described its passage as a big victory for unorganized labor. Management representatives, in contrast, had voiced strong criticism throughout the three-year drafting period but agreed to participate in order to "prevent worse." The National Association of Labor Lawyers, meanwhile, critiqued the act for its loopholes and potential ineffectiveness. Its spokesperson, Dr. Rosen, suggested that employers could void coverage by treating an employee as independent contractor, by keeping an employee for some months at less than 20 hours per week, or by firing the employee before a year of employment had passed. Plaintiff's attorney Golden of Southfield similarly noted that the law was not intended to give rights to employees in states where they had none but to neutralize employees where they do have some rights. Golden predicted that the act would go nowhere in states where employees had already been given discharge litigation rights.

As yet, only the state of South Dakota has adopted a statute based on the model act, and there are no indications of a major wave of future adoptions by other states.[299] This has surprised many observers since, in 1991, the Uniform Termination Act or similar legislation was proposed in most, if not all, state legislatures. The reluctance of most state legislatures to adopt such acts has thwarted expectations that employers would, in light of large and variable damage awards, support unjust dismissal legislation in order to clearly define property rights and reduce uncertainty.

In some respects, the failure of dismissal statutes to gain widespread acceptance can be seen as evidence for the overwhelming preference of most state legislatures and judiciaries for a flexible system in which compensatory and/or punitive damages are assigned according to the specific circumstances of a case. As concerns the evident lack of support for statutory

---

necessary to ensure that the employee performed satisfactorily on the job and therefore ruled that the dismissal was not for good cause.

[296] Meech v. Hillhaven West, Inc., 238 Mont. 21, 776 P.2d 488 (1989).

[297] Bureau of National Affairs, "Uniform Employment Termination Act," *Daily Labor Report* no 156, August 13 (1991).

[298] See William L. Mauk, "Model Termination Act is Flawed," 27 *Trial* 28, at 32 (1991). Marc Jarsulic, "Protecting Workers from Wrongful Discharge: Montana's Experience with Tort and Statutory Regimes" 3 *Employee Rights and Employment Policy Journal*, 105, at 112 (1999) also suggests that the statute significantly reduced the time it took to litigate and the size of awards.

[299] South Dakota Code Ann. §60-4-4 (1995).

solutions by employers, this can also, at least in part, be attributed to the fact that organizational concerns often override a purely economic calculus. Many managers may well be convinced that the frequent payment of dismissal awards or mandatory arbitration is more detrimental to their authority than an "occasional," and potentially costly, defeat in an unjust dismissal suit.[300]

GEOGRAPHIC DIFFUSION AND CONCEPTUAL CONSOLIDATION

Outside California, the legal possibilities of the *Petermann* decision, the first unjust dismissal suit, initially remained unexplored for some time. A similar decision to that of *Petermann* was rendered by a Michigan Appeals court in 1978, in the case of *Trombetta v. Detroit, Toledo and Ironton Railroad*; which involved an employee who refused to falsify pollution reports.[301] In 1973, the Indiana Supreme Court's ruling on *Frampton v. Central Indiana Gas* introduced the public policy exemption to that state, in the context of a worker who had filed a worker's compensation claim.[302] In 1977, the Massachusetts Supreme Court's *Fortune v. National Cash Register* decision concluded that it was not only contrary to public policy to allow an employer to dismiss an employee for exercising rights created by law but also to allow employers to terminate employees for exercising a private right spelled out in a company handbook.[303] One year earlier, in *Agis v. Howard Johnson,* a Massachusetts court had already held that where an employer's conduct in discharging an employee was extreme and outrageous, the employee could recover damages for the employers intentional infliction of mental distress.[304] In 1980, in *Pierce v. Orthopharmacutical Co,* New Jersey followed earlier California decisions by ruling in favor of a drug company employee who had objected to the submission of a drug for human testing, even though no explicit statute was available.[305] In the 1992 case of *Wider v. Skala*, the New York Supreme Court condoned a wrongful dismissal action for breach of contract in a case where no company handbook or other written evidence of a long-term employment contract was available.[306]

---

[300] Jackson and Schantz, *supra* note 294, at 102.

[301] Trombetta v. Detroit, Toledo, and Ironton RR Co., 81 Mich. App. 489, 265 NW2d 385 (1978).

[302] Frampton v. Central Indiana Gas Co., 260 Ind. 249, 297 NE2d 425 (1973).

[303] Fortune v. National Cash Register Co., 373 Mass. 96, 103, 364 NE2d 1251, 1256-57 (1977).

[304] Agis v. Howard Johnson Co., 371 Mass. 140, 355 NE2d 315 (1976).

[305] Pierce v. Ortho Pharmaceutical Corp., 84 NJ 58, 417 A. 2d 505 (1980).

[306] Wieder v. Skala, 80 N.Y.2d 628, 609 N.E.2d 105, 593 N.Y.S.2d 752 (1992). Wieder presented a novel interpretation of the notion of "implied contract" constructed not out of the employment contract but of external obligations. Wieder was employed as a commercial litigation attorney with the defendant's law firm, where he complained about the illegal conduct of an employee of the firm to his senior partners and asked them to report the issue to the Appeals Division Disciplinary Committee as required by the Professional Responsibility Association of the Bar of New York. Wieder withdrew his complaint to the bar because the firm indicated that it would discharge him if he reported the misconduct of his fellow employee. The firm nevertheless continued to employ him because he was in charge of handling the firm's most important litigation. Wieder was discharged a few days after he filed motion papers in that case. The court found no support for a public policy claim, concluding that the whistleblower law of the state was not applicable, and that no evidence for an implied contract could be found in a company handbook but suggested that in any hiring of an attorney, there is an implied understanding so fundamental to the relationship as to require no expression. Given that an attorney could face disbarment if he failed with the state's reporting requirement, the court determined that, by insisting that the employee disregard the misconduct of another employee, the firm made his further employment impossible. Concluding that Mr Wieder had stated "a valid claim for breach of

The Federal Courts, meanwhile, have indirectly contributed to the evolution of a doctrinal framework underpinning unjust dismissal litigation. In the 1985 case of *Andersen v. E and J Gallo Winery*, for instance, a district court, applying Connecticut's stringent whistleblower legislation established the liability of the employer in tort.[307]

Similarly, the Appeals Court for the Third Circuit awarded punitive damages to an employee who was wrongfully discharged in 1983 in *Woodson v. AMF Leisureland Centers*, where the employee was discharged after she refused to serve alcoholic beverages to intoxicated persons.[308] The Third Circuit concluded that even though Pennsylvania law did not expressively forbid such conduct, the protection of the employee would not constitute an unwarranted extension of Pennsylvania law.

In 1994, the legal position of the public policy exemption was further strengthened with the Supreme Court's ruling in *Hawaiian Airlines v. Grant T. Norris,* which decided that the Railroad Labor Act (RLA) *did not* preempt an aircraft mechanic's action for wrongful discharge.[309] The *Hawaiian Airlines* decision reversed a trend, which had been established by the Supreme Court's *Ingersoll Rand Co. v. McClendon*, in which the court had upheld the preemption of wrongful discharge claims by alternative statutory remedies.[310] In its 1990 *Ingersoll* decision, the Supreme Court had held that an employee's public policy action, claiming that the principal reason for his dismissal was the employer's desire to avoid contributing to or paying benefits under the employees' pension fund, was preempted by the Employer Retirement Income Security Act (ERISA). Specifically, the Court held that ERISA's explicit language and its structure and purpose demonstrates Congressional intent to preempt a state common law claim that an employee was unlawfully discharged to prevent his attainment of benefits under an ERISA-secured plan. Although a similar preemptive character could, and had, been construed from the RLA, the Supreme Court felt that the circumstances involved in *Hawaiian Airlines* justified the plaintiff's state wrongful discharge claim.

Plaintiff Norris, an aircraft mechanic, was employed by Hawaiian Airlines (HAL) in February 1987. His terms of employment were covered by a collective bargaining agreement between the carrier and the machinist and aerospace worker's union (IAMAW). Norris's mechanic's license authorized him to approve an airplane and return it into service after he made, supervised, or inspected, what he deemed to be necessary repairs. In July 1987, Norris refused to certify a maintenance record. As a consequence, the supervisor suspended Norris pending a termination hearing.

Norris reported the incident immediately to the Federal Aviation Authority. Two weeks following the incident, a Step-1 grievance hearing was held as specified in the collective bargaining agreement. At the end of the meeting, the hearing officer terminated Norris for insubordination. Conforming to collective bargaining agreement (CBA) procedures, Norris then appealed the decision and sought a Step-3 grievance hearing. Before the second hearing took place, HAL offered to suspend Norris for an unspecified time without pay but warned him that any further action of this kind would result in his immediate discharge.

---

contract based on an implied-law obligation," the court reversed a previous judgment and granted Wieder relief.

[307] Andersen v. E. and J. Gallo Winery, No. CIV. H 85-295 (JAC), 1985 WL 134. (D. Conn. Nov. 7, 1985).

[308] Woodson v. AMF Leisureland Ctrs., Inc., 842 F.2d 699, 702-03 (3d Cir. 1988).

[309] Hawaiian Airlines, Inc. v. Norris, 512 U.S. 246, 114 S.Ct. 2239, 129 L.Ed.2d 203 (1994).

[310] Ingersoll Rand Co. v. McClendon, 498 U.S. 133, 111 S.Ct. 478, 112 L.Ed. 2d 474 (1990).

In December 1987, Norris filed suit against HAL. His complaint included a claim for wrongful-discharge and torts-discharge in violation of the public policy expressed in the Federal Aviation Act and dismissal in violation of Hawaii's whistleblower act. HAL removed the action to the district court of Hawaii, which dismissed both wrongful discharge claims as preempted by the Railroad Labor Act. A second suit, naming as defendants the three HAL officers who had directed the discharge, was dismissed by a Hawaii trial court, again on grounds that it was preempted by the RLA. Norris's suit was then upheld by the Supreme Court of the state of Hawaii. In a further appeal, the US Supreme Court held that neither the RLA nor the collective bargaining agreement preempted state law causes of action on wrongful discharge. Justice Harry Blackmun ruling stated that "the most natural reading of the term 'grievances' in this context is as a synonym for disputes involving the application or interpretation of a collective bargaining agreement."[311] Since procedures regarding whistleblowing were not legally be a part of collective bargaining agreements, requirements to use the grievance apparatus could not be imposed on a whistleblower; and neither could her or his claims be relegated to collective, compulsory arbitration.

As to the second issue, namely whether the plaintiff was required to exhaust arbitral remedies under the RLA, Justice Blackmun concluded that the bargaining agreement was not the principal source of a respondent's right not to be wrongfully discharged. Specifically, Blackmun stated that in connection with Norris' claim, there existed a direct legal liability of the employer with regard to a wrongful discharge:[312]

> Here, in contrast, the CBA is not the "only source" of respondent's right not to be discharged wrongfully. In fact, the "only source" of the right respondent asserts in this action is state law tort. Wholly apart from any provisions of the CBA, petitioners had a state law obligation not to fire respondent in violation of public policy or in retaliation for whistleblowing. The parties' obligation under RLA to arbitrate disputes arising out of the application or interpretation of the CBA did not relieve petitioners of this duty.

One crucial component of Blackmun's decision was the idea that an employer was obligated by law not to fire an employee in violation of public policy. Citing the 1988 case of *Lingle v. Norge Division of Magic Chef Inc.*, Blackmun stated there was a fundamental difference between contractual claims and state or common law-dependent claims.[313] A state-law retaliatory discharge claim required the court to interpret factual issues of whether the employer was discharged unfairly under the respective doctrine of wrongful discharge:[314]

> It is observed, however, that "purely factual questions" about an employee's conduct or an employer's conduct and motives "do not requir[e] a court to interpret any term of a

---

[311] Hawaiian Airlines, *supra* note 309, at 255, 512 U.S.

[312] Hawaiian Airlines, *supra* note 309, at 259, 512 U.S. citing Andrews v. Louisville and Nashville R. Co., 406 U.S. 320, 92 S.Ct. 1562, 32 L.Ed.2d 95 (1972), where a "state-law claim of wrongful termination was pre-empted, not because the RLA broadly pre-empts state-law claims based on discharge or discipline, but because the employee's claim was firmly rooted in a breach of the CBA itself."

[313] Lingle v. Norge Division of Magic Chef, Inc., 486 U.S. 399, 408, 108 S.Ct. 1877, 100 L.Ed.2d 410 (1988). This decision itself had attracted some controversy; see, e.g., Jane Byeff Korn, "Collective Rights and Individual Remedies: Rebalancing the Balance after Lingle v. Norge Division of Magic Chef, Inc.," 41 Hastings Law Journal 1149 (1989) and also Stephanie R. Marcus, "The Need for a New Approach to Federal Preemption of Union Members' State Law Claims," 99 The Yale Law Journal 209 (1989).

[314] Hawaiian Airlines, *supra* note 309, at 262 and 263, 512 U.S.

collective bargaining agreement" ... The state law retaliatory discharge claim turned on just this sort of purely factual question: whether the employee was discharged or threatened with discharge, and if so, whether the employer's motive in discharging him was to deter or interfere with his exercise of rights ...

As to the interaction of Federal Law (such as the NLRA and the RLA) and state wrongful discharge claims, Blackmun cited the Court's earlier *Lingle*:[315]

> For while there may be instances in which the National Labor Relations Act preempts state law on the subject matter of the law in question, ... preemption merely ensures that federal law will be the basis for interpreting collective bargaining agreements, and says nothing about the substantive rights a state might provide to workers ... In other words, even if dispute resolution pursuant to a collective bargaining agreement, on the one hand, and state law on the other, would require addressing precisely the same facts, as long as the state law claims can be resolved without interpreting the agreement itself, the claim is "independent" of the agreement for preemption purposes.

Although the latter qualification of "as long as the state law claims can be resolved without interpreting the agreement itself" may have been somewhat ambiguous, Blackmun's analysis generally suggests that, in principle, state-law wrongful discharge claims should be upheld against preemptive statutes. This seems to imply a desire to eliminate the barriers to wrongful discharge litigation facing union members.[316]

The cumulation of court decisions that have modified the at-will doctrine has firmly established three specific types of exemptions from employment at-will mentioned before. [317] Today, US courts find dismissals unjust and/or award damages if the employee states a claim that falls into an acknowledged exemption from employment at-will. Accordingly, a dismissal is deemed unfair, firstly, if the employer has terminated the employee in violation of public policy, i.e., dismissed the employee because of a refusal to commit a criminal act on behalf of the employer or reported a violation of federal, state, or professional regulations. A second source of exemption from employment at-will arises where the employer's personnel policies, course of conduct, or oral promise created an implied contract for continued employment. Third, a claim for unfair dismissal can arise from an employer's breach of the covenant of good faith and fair dealing. Outside California, this doctrine has been applied largely to cases where employers dismissed workers in order to evade a pension, bonus or injury compensation payment, i.e., where evidence for employer opportunism exists.

---

[315] Hawaiian Airlines, *supra* note 309, at 263, 512 U.S. citing Lingle, *supra* note 313, at 408, 486 U.S. 399.

[316] Mendelsohn, *supra* note 250, at 16, suggests that despite the Supreme Court's decisions in Lingle and Norris, wrongful termination litigation may pose particular difficulties for unionized workers. Mendelsohn speculates that this situation has the potential of making union membership less attractive.

[317] The legal literature does as of yet not offer a consistent framework for the classification of exemptions, although the categorization of exemptions under the topics public policy, implied contract, and good faith, seems to have gained some ground. . The trend to distinguish three groups of exemptions has been strengthened by court decisions that held other claims, such as those based on discrimination, to be preempted by statute (such as state human rights acts, Title VII of the Civil Rights Act, or other federal acts, including the Employment Retirement Income Security Act). For early summaries of the above classifications, see, e.g., Mendelsohn, *supra* note 250, at 4; Richard G. Moon, "Wrongful Termination—New Claims and New Theories for Plaintiffs and Defendants," in *Labor Law Developments 1988* Chapter 9 (Southwestern Legal Foundation, ed., 1989) and Dorian A. McWhirter, *Your Rights at Work,* at 59 (1989).

UNJUST DISMISSAL LITIGATION AND JOB SECURITY

Today, the acceptance of wrongful discharge exemptions is widespread. A majority of US state courts and legislatures prohibit the discharge of workers who publicize misconduct on the part of their employer or other employees, refuse to commit illegal or unethical acts, and/or insist on their legal rights.

According to a study by David Autor, John J. Donohue III, and Stewart J. Schwab, by 2000, the courts of forty-seven states recognized one of the three exemptions from employment-at-will.[318] Specifically, in the year 2000, a total of forty-two states recognized the public policy exemption; making this the most widely recognized exemption.[319] Forty-one states recognized the implied contract exemption,[320] and eleven states the good faith

---

[318] See Autor, Donohue, and Schwab, *supra* note 291, at 34: Legal Appendix. The three states not having acknowledged any exemptions by 2000, were Florida, Georgia and Rhode Island.

[319] See Autor, Donohue, and Schwab, *supra* note 291, at 34: Legal Appendix, noting that the public policy exemption was adopted in: Alaska in Knight v. American Guard and Alert, 714 P.2d 788 (Alaska 1986); Arizona in Wagenseller v. Scottsdale Memorial Hospital, 710 P.2d 1025 (Ariz. 1985); Arkansas in MBM Co. v. Counce, 596 S.W.2d 681 (Ark 1980); California in Petermann v. Int'l Brotherhood Teamsters, 344 P.2d 35 (Cal. Ct. App. 1959); Colorado in Winther v. DEC Int'l Inc, 625 F.Supp. 100 (Colo. 1985); Connecticut in Sheets v. Teddy's Frosted Foods, 427 A.2d 385 (Conn. 1980); Delaware in Henze v. Alloy, 1992 WL51861 (Del. 1992); Hawaii in Parnar v. Americana Hotels, 652 P.2d 625 (Haw. 1982); Idaho in Jackson v. Minidoka Irrigation District, 563 P.2d 54 (Idaho 1977); Illinois in Kelsey v. Motorola, 384 N.E.2d 353 (Ill. 1978); Indiana in Frampton v. Central Indiana Gas Co, 297 N.E.2d 425 (Ind. 1973); Iowa in Northrup v. Farmland Ind., 372 N.W.2d 193 (Iowa 1985); Kansas in Murphy v. City of Topeka, 630 P.2d 186 (Kan. Ct. App. 1981); Kentucky in Firestone Textile Co. v. Meadows, 666 S.W.2d 730 (KY. 1983); Maryland in Adler v. American Standard Corp., 432 A.2d 454 (Md. 1981); Massachusetts in McKinney v. National Dairy Council, 491 F.Supp. 1108 (D.Mass. 1980); Michigan in Seventko v. Kruger, 245 N.W.2d 151 (Mich. 1976); Minnesota in Phipps v. Clark Oil and Refining Co., 396 N.W.2d 588 (Minn. Ct. App. 1986); Mississippi in Laws v. Aetna Finance Co., 667 F.Supp 342 (N.D. Miss. 1987); Missouri in Boyle v. Vista Eyewear, 700 S.W.2d 859 (Mo. Ct. App. 1985); Montana in Keneally v. Sterling Orgaine, 606 P.2d 127 (Mont. 1980); Nebraska in Ambroz v. Cornhusker Square, 416 N.W.2d 510 (Neb. 1987); Nevada in Hansen v. Harrah's, 675 P.2d 394 (Nev. 1984); New Hampshire in Monge v. Beebe Rubber Co., 316 A.2d 549 (N.H. 1974); New Jersey in Pierce v. Orthopharm. Corp, 417 A.2d 5050 (N.J. 1980); New Mexico in Vigil v. Arzola, 699 P.2d 613 (N.M. Ct. App. 1983); North Caroline in Sides v. Duke Univ., 328 S.E.2d 818 (N.C. Ct. App. 1984); North Dakota in Krein v. Marian Manor Nursing Home, 415 N.W.2d 793 (N.D. 1987); Ohio in Greely v. Miami Valley Maintenance Contractors Inc., 551 N.E.2d 981 (Ohio 1990); Oklahoma in Burk v. K-Mart Corp., 770 P.2d 24 (Okla. 1989); Oregon in Knees v. Hocks, 536 P.2d 512 (Oreg. 1975); Pennsylvania in Geary v. United States Steel Corp., 319 A.2d 174 (Pa. 1974); South Caroline in Ludwig v. This Minute of Carolina Inc., 337 S.E.2d 213 (S.C. 1985); South Dakota in Johnson v. Kreisers Inc., 433 N.W.2d 225 (S.D. 1988); Tennessee in Clanton v. Clain-Sloan Co., 677 S.W.2d 441 (Tenn. 1984); Texas in Sabine Pilot Serv. Inc. v. Hauck, 672 S.W.2d 322 (Tex. Civ. App. 1984); Utah in Berube v. Fashion Centre, 771 P.2d 1033 (Utah 1989); Vermont in Paine v. Rozendaal, 520 A.2d 586 (VT. 1986); Virginia in Bowman v. State Bank of Keysville, 31 S.E.2d 797 (Va. 1985); Washington in Thompson v. St. Regis Paper Co., 685 P.2d 1081 (Wash. 1984); West Virginia in Harless v. First National Bank, 246 S.E.2d 270, (W.Va. 1978); Wisconsin in Ward v. Frito-Lay Inc., 290 N.W. 2d 536 (Wis. Ct. App. 1980); Wyoming in Griess v. Consolidated Freight Ways, 776 P.2d 702 (Wyo. 1989).

[320] See Autor et al., *supra* note 291, at 34: Legal Appendix, noting that the implied contract exemption was adopted in: Alabama in Hoffman-LaRoche v. Campbell, 512 So.2d 725 (Ala. 1987); Alaska in Eales v. Tanana Valley Medical Surgical Group, 663 P.2d 958 (Alaska 1983); Arizona in Leikvold v. Valley View Community Hosp., 688 P.2d 201 (Ariz. 1983); Arkansas in Jackson v. Kinark Co., 669 S.W.2d 898 (Ark. 1984); California in Drzwiecki v. H&R Block, 101 Cal.Reptr. 169 (Cal. Ct. App. 1972); Colorado in, Brooks v. TWA, 574 F.Supp. 805 (Colo. 1983); Connecticut in Finley v. Aetna Life, 499 A.2d 64 (Conn. Ct. App. 1984); Hawaii in Kinoshita v. Canadian Pacific Airlines, 724 P.2d 100 (Haw. 1986); Idaho in Jackson v. Minidoka Irrigation District, 563 P.2d 54 (Idaho 1977); Illinois in Carter v. Kaskaskia Community Action Agency, 322 N.E.2d 574 (Ill. App. Ct. 1974); Indiana in Romark v. Public Service Co., 511 N.E.2d 1024 (Ind. 1987), Iowa in Young v. Cedar County Work Activity Center, 418 N.W.2d 844 (Iowa 1987); Kansas in Allegri v. Providence-St. Margaret Health Center, 684 P.2d 1031 (Kan. Ct. App. 1984), Kentucky in Shah v. American Synthetic Rubber Co., 655 S.W.2d 489 (Ky. 1983); Maine in Terrio v. Millinocket Community Hospital 379 A.2d 135 (Me. 1977); Maryland in Staggs v. Bluecross, 486 A.2d 798 (Md.Ct.Spec.App. 1985); Massachusetts in

exemptions.[321] These exemptions have generally been granted irrespective of older statutes that codify the at-will rule, which can be found in California, New York, Georgia, Louisiana, Montana, North Dakota and South Dakota. With the exception of Georgia and Louisiana, most former at-will states have adopted at least one of the exemptions from employment at-will before the 1990s.

Wrongful dismissal suits alleging any of these three exemptions or combinations thereof have been successfully filed against large multi-national firms, small local companies, and public employers.[322] Typically, the plaintiffs are individual employees who are generally not represented by unions. Workers from all levels have filed unjust dismissal suits. However, according to several analyses, supervisory and managerial employees in service occupations and the service industries seem to be somewhat overrepresented.[323] This is particularly so in connection with the implied contract exemptions, for which most state courts, including California, provide damages only for economic loss while refusing to grant punitive damages or damages for emotional distress.[324] In all causes of action, the plaintiffs are typically

---

Hobson v. McLean Hospital Corp., 522 N.E.2d 975 (Mass. 1988); Michigan in Toussaint v. Bluecross, 292 N.W.2d 880 (Mich. 1980), Minnesota in Pine River State Bank v. Mettille, 333 N.W.2d 622 (Minn. 1983); Mississippi in Bobbitt v. The Orchard Ltd., 603 So.2d 356 (Miss. 1992); Nebraska in Morris v Lutheran Medical Center, 340 N.W.2d 388 (Neb. 1983); Nevada in South West Gas Corp. v. Ahmed, 668 P.2d 261 (Nev. 1983); New Hampshire in Panto v. Moore Business Forms, 547 A.2d 260 (N.H. 1988); New Jersey in Woolley v. Hoffman-LaRoche Inc., 491 A.2d 1257 (N.J. 1985), New Mexico in Forrester v. Parker, 606 P.2d 191 (N.M. 1980); New York in Weiner v. McGraw-Hill Inc., 443 N.E.2d 441(N.Y. 1982); North Dakota in Hammond v. North Dakota State Personnel Bd., 345 n.W.2d 359 (N.D. 1984); Ohio in West v. Roadway Express Inc., 115 L.R.R.M. 4558 (Ohio. Ct. App. 1982); Oklahoma in Langdon v. Sega Corp., 569 P.2d 524 (Okla. Ct. App. 1976); Oregon in Yarzoff v. Democrat-Herald Publ. Co., 576 P.2d 356 (Ore. 1978); South Carolina in Small v. Springs Industries Inc., 357 S.E.2d 452 (S.C. 1987); South Dakota in Osterkamp v. Alkota Mfct. Inc., 332 N.W.2d 275 (S.D. 1983); Tennessee in Hamby v. Genesco Inc., 627 S.W.2d 373 (Tenn. Ct. App. 1981); Texas in Johnson v. Ford Motor Co., 690 S.W.2d 90 (Tex. Civ. Ct. App. 1985); Utah in Rose v. Allied Development, 719 P.2d 83 (Utah 1986); Vermont in Sherman v. Rutland Hospital Inc., 500 A.2d 230 (Vt. 1985); Virginia in Frazier v. Colonial Williamsburg Foundation, 574 F.Supp. 318 (E.D.Va. 1983); Washington in Roberts v. Atlantic Richfield Co., 563 P.2d 764 (Wash. 1977); West Virginia in Cook v. Hecks Inc., 342 S.E.2d 453 (W.Va. 1986); Wisconsin in Ferraro v. Koelsch, 368 N.W.2d 666 (Wisc. 1985); Wyoming in Mobile Coal Producing Inc. Co. v. Parks, 704 P.2d 702 (Wyo. 1985).

[321] See Autor, Donohue, and Schwab, supra note 291, at 34: Legal Appendix, noting that the good faith exemption was adopted in: Alaska in Mitford v. Lasala, 666 P.2d 1000 (Alaska 1983); Arizona in Wagenseller v. Scottsdale Memorial Hosp., 710 P.2d 1025 (Ariz. 1985); California in Cleary v. American Airlines, 168 Cal.Rptr. 722 (Cal. Ct. App. 1980); Connecticut in Magnan v. Anaconda Indus., 479 A.2d 781 (Conn. Super. Ct. 1980); Delaware in Merril v. Crothall American, 606 A.2d 96 (Del. Sup. Ct. 1992); Idaho in Metcalf v. Intermountain Gas Co., 778 P.2d 744 (Idaho 1989); Louisiana in Barbe v. A.A. Harman and Co., 719 So.2d 462 (La. 1998); Massachusetts in Fortune v. National Cash Register Co., 364 N.E.2d 1251 (Mass. 1977); Montana in Gates v. Life of Montana Insurance Co., 638 P.2d 1063 (Mont. 1982); Nevada in K-Mart Corp. v. Ponsock, 732 P.2d 1364 (Nev. 1987); Wyoming in Wilder v. Cody County Chamber of Commerce, 868 P.2d 211 (Wyo. 1994).

[322] Mendelsohn, *supra* note 250, at 1, reports on a survey of 120 California jury trials between 1980 and 1986, noting that about one third of all defendants were large corporations employing over 10,000 employees, while only 18 percent of sample defendants employed fewer than 100 workers; see James Dertouzos, Elaine Holland and Patricia Ebener, "The Legal and Economic Consequences of Wrongful Termination," *RAND Institute for Civil Justice Report R-3602 ICJ*, at 21 (1988).

[323] Dertouzos, Holland and Ebener, ibid., at 21, note that in their survey of jury trials the average age of wrongfuly terminated employees was 45, their average wage was $36,000, and 13 percent of the sampled employees were in upper management positions.

[324] David J. Jung, "Jury Verdicts in Wrongful Termination Cases," *Report by the Public Law Research Institute at Hastings College of the Law*, at section IV (1997), reports on a survey of 639 California jury verdicts between 1992 and 1996, noting that 49 percent of implied contract plaintiffs were executives, middle managers, or professionals. When these plaintiffs won, their average award amounted to $724,721, which significantly exceeded the average of $172,856 that non-managerial employees were able to achieve. See also David J. Jung and Richard Harkness, "The Facts of Wrongful Discharge," 4 *The Labor Lawyer* 257, at 260 (1988), for an

represented by private attorneys who work on a contingent fee basis; that is, the attorney is compensated by a percentage of the award, and remains uncompensated if the lawsuit fails. [325] Because attorneys' risks in accepting a contingency fee remuneration can be higher than in conventional law suits, the typical compensation rates of contingency contracts tends to exceed the payments involved in typical fee-for-service contracts. [326]

Estimates on the full extent of unjust dismissal litigation have proven notoriously difficult, primarily because recorded jury verdicts represent only a small fraction of all civil cases filed. Accordingly, Brian Ostrom and Neal Kauder have suggested that of the less than three percent of tort cases that are resolved by jury trial, plaintiffs won 49 percent of the time and received a median award of $51,000. [327] Using an uptake rate of five percent, Lewis Maltby estimated that in the late 1980s, about 1,240 unjust discharge claims had been filed annually. [328] Given that 154 verdicts were recorded for California for 1995, and 144 for 1996, and using a more appropriate uptake rate of three percent, this would suggest that during the mid-1990s, between 4,800 to 5,100 wrongful discharge cases were filed annually in California courts. [329]

Several surveys have suggested that unjust dismissal suits have been characterized by high plaintiff success rates and exceptionally sizable awards to employees. [330] *Jury Verdicts Weekly*, for instance, reported that during the period from October 1981 to November 1987, the plaintiffs prevailed in almost 66 percent of all wrongful discharge suits tried before California juries. [331] Susan Mendelsohn cites an unpublished survey compiled in 1988 from *Jury Verdicts Weekly*, which estimated awards for the period between October 1981 to November 1987, as exceeding the company's last offer by 1,497 percent and the settlement

---

earlier survey of California verdicts, which revealed a 70 percent plaintiff success rate, with an average award of $486,812 and a median award was $124,150.

[325] In their survey of 1980 to 1986, of California jury verdicts, Dertouzos, Holland and Ebener, *supra* note 322, found defense billings to amount to over $80,000 or about 40 percent average final payout ($208,000) with costs rising between 15 and 24 percent annually.

[326] See, e.g., Carl E. Person, "Fired, Laid Off or Demoted? Your Legal Options," *Law Mall* revised June (1994) at <www.lawmall.com/pamphle1.php> accessed February 2012. Person suggested that, given a fee and costs of $175 per hour and an approximate workload of 200 hours, amounting to $35,000 in total costs, lawyers should not take on contingency contracts in which a recovery of at least $50,000 is not possible.

[327] Brian J. Ostrom and Neal B. Kauder, *Examining the Work of State Courts, 1994: A National Perspective from the Court Statistics Project*, at 8 (1994).

[328] Maltby (1990), *supra* note 253, at 51. Maltby's estimate was based on 63 verdicts, which were recorded in 1987, in the unpublished report "Analysis of Reported California Wrongful Discharge Jury Verdicts Calendar Year 1987" conducted by the San Francisco Law Firm Schachter, Kristoff, Ross, Sprague and Curriale. Maltby's uptake rate of five percent is identical to that of the earlier report by Dertouzos, Holland and Ebener, *supra* note 322. It is likely that uptake rates post-1990 conform to the three percent national average on account of the fact that the high rate of employee plaintiffs winning cases encouraged employers to settle out of court.

[329] Jung (1997), *supra* note 324, at section III, reports that looking at the five-year period from 1992 to 1997, complaints alleging unlawful termination of employment filed with the California Department of Fair Employment and Housing by employees wishing to sue under the Fair Employment and Housing Act increased by an average of 7.8 percent each year. Jung also reports that the number of jury verdicts in California wrongful termination cases reported in the Lexis-Nexis Database "increased by almost 75 percent between 1993 and 1994," but was then constant in later parts of the 1990s.

[330] Record awards include Schultz v. Advocate Health and Hospital Co., No. 01C-0702 (N.D. Ill Oct 20, 2002), in which $11.65 million were awarded to a man who was wrongfully discharged for claiming his rights under the Family Medical Leave Act (FMLA). In McKenzie v. Miller Brewing Co., Docket No. 97-3572, 2000 Wisc. App. 48, the court struck down an earlier $26 million jury verdict to a plaintiff who claimed that he had been wrongfully dismissed after having been given false promises of continuous employment.

[331] This estimate is recorded in Mendelsohn, *supra* note 250, at 7. Maltby, *supra* note 253, at 52, cites a Schachter, Kristoff, Ross, Sprague and Curriale report as estimating the percentage of employers winning wrongful discharge cases at 61 percent.

demands of employees by 187 percent on average. The plaintiff's settlement demands ranged from \$5,875,000 to zero; the settlement offers ranged from \$760,000 to zero; and the verdicts from \$8,000,000 to zero. The mean compensatory and punitive damages amounted to about \$630,000, and the median award was \$60,000, this difference between mean and median being due to some exceptionally high awards.[332] These estimates broadly match the picture given by a 1988 RAND study, which, based on a survey of 120 California jury verdicts between 1980 to 1986, suggested that plaintiffs prevailed in 68 percent of cases and won average initial jury awards of \$650,000.[333]

A study by the California Employer Association for the years 1994/95, yielded a lower estimate of the average settlement of about \$440,000. While this may have reflected an actual decrease in the size of awards, the lower figure may be also be due to the exclusion of cases with high punitive awards, which the CAE ignored in its calculations.[334] In the hitherto most extensive study of wrongful discharge verdicts, which analyzed 639 California cases from 1992 to 1996, Jung found that in California, plaintiff success rates fluctuated between 47 percent and 57 percent over the years, with punitive damages being awarded in seven percent to ten percent of cases. As concerns the size of awards, Jung found median compensatory awards to fluctuate between \$150,000 and \$270,000 and median punitive damages between \$150,000 and \$560,000 over the years investigated.[335]

While these figures indicate a high degree of fluctuation in the size of jury awards, which appears to be driven by the presence of a small number of very high awards, they seem to suggest that unjust dismissal litigation can be lucrative for both the employee and attorney provided that the dismissed employee earned a substantial wage. This is illustrated by the following calculation, which has appeared on the Internet *Legal Mall* in 1996. Assuming that a middle manager, age 40, earning \$100,000 per year was improperly terminated, this manager could claim 25 years at \$100,000 minimum, or accounting for inflation \$100,000 in year one and approximately \$400,000 in year 25. This would average at about \$250,000 annually or a total of \$6,250,000 in total salary losses. If successful, a jury would typically also add attorney's fees and costs but make a deduction for the right of receiving this income now. Income taxes would ordinarily not be deducted because the employee would still have to apply on the settlement in many instances. The defendant would be arguing that in 25 years, the plaintiff should get a job, and that perhaps two years would be an appropriate time in which the plaintiff should find re-employment, yielding a sum of about \$250,000, all factors taken into account. At this stage, arguments about how much damage had been done to the employee's reputation, emotional state, etc., would have to be heard. If the jury settled on somewhere in the middle, the award would amount to approximately 2.5 million; if it were to settled at the lower end, the manager could still receive in excess of \$200,000.[336]

Despite evidence about the exceptional size of some awards to plaintiffs and the high success rates of unjust dismissal suits, it is unclear whether the threat of these suits creates a genuine deterrence effect for employers. Whereas studies of the 1970s and 1980s, identified a

---

[332] Mendelsohn (1990), *supra* note 250, at 7.

[333] Dertouzos, Holland and Ebener, *supra* note 322, at vii.

[334] The California Employer Association estimate was calculated by T. Dowalls of Littler, Mendelson, Mathieson, Fastiff, Tichy and Mathieson, and appeared on the Internet in connection with a CAE briefing and workshop.

[335] Jung (1997), *supra* note 324, at section IV.

[336] The numerical example appears in Person, *supra* note 325, and as such reflects the experiences of a practicing New York attorney during the 1990s.

reduction of planned dismissals due to grievance arbitration,[337] no comparable evidence on private unjust dismissal litigation is currently available.[338] An award of $60,000, the median identified in Brown's survey, arguably would be unlikely to have a substantial impact on a medium size service sector firm with typical profits in excess of $5 million, where it would amount to less than 1.2 percent of the profits. Since most companies willing to do so should be able to settle out of court, the high awards reported in many jury trials, in any case, are likely to be the exception rather than the rule.

Perhaps more importantly, following the establishment of wrongful discharge litigation, there is now a growing industry of insurance and human resources consultants who have devised means for neutralizing the threat of dismissal litigation.[339] As yet, there is no concrete evidence as to how effective these measures are, albeit that the historical record would suggest that employers' superior access to resources will eventually ensure a reassertion of management rights. In addition to these personnel-management-based defenses, recent research has linked the adoption of at-will exemptions in certain states to the growth of their temporary help sector. Accordingly, David Autor has cautiously suggested that a one percent increase in unionization in adopting states correlated, on average, to a 2.6 percent increase in a state's temporary help sector.[340] While this relationship does not by itself suggest that at-will exemptions acting as a constraint on on labor market flexibility will lead to an unexpected growth in temporary employment contracts, it stands to reason that where employers feel genuinely threatened by these new legal possibilities of employee protection, they will give preference to contracting relationships that reduce the threat of dismissal litigation.

Irrespective of the question as to whether unjust dismissal litigation represents a genuine deterrent to the unfair and excessive dismissal of employees in the private sector, there is little doubt that the rise of unjust dismissal litigation did sharpen the debate on employment protection deficits in the US labor market. With precedents of significant awards to employees who were unfairly dismissed, there is no longer a presumption that firing decisions fall out with the orbit of established norms of human and civil rights or the prevalent understanding of contractual obligations. Whether this sea change will translate itself into concrete legislative action, however, is unpredictable. To be clear, there is widespread awareness of the problems that the *status quo* is creating both for unionized and non-unionized workers.[341] A recent article by Estlund, for instance, has highlighted the need to replace limited remedies for unjustly dismissed workers under the NLRA with a private right

---

[337] See, e.g., Richard B. Freeman, "The Effect of Unions on Worker Attachment to Firms," *National Bureau of Eocnomic Research Working Paper Series,* Working Paper No. 400, at 40 and 41 (1979), which concludes at that "trade unionism is associated with significantly greater job tenure and conversely with significantly lower probabilities of separation," which, in turn, can be attributed to "to grievance systems and specific work rules like seniority" or more generally the "industrial jurisprudence mode of operation."

[338] Matthias P. Beck, "Public Policy Exemptions, Whistleblower Statutes, and Government Worker Layoffs: A Case of Adverse Effects?" 24 *Journal of Collective Negotiations in the Public Sector* 1 (1995) suggests that dismissal rates in states with strong wrongful discharge regimes tend to be higher on account of the tendency of employers to dismiss employees in batches, so as to avoid litigation.

[339] See, e.g., Susan Bisom-Rapp, "Bulletproofing the Workplace: Symbol and Substance in Employment Discrimination Law Practice," 26 *Florida State Law Review* 959 (1990) for a thoughtful overview of litigation prevention strategies and their implications on the workforce.

[340] David H. Autor, "Outsourcing at-will: The Contribution of Unjust Dismissal Doctrine to the Growth of Employment Outsourcing," 21 *Journal of Labor Economics* 1, at 27 (2003).

[341] See, e.g., Eugene Scalia, "Ending Our Anti-Union Federal Employment Policy," 24 *Harvard Journal of Public Policy* 489 (2000) for a passionate plea in favor of an overhaul of U.S. employment law.

of action for anti-union discharges.[342] In all likelihood, some of these reform proposals will eventually be implement in some form. However, given the obstacles created by antiquated provisions within the NLRA and the unwillingness of legislators to acknowledge a greater need for regulation in the non-unionized workplace it is questionable whether initiatives aimed at creating the type of comprehensive dismissal regulation found elsewhere in advanced industrialized countries will succeed in the US without significant political leadership and support. If we were to review the principal causes of the under-protection of US workers, such as the strength of the discourse on managerial prerogatives and their support by the courts, the fact that the NLRA was the first statute providing a significant restriction on dismissals, placed dismissal protection within the contentious framework of union organizing efforts, and, lastly, the focus of past union efforts on the plant level management of dismissals—then there is little evidence that these inhibiting factors have changed significantly. This can be taken to suggest that future change could be difficult, but it can also be seen to imply that if potential social benefits from such changes are significant and accrue to a large share of the population, much delayed reforms may indeed find considerable grassroots support.

---

[342] See Cynthia L. Estlund, "The Ossification of American Labor Law," 102 *Columbia Law Review* 1527, at 1557 (2002).

CONCLUSION

At its core, this monograph has explored the lengthy processes though which the US political economy of dismissals was created. In this context, it has been argued that the US is now the last industrialized country that does not have comprehensive dismissal legislation[343] and that the existing US regime of dismissal protection is characterized by a high degree of fragmentation. To recapitulate, existing employees' rights statutes protect particular groups of the US workforce against certain types of dismissals but effectively cover only a small fraction of the workforce. In the past three decades, the protection of employees from discharge, moreover, has if anything decreased. Union densities have declined, eroding the discharge protection that has traditionally been provided through just-cause rules and the grievance and arbitration apparatus of the unionized workplace.

Broadly speaking, the absence of such regulation affects two principal groups of employees. First, it affects employees whose dismissal is based on their personal characteristics, skills, or actions. Employees may be singled out for dismissal because management perceives them as incompetent or their skills as inadequate, but equally, individual dismissals may occur in retaliation of legitimate workers' actions such as the objection to unethical or criminal activities by the employers.[344] Intrinsically related to the US anomaly of limited dismissal regulation has been the phenomenon of intensifying unjust dismissal litigation, which the US has experienced over the last three decades. Partly due to the absence of comprehensive unjust dismissal legislation and reduced coverage by collective bargaining agreements, the US courts have faced a continuous increase in private common law unjust dismissal suits.[345] Employers in the US have responded to this rise in dismissal suits by devising an elaborate set of litigation-avoidance strategies.[346] These strategies range

---

[343] See, e.g., Henry H. Peritt, Jr., *Employee Dismissal: Law and Practice,* at section 2.1 (1987).

[344] In one of the earliest estimates of this kind, Theodore St. Antoine, "Changing Concepts of Worker Rights in the Workplace," 473 *Annals of the American Academy of the Political and Social Sciences* 108, at 108 and 110 (1984) approximately 70% of all U.S. workers have no guarantee against arbitrary dismissal. A briefing paper the American Civil Liberties Union estimated that at least 200,000 Americans were unjustly fired in the U.S. each year; see American Civil Liberties Union, "The Rights of Employees," *Briefing Paper Number 12* (1996?) <www.scpetictank.org/files/aclu/12pap.htm, accessed 26 February 2012>.

[345] See, e.g., Jonathan D. Glater, "Layoffs Herald a Heyday of Lawsuits," *New York Times,* January 30 (2009) noting an increase in termination related lawsuits in New York courts.

[346] For an overview of the strategies from an academic perspective see, Susan Bisom-Rapp, "Discerning from Substance: Understanding Employer Litigation Prevention Strategies," 3 *Employee Rights and Employment Policy Journal* 1 (1999). Practitioner articles recommending specific litigation avoidance include, among many others, James G. Frierson, "How to Fire without Getting Burnt," 67 *Personnel* 44 (1990), recommending an interviewing and hiring strategy that eliminates potentially "troublesome" employees, explicit company policies and documents that emphasize the at-will nature of employment and pay and promotions procedures

from disclaimers to be signed by the employee at the time of employment, fixed-term routine contract revisions, to the creation of in house dismissal-arbitration councils. In addition, insurance firms are now offering policies that protect firms against the liabilities of wrongful termination suits.

The second group of workers affected by the absence of dismissal regulations includes employees whose discharge is the result of a strategic management initiative or of economic pressures. In contrast to the UK, Germany, and a host of other advanced industrialized nations, US workers have no statutory entitlement to severance pay. Perhaps more important is a less tangible aspect of the US discharge regime, namely the limits placed on the involvement of employee organizations in influencing or preventing redundancies. US courts, over the last five or more decades, have effectively protected the rights of employers to close branches and dismiss workers with little or no interference from unions.[347] In contrast to European co-determination schemes, the ability of US unions to influence, or prevent, decisions on redundancies, therefore, is very limited.

Comparisons of dismissal regimes of this kind, needless to say, are underpinned by normative assumptions, namely the idea that comprehensive systems for the protection of workers from unfair, capricious or unnecessary dismissals are socially beneficial. Rather than taking this view, which has indeed informed much of the previous analysis. for granted the following section provides a discussion of why, contrary to the assumptions of neoclassical economics, dismissal protection should be considered socially desirable.

AN EXCURSE ON THE ECONOMICS
OF DISMISSAL RESTRICTION

Whereas much of the industrial relations implicitly assumes that the restriction of dismissal *per se* is a desirable social good, this is not the case for most neoclassical economic analysis. In the prototypical neoclassical view, the right of employers to dismiss a worker, at least on a macro-level, contributes to an efficient allocation of resources. Under perfect competition, the employer adjusts the quantity of labor demanded to a given wage rate. In

---

that state that these company rules apply to all employees; Mark J. Keppler, "Halting Traffic on the Road to Wrongful Discharge - Avoiding Wrongful Discharge Suits," 67 *Personnel* 48 (1990) recommending the use employee handbooks as a legal defence and the use of in-house dispute resolution procedures; Lisa Jenners, "Employment-At-Will Liability: How Protected are You," 71 *Human Resource Focus* 11 (1994) recommending that employers "sanitize" written documents so that promises may not be construed from any of these documents as well as warning employers not to make any oral employment guarantees during conversations. Paradoxically, some research now suggests that strategies adopted in light of the threat of lawsuits have a negative impact on employment relations. See, e.g., Raymond L. Hilgert, "How At-Will Statements Hurt Employers," 67 *Personnel Journal* 75 (1988) suggesting that the at-will statements that are today included in many employment contracts as a condition of employment are unnecessary and over-reactive; Catherine C. Schwoerer and Benson Rosen, "Effects of Employment-at-will Policies and Compensation Policies on Corporate Image and Job Pursuit Intentions," 74 *Journal of Applied Psychology* 653 (1989). See also Randy Myers, "Protecting Against Employment Perils," 82 *Nation's Business* 65 (1994) describing the evolving insurance industry, which provides coverage in case of wrongful discharge litigation and discussing insurance options available to management.

[347] See especially James B. Atleson, *Values and Assumptions of American Labor Law* (1983) for an analysis of judicial bias against union involvement in plant closure and relocation decisions; as well as Katherine van Wetzel Stone, "The Post-War Paradigm in American Labor Law," 90 *Yale Law Journal* 1509 (1981) regarding issues surrounding concession bargaining and employer union collaboration.

other words, employment in a specific sector "a" is increased, so long as the last worker's marginal productivity equals the wage the employer is required to pay her or him. If wages rise too fast, say because productivity in other sectors rises faster than in sector "a", the employer will start dismissing workers (or in a less extreme case, stop hiring them). Over time, an optimal level of fluctuation will be achieved, which will ensure that employees are allocated to the most productive sectors of the economy.[348]

Job-security enhancing, employment-protection legislation, according to neoclassical analysis, can hamper this process and create inefficiencies or "rigidities." Such rigidities are said to arise as part of the expansion of the government and its increasing interventionist role in the economy. Together, rigidities and interventions can reduce geographical mobility, skill/occupational mobility, job mobility, and the sectoral reduction of wages to market clearing levels. In a pure market economy, reduced mobility results in an inefficient reduction of factor movements, which, in the long run, reduces the productivity and competitiveness of a country.

While these ideas appear to be superficially plausible, it must be understood that advanced industrial economies have long ceased to be pure market economies (if they ever were that in the first place). Thus it can be argued that once the state undertakes measures to support unemployed workers, the dismissal of employees itself is no longer purely a matter of what benefits an individual firm. Accordingly, under a system of unemployment insurance and welfare payments, an employer externalizes much of the costs of a dismissal to society. Displaced workers can add to unemployment insurance expenses and welfare payments, without the dismissing employer paying for it. With the company not bearing the true costs of dismissals, additional distortions in the allocation of resources can rise. More workers are likely to be employed industries that are likely to experience frequent job loss than is socially efficient, and dismissals are likely to occur more frequently than if employers were accountable for at least a part of their cost. Ultimately, therefore, on a macro-level, the question whether restriction on dismissals are beneficial is at the very least difficult to decide.

An alternative route to the assessment of dismissal regulation is to look not at the economy as a whole but at the operation of the firm. A firm's efficiency may be improved if the employer has the right to dismiss employees at-will, but such a solution can also encourage employer opportunism and may have trade-offs with respect to equity issues. Favorable views of the employment-at-will are typically based on a rigid application of the neoclassical theory of the firm and the market. The neoclassical paradigm implies that markets are the most effective mechanism for operating the labor market. Any deviation from market processes in deciding economic outcomes, such as the enactment of dismissal protection legislation, is assumed result in inefficiencies. In the concrete context of dismissal regulation, two principal types of inefficiencies are assumed to arise, once the employers' right to fire at-will is restricted; namely, increases in monitoring costs and organizational inefficiencies. Counter-arguments meanwhile often stress issues arising from the power asymmetry of worker and employer.

The first type of inefficiency results from increases in monitoring costs due to a reduction of the deterrence effect of dismissal. Neoclassical analysis typically assumes that the

---

[348] Bernhard Okun and Richard W. Richardson, "Regional Income Inequality and Internal Population Migration," 9 *Economic Development and Cultural Change* 128 (1961).

unadulterated right to dismiss keeps monitoring costs at a minimum.[349] Knowledge that each party can renounce the agreement accordingly decreases the chances that a worker will not put forth the expected levels of performance and that employers will not proffer the promised compensation. Since employee shirking can be costly and monitoring is often impossible, the freedom of the employer to dismiss ensures output. An alteration of this contract format through a restriction of dismissals undermines the threat of a dismissal and can ultimately reduce output in existing firms, hinder the creation of new firms, or lead the employer to hire fewer workers.[350]

A second type of inefficiency is said to arise from the organizational implications of restrictions on employers' dismissal rights.. Since restrictions on firing for reasons of redundancies cannot be completely separated from restrictions on unjust dismissal, interference with the right to dismiss, and particularly the imposition of penalties, are said to result in excess employee capacities (quantity decision) as well as inflexibilities regarding the choice of the workforce (quality decisions). As an exponent of this view, the renowned Chicago economist Gary Becker has warned against the "the courts' becoming a pink slip police."[351] He suggests that court policing of dismissals erodes managerial property rights and, in the long run, eliminates incentives for the creation for the creation of new firms.

Arguing along these lines, Arnold Picot and Ekkehard Wenger (1988), additional problems arise when employees exploit available restrictions on dismissal. Picot and Wenger suggest that[352]

> If employees have protective rights there is no guarantee that these rights cannot be exercised in order to expropriate the employer. Protection against dismissal, for example, may reduce work effort because the employer cannot fire 'at-will' ... The ensuing moral hazard problems are a strong argument in favor of short-term termination rights.

Like many orthodox neoclassical analyses, this quote reflects an asymmetrical and perhaps biased view of the employment relationship. The protection of employees from dismissals is viewed as expropriation or as a deviation from some natural state, whereas little or no attention is paid to the problems created for dismissed employers. Not surprisingly, the previous arguments have been countered early on by arguments that stress the generic differences between a conventional contract and an employment contract, and the special position of the employee vis a vis the employer in a firm, respectively (see,e.g., the discussion of John Commons's work in chapter 1).

In essence, most first-generation arguments in favor of dismissal regulation rest on the notion that employment contracts are conducted on the basis of a power asymmetries. The contemporary literature cites two principal sources of such power asymmetries. Firstly, employer's financial resources considerably exceed those of employees. As a rule, the adverse effects of quits are therefore unlikely to endanger the financial well-being of an employer.

---

[349] See, e.g., Richard A. Epstein, "In Defense of the Contract At- Will," 51 University of Chicago Law Review 947 (1984) for an overview of efficiency arguments in favor of employment-at-will.

[350] See, e.g., John T. Addison, "Job Security in the United States: Law, Collective Bargaining, Policy, and Practice," 24 *British Journal of Industrial Relations* 381 (1986).

[351] Gary S. Becker, "The Court's Shouldn't Become Pink Slip Police" *Business Week* 14, August 28 (1989).

[352] Arnold Picot and Ekkehard Wenger, "The Employment Relation from the Transaction Cost Perspective," in *Management under Differing Labor Market and Employment Systems* 29, at 32 (Guenther Dlugos, Wolfgang Dorow and Klaus Weiermair eds., 1988).

Employees, in contrast, depend on their jobs for their financial well-being, and cannot effectively use the threat of quitting. Secondly, since skills are not perfectly transferable, employees can face long job searches or incur wage losses due to inadequate matching. Employers, meanwhile—depending on the business cycle—can recruit from a more or less extensive pool of possible future employees, thus facing short replacement periods and/or replacement losses.

Although convincing at first sight, more recently, power asymmetry arguments have been subject to some criticism. Opponents of power asymmetry arguments have argued that unless employers have an interest in dismissing workers beyond economic rationality, the presence of power asymmetries does not explain why an employer would take advantage of this position in a manner that would warrant legal intervention.[353] If decisions are ruled by economic rationality on both the employer's and the employee's side, a profit-maximizing employer is said to have nothing to gain from an unjust dismissal. Discharges will therefore be limited to those instances where they are necessitated by economic circumstances or the personal characteristics of employers. This conduct will be enforced by the possibility of reputational damages, which helps create an additional incentive for employers to discharge on justifiable grounds only.

Responding to such objections, more recent arguments in favor of restrictions on the at-will right of employers have reversed the "shirking" and "opportunism" argument—applied earlier in defence of employment-at-will. Here, the presence of implicit contracts is used as justification of a restriction of the dismissal rights of employer. In the traditional model of the labor market, the employer pays a worker the value of her or his marginal product for each pay period. Efficiency wage models, however, assume that any single pay period's wage is insufficient to deter shirking.[354] According to Becker and Stiglitz, this problem can be resolved by compensation schemes where the employee pays the employer a bond upon taking a job.[355] Bond schemes of this kind are impractical mostly because workers are unable to borrow sufficient funds at the start of their jobs. The practical alternative to bonds posted at the beginning of an employment, lies in a wage structure that internalizes the "bond effect." Such wage structures typically defer a part of a worker's wage to later periods of her or his employment. In terms of the employment contract, this means that the worker is offered a more or less steep age-wage profile, which provides wages below the worker's marginal product for the early years of her or his employment and wages above the marginal product for the later years.

By shifting proportionally more compensation to later years, the employer raises the cost of termination to the worker. If dismissed, the employee loses his accumulated deferred wages in escrow. The worker therefore has greater incentive to put in an effort throughout her or his working life. This scheme as a whole, nevertheless, is preferable to the employee, as she or he is likely to be paid the higher wage associated with the employee's assumption of continual higher effort.

---

[353] Anonymous, "Note: Employer Opportunism and the Need for a Just-Cause Standard," 103 *Harvard Law Review* 510, at 511 (1989).

[354] See, e.g., Herbert Gintis and Tsuneo Ishikawa, "Wages, Work Intensity and Unemployment in Competitive Labor Markets," 1 *Journal of Japanese and International Economics* 195 (1987).

[355] Gary Becker and George J. Stigler, "Law Enforcement, Malfeasance, and Compensation of Enforcers," 3 *Journal of Legal Studies* 1 (1974).

With regard to dismissal and employer shirking, the difficulty with such a scheme is how the total amount of deferred wages changes over time. In the early years of the job, when wages paid are below the employee's productivity level, the total amount of deferred benefits rises, reaching a maximum around the mid-period of employment. Following this reversal point [R], the amount of benefits is paid off, as wages rise above the marginal product of the worker. If the firm discharges a worker at or after the reversal point [R], that is during the second half of the job, it not only avoids paying the extra cost of the disincentive payments but also incurs the wage savings it has accumulated from the time it hired the employee. In a world in which no market or legal constraints operate, a firm hence has a rational incentive for the dismissal of a productive worker for no cause. Therefore, dismissal protection can be an imperative, particularly for those workers who are in a long-term relationship with a firm.

Despite the apparent imperative for a restriction of the doctrine of employment-at-will, which ensues from the combination of a prevalence of deferred benefit systems with the incentive to dismiss unjustly, this justification of restrictions argument is not entirely unproblematic. Thus the Chicago law professor Epstein has suggested in a 1984 article that the firm's concern with its reputation in the labor market will prevent such opportunistic discharges.[356] Epstein argues that workers have access to information about opportunistic firms, which will ensure that firms with a history of opportunistic conduct will run out of business. In a not untypically circular Chicago school argument, Epstein hypothesizes that if reputation would not discipline opportunism, workers would negotiate for restrictions on dismissals; given that such clauses are rare or completely unknown, opportunism must also be negligible.

This view is mirrored in a 1987 working paper by Williamson, where the author argues that managerial self-interest itself will limit "downward opportunism." Says Williamson:[357]

> I submit, however that just as a responsible labor union will examine the merits of worker complaints (worker opportunism) before bringing them forward through the grievance machinery (Williamson, 1985, pp. 155-56), so will managers be deterred from abusing workers who developed firm specific capital ...

Williamson, accordingly, assumes that managerial opportunism exists but then suggests that a firm's interest in preserving firm specific capital will militate against the exercise of this opportunism. One of several problems with this argument is that a firm's relative valuation of an individual's firm specific capital might vary and/or decline. Previously acquired firm-specific skills might become obsolete, encouraging the firm to unjustly dismiss a worker, if the firm assesses the value of these skills as below the gains it can make from a discharge.

Problems also arise from issues of information acquisition and transparency. Thus a 1989 Note in the *Harvard Law Review* centres its argument in favour of dismissal protection on the argument that transaction costs are likely to weaken reputational restraints on managerial misconduct.[358] The job searcher cannot easily obtain information about a firm's personnel relations, because the applicant is likely to feel inhibited from asking a potential employer

---

[356] Epstein, *supra* note 349, at 982.

[357] Oliver E. Williamson, "Transaction Cost Economics: The Comparative Contracting Perspective," *Yale Law School Program in Law and Organization, Working Paper* No. 55, at 6 (1987).

[358] Anonymous, *supra* note 353, at 523 and 528. See also Paul Fenn, and Christopher Whelan, "Job Security and the Role of Law: An Economic Analysis of Employment-At-Will," 20 *Stanford Journal of International Law* 353, at 372 (1984).

about employment practices. Firms may moreover deliberately project a false image of job security and steady employment relations.

A perhaps even greater difficulty in judging the appropriateness of dismissal regulation arises from the questions about cost and efficiency of such regulations. Whereas some research suggests that employees should be protected against discharges by a European style just-cause standard,[359] others question whether efficiency considerations do in fact justify proposals advocating such regulation.[360] This is also the line taken in the 1989 *Harvard Law Review* Note on at-will employment, where the authors suggest that a trade-off exists between the costs of unjust dismissals, and the costs of legal enforcement of dismissal standards. The Note explains:[361]

> From a purely efficiency based perspective, the fact that ... employer opportunism exists does not necessarily justify a general good cause standard. Remedying opportunism does achieve efficiency gains ... Such benefits, however, come only at a cost. Where the fact finder can collect information and evaluate claims easily ... a judicial remedy may be appropriate ... Reasonable solution may thus be limited exceptions like the public policy, implied contract, and faith exception. However in the general case the employer's motive is only implicit, information for the fact finder make the remedy much more costly.

The dilemma involved in weighing potential gains from the enforcement of legislation, which prevents opportunistic discharges again enforcement costs (narrowly or broadly defined), is likely to remain unresolved as neither gains nor costs can be accurately assessed.[362] Therefore, some studies have taken a different route from the traditional cost benefit approach, which seems to underpin much of the literature on dismissal litigation. Such approaches explore wrongful discharge litigation from a rights perspective, rather than a cost perspective. Hypotheses based on the rights or property rights approaches are particularly suggestive in the context of opportunistic dismissals after the "reversal point," as they directly address questions as to how to protect accumulated property rights, such as the deferred wage of employees.

Conceptually this also offers an opportunity to depart from arguments that attempt to base normative conclusions with regard to employment regulation on notions of employee shirking. Apart from the bias implied in the predominant application of the idea of shirking to employees, the argument is suffering from conceptual weaknesses. In some cases, shirking arguments take recourse in tautology. Because workers shirk, they must be monitored. Workers, in turn, shirk because monitoring is impossible.[363] In others, evidence for shirking is

---

[359] See, e.g., Cornelius J. Peck, "Unjust Discharges from Employment," 40 *Ohio State Law Journal* 1 (1979).

[360] William B. Gould, "Stemming the Wrongful Discharge Tide: A Case for Arbitration," 13 *Employee Relations Law Journal* 404, at 417 (1987), opposes the introduction of a general just-cause standard on administrative grounds but supports the creation of Canadian-style industrial court system in the U.S..

[361] Anonymous, *supra* note 353, at 528.

[362] The merits of dismissal regulation have been debated in American legal journals for some time. See, e.g., the early contributions by Clyde W. Summers, "Individual Protection Against Unjust Discharge" 62 *Virginia Law Review* 481 (1976); Lawrence E. Blades, "Employment-At-Will vs. Individual Freedom: On Limiting the Abusive Exercise of Employer Power" 76 *Columbia Law Review* 1404 (1967); Joan M. Krauskopf, "Employment Discharge: Survey and Critique of the Modern At-Will Rule" 51 *University of Missouri Kansas City Law Review* 189 (1983); and Peter Linzer, "The Decline of Assent: At-Will Employment as a Case Study of the Breakdown of Private Law Theory" 20 *Georgia Law Review* 323 (1986).

[363] Regarding the problem of such tautologies, see, e.g., Kate Cartier, "The Transaction Cost and Benefits of the Incomplete Contract of Employment," 18 *Cambridge Journal of Economics* 181 (1994).

largely, if not exclusively, anecdotal. The latter is the case in the above-mentioned Harvard Note, which highlights the reliance of this literature on dubious sources such as Gerald Mars' 1982 monograph *Cheats at Work*.[364]

The principal objection to notions of shirking, cheating or opportunism, however, is not their conceptual weakness but their negative bias. While these behaviors may exist in the workplace, the idea that shirking is widespread rests on a questionable view of human behavior as well as a lack of objectivity.[365] In theory, this is the case for both the assumption of employer, and employee shirking. In practice, however, the presence of a strong economic incentive to shirk or act opportunistically on the employer side, and the absence thereof on the employee side, renders arguments about employer shirking perhaps more credible. Arguments about employer opportunism derive their fortitude not from the imposition of unwarranted behavioral assumptions but rather the realization of the existence of real economic incentives to act opportunistically. The dismissal of an employee past the reversal point may, for the employer, represent little more than a "cost-saving opportunity," which is likely to carry little or no social taboo in some areas of the business world. Given existing laws, most instances of such employer conduct will also carry no penalty; since as long as the employer's conduct does not fall within any of the relatively narrowly described categories the law is inapplicable. The "opportunistic" worker, in contrast, is subject to the threat of discipline through dismissal. In addition, she or he will often lack any real economic incentive to shirk or act opportunistically. Not conducting the work required during the time on the job in most cases does not provide workers with additional income, and a reluctance to perform at one's level of ability is unlikely to yield monetary or other advantages to an individual employee. Conscientious behavior in unsupervised work, meanwhile, may reflect respect for oneself, for the contract, for other workers or the employer; or responsibility for standards or rules of a professional organization. It can ensue from the sense of identity, craftsmanship, or satisfaction that work can confer.[366]

This asymmetry in the incentive structures *per se* could justify an asymmetric treatment of dismissals, in which the discharge of a long-tenured employee would be treated more suspiciously than an employer's claim that the worker shirked and was dismissed for justifiable grounds. Despite marked differences in the incentives structure, arguments about employer opportunism alone, however, do not yield an effective guideline as how to regulate dismissals. This is the case not only because of the costs of the enforcement of potential legislation of such a standard but also because of the inherently implicit nature of the contractual arrangements. This implicitness extends to the characteristics of the non-linear wage contract, as well as the unexpressed performance standards imposed on the workers. The following section will discuss, albeit on a very provisional level, how a justification of dismissal regulation could be constructed without relying on notions of opportunism or shirking. This argument relies heavily on property rights approaches.

The property rights view of job security then is based on a substantial critique of notions of shirking, and more broadly, the traditional neoclassical model of the firm. This traditional

---

[364] See Gerald Mars,' *Cheats At Work: An Anthology of Workplace Crime* (1982) as discussed in Anonymous, *supra* note 353, which describes the dubious example of British bus drivers who accelerate in order to pick up as few passengers as possible and to earn an extra tea break.

[365] See Cartier, *supra* note 363, at 185.

[366] See, e.g., Eliot Freidson, "Labors of Love in Theory and Practice: A Prospectus," in *The Nature of Work* 149 (Kai Erikson and Steven Vallas eds., 1990).

neoclassical model of the firms assumes that employees as an economic and legal group are distinct and clearly distinguishable from the owner/managers of the firm. This approach reflects the neoclassical model of the firm, wherein, as stated by Kenneth Arrow:[367]

> ... workers are not part of the firm. They are purchased on the market, like raw materials or capital goods. Yet they (or some of them) carry the information base ... they are neither owners nor slaves.

In the neoclassical model, workers are excluded from the stakeholders of the firm. They are assigned no role in managing the firm or themselves or in monitoring the quality of output or the characteristics of the labor process. Perceiving workers as factor input, the neoclassical model rejects any worker claims of property rights in the firm. This rejection is understood to be justified on several conceptual and even "ethical" grounds. Central to it is a view that places uncertainty at the center of the activity of the firm.

According to the traditional neoclassical model of the firm, the organization of the firm is based on an implied contract to allocate risk asymmetrical between the employer and employee. In this context, workers surrender discretion to their employer in exchange for the avoidance of risk, and are consecutively "guaranteed" an individually or collectively negotiated wage.[368] As a result of the asymmetric contract, owner/managers are assigned supervisory functions in the firm. This is necessary, because contract performance by the worker cannot be guaranteed. Compliance with contractual obligations is enforced by monitoring, influenced through the terms of the wage bargain, or subtly conditioned by working conditions, mutual control or other such means.

Following the neoclassical dictum of voluntary choice and exchange, employees submit to this exchange voluntarily. Models of managerial and entrepreneurial activity propose that each individual makes a career choice by comparing entrepreneurial income to earnings from non-entrepreneurial employment. This decision depends on the individual's "endowment with entrepreneurial characteristics." The exercise of entrepreneurial skills, is—despite evidence to the contrary—said to be invariable linked to risk taking by the entrepreneur; which then is taken to justify the exclusion of workers from stakeholder status.

The problems of this neoclassical division of manager and worker are substantial. The essentially "pseudo-ethical" justification of a division of reward between the higher risk taker who receives greater rewards, and the lower risk taker whose rewards are limited, is at best antiquated and at worst manipulative. The job loss of workers typically poses a greater threat to the economic well-being of the worker than does—given contemporary legal and institutional arrangements—bankruptcy to the employee.

Apart from this political bias, the neoclassical view of the division between employer and employee is intellectually inconsistent as regards dismissals and job security in particular.

Firstly, if managers are required to monitor the performance of the worker under the contract; i.e., screen that the work required is performed, workers should have an equal incentive and/or right to monitor the performance of managers, as managerial performance will impact dramatically on their future ability to perform under the contract. In other words,

---

[367] Kenneth Arrow, "Information and the Organization of Industry," Lectio Magistralis, Catholic University of Milan, at 7 (1994).

[368] See, e.g., Armen Alchian and Harold Demsetz, "Production, Information Costs, and Economic Organization," 62 *American Economic Review* 777 (1972).

if managerial authority is justified by risk taking, the risk of job loss encountered by individuals should at least to some degree authorize workers to exercise some control over managerial decisions.

Secondly, if managerial rewards are justified because of the managers' distinct entrepreneurial activities, workers whose input into the firm is innovative and entrepreneurial should be granted managerial status, if only on efficiency grounds (i.e., in order to allow them to implement their innovation effectively).

Thirdly, if firm-specific skills account for a substantial increase in the productivity and profits of the firm, the worker's property in these skills should be protected, particularly if they will not be rewarded elsewhere or have not been adequately remunerated by the firm. A conceptual alternative would therefore propose an approach whereby rights within the firm are defined not by an a priori distinction between employer and employee but rather by a property rights-based and therefore incentive compatible assignment of rights. Accordingly, property rights theory would define as a firm's owners those persons who share two rights: the right to control the firm and the right to appropriate the firm's residual earnings. Moreover, there would be recognition that many firms are owned by persons who also supply the firm with some factor of production, usually capital. Accordingly, a legal analogy could be said to exist, as has been argued by the economist Henry Hansman, between the producer cooperative and the business corporation.[369] In the producer cooperative, say a dairy cooperative, ownership rights are held exclusively by virtue of the fact that the farmer sells milk to the firm. Not all farmers who sell milk to the firm need be owners, since the firm may purchase some milk from non-members who are simply paid a fixed price but do not exercise control over the firm or participate in the division of residual earnings.

In the typical cooperative, the members engage in continuous exchanges and vary their volume of transactions with the firm.[370] In contrast to the Knightian entrepreneur, who is also the primary innovator in the firm, ownership in the cooperative is assigned to persons who have the transactional relationship of a resource supplier to the firm. The reason for this is that the ownership relation is used to mitigate some of the costs that would arise in the case of contracting. The advantage of assigning ownership to the supplier of resources extends to issues of market power, as well as *ex post* market power or lock-ins. In terms of market power, this ownership by resource suppliers reduces efficiency losses associated with the setting of input prices above marginal costs. *Ex post* market-power benefits arise from the fact that owner-suppliers of capital, or other resources, must make transaction specific investments upon entering into the transactional relationship. Once such a transactional relationship has been entered into, exit becomes costly—a situation that can be exploited by the firm, unless it is at least partially controlled by the owner-suppliers of resources. Ownership of the firm by the supplier or investor reduces such incentives for opportunistic behavior. A final advantage of the above system lies in the possible reduction of managerial opportunism can be reduced because of the owners' incentive in exercising control.[371]

The crucial issue involved in the cooperative analogy then is that ownership need not be, and frequently is not, associated with the actual investment of a lump sum of capital, the provision of raw material, or an intermediate product. In other words, the distinction of

---

[369] See Henry B. Hansman, "Towards A General Theory of Corporate Ownership," Yale Law School, *Program in Law and Organization, Working Paper* No. 74, at 4 (1988). .

[370] See Hansman, ibid., at 8.

[371] Hansman, ibid., at 11.

investor owners according to the amount, timing, and nature of the resource provided to the firm has no legal bearing on ownership rights. Conversely, property rights do not depend on the amount, timing, and nature of the resource provided. Key to the property rights claim is that a resource has been provided consistently over time on which the firm's performance crucially depended and for which the provider was not compensated at the market rate at the time.

By supplying the input of her or his labor continuously to the firm, the worker thus can be assumed to have acquired a property right in the firm. Some property rights analysis would suggest that any worker continuously employed for a given time period has acquired such a property right. This being the case primarily because the job has enabled an employee to "achieve social status, personal opportunity, and power," which in turn has benefited the firm. Dismissal from the respective job endangers these achievements and therefore must be compensated for—say by a severance payment.

A second, less radical view, qualifies this analysis. Workers acquire a compensable property rights in their job if the compensation they received does not account fully for the work done. This will typically be the case if the worker is paid on the basis of a non-linear wage contract and has been dismissed before completion of lifetime employment. It is also the case if the worker has acquired substantial firm-specific skills the acquisition of which helped the firm to increase productivity but that cannot be transferred to other firms. Since foregone earnings in an implicit contract situation, and those lost through the non-transferability of skill cannot be immediately valued, an approximation rule has to be applied. One simple rule of thumb would be to approximate these losses through the payment of a sum that rises with tenure, as well as the individual workers earnings, up to a certain number of years.

Contrary to the approach adopted in the *Harvard Law Review Note*,[372] the property rights approach implies that a discharged employee, having completed a fixed spell of employment, should be compensated in any case irrespective of the justification of the nature and motives of the discharge. The advantage of this approach as compared the current system of dismissal litigation is twofold. First, granting such a severance pay to all, or to most, workers who were dismissed reduces monitoring and litigation costs, which may be socially unproductive. Second, given that these severance costs are substantial enough, the requirement of such payments is likely to reduce employer incentives to act opportunistically in the context of a non-linear age-wage profile (especially as the chance of employees going without such a payment is eliminated). Thirdly, given that firms dismiss workers in excess of the social optimum because the costs of dismissal are externalised, a general severance requirement would allocate costs of dismissal more efficiently.

Severance payments are, of course, only one of many measures through which the problem of unjust, capricious and unnecessary dismissals can be addressed. Indeed, the literature on this topic proposes and discusses a host of possible approaches ranging from a general "just-cause standard," applying to all workers, to the universal provision of arbitral remedies once a dismissal has been identified as questionable. The purpose of this monograph is not to discuss these alternatives in detail nor to engage in a complex technical discussion as to how this problem could best be solved. Instead it is the goal of this work to merely stimulate a discussion on an issues which continues to carry considerably, and perhaps

---

[372] Anonymous, *supra* note 353.

heightened, policy relevance. Having provided a historical overview of developments in this area, this analysis will conclude with a brief "Afterword" that will discuss potential reasons for the relative stability of the flawed US dismissal protection alongside some of the factors that might allow this inertia to be overcome.

AFTERWORD:
EXCEPTIONALISM REVISITED

The notion of American exceptionalism has remained a powerful element in the debate on US labor relations. Past analyses have attributed the comparatively loose regulation of the US labor market to various manifestations of exceptionalism including the frontier spirit of a "class-less" society, the absence of strong socialist/social democratic parties, to the conservativeness of the US courts.[373] In this context some core claims of exceptionalism have rested on the allegedly anomalous position of US unions, and most notably, the absence of powerful political party-union alliances and the resultant lack of integration of unions into the state apparatus.[374]

Specifically, the labor historian William Forbath attributes the phenomenon of weak union integration and a concomittant lack of employment regulation to the fact that from 1900 to 1930, a number of anti-strike degrees pitched labor's energies on repealing judge-made law; thus establishing "the central anti-statist politics" of the US labor movement. Relying implicitly on notions of path-dependency, Forbath's conclusion to his *Law and the Shaping of the American Labor Movement* argues that the anti-statist leanings of US labor leaders have been continuously reinforced until today and, in so doing, prevented a political repositioning of US labor in a corporatist sense. Says Forbath:[375]

> From the labor movement's perspective, the nation's labor law has largely failed over the past two decades to protect union organizing or to defend existing unions from a new open shop movement on the part of the employers in many unionized sectors. So great is organized labor's discontent that one has begun to hear labor leaders mooting, half-seriously, the desirability of a "deregulation" of labor relations. One hears, in other words, strong echoes of the anti-statism of the Gompers era.

The evidence presented here, in connection with job protection, does not contest Forbath's analysis; rather it extends the notion of US exceptionalism into a different direction. Exceptionalism, admittedly, is evidenced in the way the US, as a state, situates organized labor. The absence of Swedish, French, German, or even Canadian style political alliances

---

[373] Aristide Zolberg, "From One Exceptionalism to Many: American Working Class Formation in Comparative Perspective" *Why is there no Socialism in the United States* 101 (Jean Heffer and Jeanine Rovet, eds., 1988).

[374] Derek Bok, "Reflections on the Distinctive Character of American Labor Law," *84 Harvard Law Review* 1394 (1971), and Joel Rogers, "Divide and Conquer: Further Reflections on the Distinctive Character of U.S. Labor Law," 1990 *Wisconsin Law Review* 1 (1990).

[375] William E. Forbath, *Law and the Shaping of the American Labor Movement*, at 172 (1991).

whose principal goal is the support of the collective bargaining efforts of unions is a marked feature of US politics and labor relations. However, in terms of analytical locus the characteristics of these alliances only provide partial proof of "the unusual." If we assume that exceptionalism is primarily about individuals in similar societies having dissimilar rights, then the weak positioning of US unions alone provides incomplete evidence of something being unexpected or "outside the norm." In theory, at least, one could imagine an industrial relations system which assigns a weak political position to unions, but rigorously enforces individual employment rights through systems of external arbitration or litigation; thus creating all the requisite elements for a balancing of power between capital and labor. If this imaginary system produced results very similar to a strongly unionized collective bargaining system, then there would be no exceptionalism of outcomes and, unless there are unforeseen changes, it might be hard to convince others of the relevance of the existing exceptionalism of processes. In other words, for a theory of exceptionalism to be credible, it must account for the possibility of the different institutional pathways leading ultimately to similar outcomes. Conversely, if exceptional outcomes are to be credibly explained this should encompass at least an attempt to survey several of the institutional frameworks which have contributed to the respective outcome.

Looking at the issue of job security, this study has attempted to provide a picture that takes into account the various institutional sources on which US workers can draw in seeking to protect themselves against arbitrary and unjust dismissals. In doing so, this study has suggested that few of the classical interpretations of US exceptionalism provide a credible and comprehensive narrative for the absence of strong job protection measures in the US labor markets. Granted, there is evidence of conservative tendencies amongst the courts who interpreted statutory legislation such as the NLRA. Equally, there is evidence of short-termism and anti-statism amongst the US union leadership. However none of this is absolute or indisputable. Thus, the same Supreme Court, which limited the bargaining power of unions under the NLRA, also protected union leaders from overgeneralizing anti-racketeering statutes that had been partially born out of the anti-democratic spirit of the cold war. Even more so, the rise of exemptions to the at-will doctrine during the Reagan presidency belies some of the allegations that claim that US courts are nothing more than the political pawns of an anti-labor lobby. Similarly, US trade unions, which have often stood accused of having neglected legislative avenues to job security-enhancing measures, meanwhile, must be credited with creating plant-based job protection systems that provided significant levels of job protection for union workers, albeit only for a few decades. If we were to take this timeline of events seriously, then unions stand, if anything, only accused of a tactical error that was based on the assumption that trade union coverage would continue to expand, thus making unnecessary a strengthening of individual employment rights. Perhaps, then, against the backdrop of union successes in the 1950s and 1960s, there is less evidence for anti-statism than there is for pragmatism and a lack of foresight.

Nonetheless, the narrative presented here describes a series of events in which the actions of courts, unions and employers conspired to deprive US workers from protection against dismissals to a degree that eventually encouraged courts to re-introduce some rudimentary doctrines of wrongful discharge. Taken at face value, none of this makes for good theory; not even good institutionalist theory. Equally, none of this allows for the identification of "heroes," while providing ample evidence for opportunism. This opportunism ranges from nineteenth and early twentieth century courts, which acted as handmaidens to business interests to a New Deal administration that sought to provide space for the orderly expansion of collective bargaining for the sake of economic stability, but was unwilling to introduce even a semblance of co-determination. It includes powerful postwar unions that were apparently able to enhance the job security of their members as long as the US manufacturing economy prospered, without showing much concern for individual employment rights as well as employers that used every opportunity to preserve the managerial prerogative, even in context were consensual arbitral solutions would have been more suitable to their interests. It also covers individual litigants and lawyers who, driven by prospects of substantial awards, exploited the possibility of wrongful discharge litigation to a level that may well have damaged the integrity of judicial processes.

One way of re-conceptualizing the weakness of job protection as a US exceptionalism is not to attribute events to a single *leitmotiv*, such as the alleged anti-statism of the US union leadership, but rather to contradictions and institutional indeterminacy as an explanation in its own right. Such an analysis of labor regulation in terms of inherent contradictions has been advocated both by orthodox Marxist scholars as well as neo-Marxist scholarship. At its most elementary level, the concept of the inherent contradictions of labor regulation relates to the desire of this type of regulation to legitimize the existing order, while allowing for the articulation of working class interests; all of which gives rise to contradictory tendencies both within and between different spheres of labor regulation. Citing *Le Droite Capitaliste du Travail* by Collin et al., the Russian political scientist Igor Kiselev notes to this effect that:[376]

> ...The rules of bourgeois labor law "on the one hand, legalize the existing order, and on the other, are the results of a struggle aimed at a more or less radical change in the existing system." ...All this explains the existence in bourgeois law of opposing tendencies differing in character and the orientation of their provision.

Implied in Kiselev's analysis, as in much of the writings of neo-Marxist scholars, is the notion that, in capitalist states, multiple, overlapping and inconsistent sub-systems of labor regulation—such as centralized collective bargaining, local bargaining, collective litigation and individual litigation—coexist; whereby there stability is predicated on the condition that they do not, cumulatively, alienate the interests of either capital or of co-opted labor.

Applying this theoretical approach to job security regulation is necessarily tentative and speculative undertakings. However, the notion of contradictory labor regulation systems prevailing as long as they reasonably accommodate key interests provides an implicit rationale for the divergence of regulatory set-ups. Specifically, it can be argued that with stability of regulatory systems resting on either the explicit or implied consensus of capital a conundrum of regulatory subsystems can evolve over time either by assigning a dominant role to whichever element of the these subsystems most suitably accommodates these interests or by maintaining a palatable balance between existing systems.

Following the tenets of regulation theory, it can be argued that liberal corporatist systems which employ centralized collective bargaining present one of the more frequent developmental trajectories of labor regulation for the accommodation of the governance

---

[376] Igor Kiselev, *State Monopoly Capitalism and Labor Law*, at 51 (1988), citing Francis Collon, Regine Dhuquois, Pierre-Herbert Goutierre, Antoine Jeammand, Gerard Lyon-Caen, Albert Roudil, *Le Droite Capitalist du Travail*, at 117 (1980).

needs of advanced capitalist states.[377] In liberal corporatist systems, centralized collective bargaining is given an explicitly dominant place amongst other sources of labor regulation on account of the establishment of a close bargaining partnership between core unions, employer associations and the state. Whilst liberal corporatist systems are characterized by more expansive welfare state provisions, they are typically less supportive of individual employment rights and, as a whole, seek to restrict in one form or another individual litigation. In addition, classical liberal corporatist systems tend to limit local level bargaining and plant level militancy, often by assigning state-type policing powers to the national trade union leadership.

Less frequent than liberal corporatist systems of labor regulation are micro-corporatists systems. Micro-corporatists systems are characterized by a situation where employment protection and employment rights evolve from plant level or local bargaining. Like liberal corporatist systems, micro-corporatists systems are usually unsupportive of individual employment litigation. At the same time, however, they are adverse to central guidance either in matters of wage and effort bargaining, or in matters of job rights. This unwillingness to submit to a central or national strategy typically emanates from the ability of micro-corporatist bargainers to exploit regional or sectoral inequalities.[378] As a consequence, micro-corporatist systems erode once their principal agents cease to be able to exploit inequalities effectively, and/or if centralized systems provide them with more advantageous frameworks for accommodating conflicting and contradictory demands. While each of these systems embodies contradictions, they are often able to secure their survival over extended periods of time on account of their ability to match the governance of certain socio-political and economic environments.

The second variant of indeterminate labor regulations system is rarer than various variants of corporatism. Indeterminate systems derive their stability not from giving a dominant place to any of the potential sub-systems of labor regulation but rather from giving an equal or near-equal place to several sources of weak labor regulation; thus providing the promise, or illusion, of an expansion of future rights in one or another sub-systems. Indeterminate systems generally appear in parallel with multi-centrist political systems where it is difficult to identify a suitably limited group of participants for a corporatist set-up. Apart from this, the preservation of an indeterminate system appears to correspond with the presence of strong systems of constitutional governance, which limit both the possibility of exceedingly close interest group-government partnerships as well as the subjugation of individual rights, however narrowly and prejudicially defined, by corporatist coalitions.

One of the key speculative findings of this research monograph is that the US system of labor regulation closely mirrors the characteristics of an indeterminate system where the existence of several weak sources of employment protection militates against demands for major reform: allowing a relatively unsatisfactory level of under-regulation to persist against calls for greater employment regulation.

This, by itself, does not bode well for the possibility of a future reform of the contemporary system that governs US workplaces. However, the literature on successful

---

[377] Walter Korpi and Michael Shalev, "Strikes, Power and Politics in the Western Nations, 1900-1976," 1 *Political Power and Social Theory* 117 (1980); and Walter Korpi and Michael Shalev, "Working Class Mobilization and American Exceptionalism," 1 *Economic and Industrial Democracy* 31 (1980).

[378] Lars Calmfors and John Driffill, "Bargaining Structure, Corporatism and Macroeconomic Performance," 6 *Economic Policy* 31 (1988).

changes in regulatory environments suggest that reform is possible when there is strong policy commitment and when there are discernible net gains from continued reform. Accordingly, a study by Jose Edgardo Campus and Hadi Salehi Esfahani, which investigated the prerequisites of successful policy reform in the context of public enterprise reform, has argued that fundamental political reforms are possible even when such reforms disrupt social pacts and their benefits will be delayed. Said Campus and Esfahani:[379]

> The political economy of policy reform is rich with issues that scholars have only recently begun to confront. Though we have focused on public enterprise reform in this paper, in the process, we have identified some basic issues that are common to all kinds of reforms. Reform, as we argue, disrupts social pacts and thus carries with it potentially huge political costs. Thus the potential gains must be large enough for regime leaders to be able to compensate some of the losers and/or to build alternative bases of support. Assuming there are net gains to be made, leaders face still another problem. Because the gains materialize later in the reform process while the costs are borne earlier, institutional mechanisms need to be established in order to make policy reversals costly. Only in this way can the gains and thus the compensations and benefits be guaranteed.
>
> … it may be possible to identify countries in which the reform might reasonably succeed and those in which it would most likely fail. Countries in which potential gain-cost ratio is high and where credible commitment mechanisms can be established would fall in the first category.

Applying this framework, it could be argued that the potential gains from significantly reducing the ability of US employers to engage in unnecessary and capricious dismissals of employees that ultimately aggravate instability in the labor market could be substantial; exceeding the costs such measures might have in terms of an increased inflexibility in the labour market.

In addition to these immediate gains, there would be significant long-term gains in terms of a much-needed increase in human capital investment, which would result both from the efforts of individual workers who no longer abstain from such training, and the efforts of employers who are required to show a greater commitment to their workforce. Crucial for such a strategy of "deflexibilization" to succeed, meanwhile, would be an ongoing awareness of either the benefits of these reforms or alternatively the costs of not undertaking them, as well as significant policy commitment to their implementation.

Crucial, also, is the choice of a point in time when the benefits supporting a decision in favour of reform, as well as the costs of non-reform, are particularly noticeable. In the view of this author, such a point in time may well have been reached as a consequence of the 2007 crisis. This makes it imperative for those progressive forces who have, for some time, sought a fundamental change in the US labor regulation to seize the initiative and to advocate and promote mnecessary regulatory change at a time when it is needed most and its absence is felt most painfully by those facing a continuous threat of employment insecurity and unemployment.

---

[379] See Jose Edgardo Campus and Hadi Salehi Esfahani, "Credible Commitment and Success with Public Enterprise Reform," 28 *World Development* 221, at 237 (2000).

REFERENCES

Addison, John T. "Job Security in the United States: Law, Collective Bargaining, Policy, and Practice," 24 *British Journal of Industrial Relations* 381 (1986).

Alchian, Armen and Harold Demsetz, "Production, Information Costs, and Economic Organization," 62 *American Economic Review* 777 (1972).

Allen, Stephen G., "Union Work Rules and Efficiency in the Building Trades," 4 *Journal of Labor Economics* 212 (1986).

Anonymous, "Editorial: Downsizing," *New York Times* 14, 25 February (1996).

Anonymous, "Learning to Cope" *The Economist* 13, 6 April (1996).

Anonymous, "Note: Employer Opportunism and the Need for a Just-Cause Standard," 103 *Harvard Law Review* 510 (1989).

Anonymous, "Note: Remedies and Measure of Damages in Employment Contracts," 7 *Columbia Law Review* 408 (1907).

Anonymous, "Fire and Forget" The Economist 51, April 20 (1996).

Anonymous, "Note: Drafting Problems and the Regulation of Featherbedding—An Imagined Dilemma," 73 *Yale Law Journal* 812 (1964).

Anonymous, "Note: Featherbedding and Taft-Hartley," 52 *Columbia Law Review* 1020 (1952).

Appleby, Joyce, *Capitalism and a New Social Order* (New York, NY: New York University Press, 1984).

Arrow, Kenneth "Information and the Organization of Industry," *Lectio Magistralis* (Milan: Catholic University of Milan, 1994).

Atleson, James B., "Wartime Labor Regulation, the Industrial Pluralists, and the Law of Collective Bargaining" in *Industrial Democracy in America: The Ambiguous Promise* 164 (Nelson N. Lichtenstein and Howell Harris, eds, Cambridge: Cambridge University Press, 1993).

Atleson, James B., *Values and Assumptions of American Labor Law* (Amherst, MA: University of Massachusetts Press, 1983).

Austin, Aleine, *The Labor Story: A Popular History of American Labor*, 1786-1949 (New York, NY: Coward-McCann, 1949).

Autor, David H., "Outsourcing At-will: The Contribution of Unjust Dismissal Doctrine to the Growth of Employment Outsourcing," 21 *Journal of Labor Economics* 1 (2003).

Autor, David, John J. Donohue III, and Stewart J. Schwab, "The Costs of Wrongful Discharge Laws," *National Bureau of Economic Research Working Paper Series*, Working Paper No. 9425 (Cambridge, MA: NBER, 2001).

Barenberg, Mark, "The Political Economy of the Wagner Act: Power, Symbol and Workplace Cooperation," *Harvard Law Review*, 1381 (1993).

Batt, F. Raleigh, *The Law of Master and Servant* (London: Pitman, 3rd edition, 1939).

Beal, Edwin F., Edward D. Wickersham and Philip K. Keinast, *The Practice of Collective Bargaining* (Homewood, IL: Irwin, 5th edition, 1976).

Beck, Matthias P., "The Law and Economics of Dismissal Regulation: A Comparative Analysis of US and UK Systems," in Law and Economics and the Labour Market 92 (Gerrit de Geest, Jacques J. Siegers, Roger van den Bergh, eds., Cheltenham: Edward Elgar, 1999).

Beck, Matthias P., "Public Policy Exemptions, Whistleblower Statutes, and Government Worker Layoffs: A Case of Adverse Effects?" 24 *Journal of Collective Negotiations in the Public Sector* 1 (1995).

Beck, Matthias P., "Union Agendas and the Disintegration of Job Stability—an Institutional Perspective," 5 *Journal of Interdisciplinary Economics* 79 (1994).

Becker, Gary S. and George J. Stigler, "Law Enforcement, Malfeasance, and Compensation of Enforcers," 3 *Journal of Legal Studies* 1 (1974).

Becker, Gary S. "The Court's Shouldn't Become Pink Slip Police" Business Week 14, August 28 (1989).

Bellace, Janice R., "A Right of Fair Dismissal: Enforcing a Statutory Guarantee," 16 *University of Michigan Journal of Law* 207 (1983).

Benjamin, Aaron, "Governmental Restraints on Featherbedding," 5 *Stanford Law Review* 680 (1953).

Bimba, Anthony, *The History of the American Working Class* (New York, NY: International Pub., 1936).

Bisom-Rapp, Susan, "Bulletproofing the Workplace: Symbol and Substance in Employment Discrimination Law Practice," 26 *Florida State Law Review* 959 (1990).

Bisom-Rapp, Susan, "Discerning from Substance: Understanding Employer Litigation Prevention Strategies," 3 *Employee Rights and Employment Policy Journal* 1 (1999).

Blackstone, Sir William, *Commentaries on the Laws of England*, Book 1 (made available in electronic form by the University of Adelaide Library, originally published as Oxford: Printed at the Clarendon Press, 1769).

Blades, Lawrence E., "Employment-At-Will vs. Individual Freedom: On Limiting the Abusive Exercise of Employer Power" 76 *Columbia Law Review* 1404 (1967).

Blair, Margarete M., *Ownership and Control: Rethinking Corporate Governance of the 21st Century* (Washington, DC: Brookings Institution, 1995).

Bloch, Robert E., "The Disclosure of Profits in the Normal Course of Collective Bargaining: All Relevant Information Should Be on the Table," 2 *Labor Lawyer* 47 (1986).

Bluestone, Barry, and Bennett Harrison, *The Deindustrialization of America: Plant Closings, Community Abandonment and the Dismantling of Basic Industry* (New York, NY: Basic Books, 1982).

Bok, Derek C. and John T. Dunlop, *Labor and the American Community* (New York, NY: Simon and Schuster, 1970).

Bok, Derek C., "Reflections on the Distinctive Character of American Labor Law," 84 *Harvard Law Review* 1394 (1971),

Bonnett, Clarence E., "The Yellow Dog Contract in Its Relation to Public Policy," 7 *Tulane Law Review* 315 (1932-1933).

Brannon, Henry, *A Treatise on the Rights and Privileges Guaranteed by the Fourteenth Amendment to the Constitution of the United States* (Cincinnati, OH: Anderson, 1901).

Bratton, William W. Jr., "The New Economic Theory of the Firm: Critical Perspectives from History Bratton," 41 *Stanford Law Review* 1471 (1989).

Brown, Peter M. and Richard S. Peer, "Anti-Racketeering Act: Labor and Management Weapon Against Labor Racketeering," 32 *New York University Law Review* 965 (1957).

Brown, Ray A., "Police Power: Legislation for Health and Personal Safety," 42 *Harvard Law Review* 868 (1929).

Burck, Gilbert, "The Great Featherbedding Fight" 63 *Fortune Magazine* 151 March (1960).

Burck, Gilbert, "The Great Featherbedding Fight" in *Readings in Labor Economics* 424 (Gordon F. Bloom, Herbert R. Northrup and Richard L. Rowan, eds., Homewood, IL: Irwin, 1963).

Bureau of Labor Statistics, "Extended Mass Layoffs in 2009," *Report* No. 1025 (Washington, DC: Bureau of Labor, 2010).

Bureau of National Affairs, "Disciplinary Practices and Policies," *Personnel Policies Forum,* Survey No. 42 (Washington, DC: BNA, 1957).

Bureau of National Affairs, "Uniform Employment Termination Act," *Daily Labor Report,* No. 156, August 13 (Washington, DC: BNA, 1991).

Burn, Richard, *The Justice of the Peace and Parish Officer,* Volume V (London: Sweet and Maxwell, 26th edition, 1831).

Bye, Raymond T. and William W. Hewett, *Applied Economics: The Application of Economic Principles to the Problems of Economic Control* (New York, NY: F.S. Crofts, 1947).

Calmfors, Lars and John DRIFFILL, "Bargaining Structure, Corporatism and Macroeconomic Performance," 6 *Economic Policy* 31 (1988).

Campus, Jose Edgardo and Hadi Salehi Esfahani, "Credible Commitment and Success with Public Enterprise Reform," 28 *World Development* 221 (2000).

Capelli, Peter and Robert A. McKersie, "Labor and the Crisis in Collective Bargaining," in *Challenges and Choices Facing American Labor* 227 (Thomas A. Kochan ed., Cambridge, MA: MIT Press, 1985).

Carlson, Alan and Bruce Phillip, "Due Process Considerations in Grievance Arbitration Proceedings," 2 *Hastings Constitutional Law Quarterly* 519 (1974).

Carrington, Frederick A., and Joseph Payne, *Reports of Cases Determined at Nisi Prius, in the Courts of King's Bench and Common Pleas and on the Circuit, From the Sittings in Easter Term 1825 to the Sittings in Trinity Term, 1827,* Volume II (London: Sweet and Maxwell, 1827).

Cartier, Kate, "The Transaction Cost and Benefits of the Incomplete Contract of Employment," 18 *Cambridge Journal of Economics* 181 (1994).

Caunce, Stephen, "Farm Servants and the Development of Capitalism in English Agriculture," 45 *Agricultural History Review* 49 (1997).

Chitty, Joseph, *Chitty's Treatise on the Law of Contracts* (London: Sweet and Maxwell, 19th edition, 1937).

Classen, Timothy J. and Richard A. Dunn, "The Effects of Job Loss and Unemployment Duration on Suicide Risk in the United States: A New Look Using Mass-Layoffs and Unemployment Insurance Claims," 21 *Health Economics* 338 (2012).

Collon, Francis, Regine Dhuquois, Pierre-Herbert Goutierre, Antoine Jeammand, Gerard Lyon-Caen and Albert Roudil, *Le Droite Capitalist du Travail* (Grenoble Presses Universitaires de Grenoble, 1980).

Commons, John R., *Institutional Economics* (New York, NY: Macmillan, 1934).

Commons, John R., "Institutional Economics," 26 *The American Economic Review* 237 (1936).

Commons, John R., *Legal Foundations of Capitalism* (New York, NY: Macmillan, 1924).

Commons, John R., and John B. Andrews, *Principles of Labor Legislation* (New York, NY: Harper Bros., 4th revised edition, 1936).

Corbin, Arthur L., *Cases on the Law of Contracts: Selected from Decisions of English and American Courts* (St. Paul, MN: West Pub., 1921).

Corman, Calvin W., "The Partial Performance Interest of the Defaulting Employee - Part One," 38 *Marquette Law Review* 61 (1954).

Corrada, Roberto L., "The Arbitral Imperative in Labor and Employment Law," 47 *Catholic University Law Review* 919 (1998).

Corwin, Edward "Standpoint in Constitutional Law" in *The Bacon Lectures on the Constitution of the United States: Given at Boston University 1928-1938* (Multiple Authors, Worcester, MA: Heffernan Press, 1939).

Cox, Archibald, and John T. Dunlop, "Regulation of Collective Bargaining by the NLRB," 63 *Harvard Law Review* 389 (1950).

Crompton, Charles John, Roger Meeson and Henry Roscoe, *Reports of Cases Argued and Determined in the Courts of Exchequer, From Easter Term, 5 Will. IV. to Michaelmas Term, 6 Will IV. Volume II* (London: Sweet and Maxwell, 1836).

Cross, Adam Corey "Companies starting to Hire Back after Mass Layoffs," *Fiscal Times*, January 27 (2011).

Cross, James A., *A Shameful Business: The Case for Human Rights in the American Workplace* (Ithaca, NY: Cornell University, 2010).

Crump, Douglas W., William M. Rees, and Paul N. Todd, "Constructive Dismissal Construed: The Court of Appeal Digs for Clarity," 41 *Modern Law Review* 581 (1978).

Dalton, Michael, *The Country Justice* (London: Printed by William Rawlins and Samuel Rycroft, assigns of Richard and Edward Atkyns, 1690).

De Noyer, Dena "Comment: Remedying Anticipatory Repudiation—Past, Present, and Future?" 52 *Southern Methodist University Law Review* 1787 (1999).

Dertouzos, James, Elaine Holland, and Patricia Ebener, "The Legal and Economic Consequences of Wrongful Termination," *RAND Institute for Civil Justice Report R-3602 ICJ* (Santa Monica, CA: RAND Corporation, 1988).

Dicey, Albert V., *Lectures on the Relation between Law and Public Opinion in England during the Nineteenth Century* (London: Macmillan, 1919).

Elkouri, Frank, and Edna Asper Elkouri, *How Arbitration Works* (Washington, DC: Bureau of National Affairs, 3rd edition, 1973).

Epstein, Richard A. "In Defense of the Contract At-Will," 51 *University of Chicago Law Review* 947 (1984).

Ernst, Daniel R., "Free Labor, the Consumer Interest and The Law of Industrial Disputes, 1885-1990," 36 *The American Journal of Legal History* 19 (1992).

Estlund, Cynthia L., "The Ossification of American Labor Law," 102 *Columbia Law Review* 1527 (2002).

Estreicher, Samuel "Unjust Dismissal Laws: Some Cautionary Notes" 33 *American Journal of Comparative Law* 310 (1985).

Fearon, Peter, *War, Prosperity and Depression-The US Economy 1917-45* (Lawrence, KS: University of Kansas Press, 1987).

Feinman, Joey, "The Development of the Employment-At-Will Rule," 20 *American Journal of Legal History* 118 (1976).

Feller, David E., "A General Theory of the Collective Bargaining Agreement," 61 *California Law Review* 663 (1973).

Fenn, Paul and Christopher Whelan, "Job Security and the Role of Law: An Economic Analysis of Employment-At-Will," 20 *Stanford Journal of International Law* 353, at 372 (1984).

Fitch, John A., *The Causes of Industrial Unrest* (New York, NY: Harper Bros., 1924).

Flaim, Paul O., and Ellen Sehgal, "Displaced Workers of 1979-83: How Well Have They Fared?" 108 *Monthly Labor Review* 3 (1985).

Flanagan, Robert J., *Labor Relations and the Litigation Explosion* (Washington, D.C.: Brookings Institution, 1986).

Forbath, William E., "Ambiguities of Free Labor: Labor and the Law in the Gilded Age," 1985 *Wisconsin Law Review* 767 (1985).

Forbath, William E., *Law and the Shaping of the American Labor Movement* (Cambridge, MA: Harvard University Press, 1991).

Fredrikson, Mary E. and Timothy P. Lynch, "Labor: The Great Depression to the 1990s," in *Encyclopedia of American Social History* Vol. II 1488 (1990).

Freedland, Mark, *The Personal Employment Contract* (Oxford: Oxford University Press, 2003).

Freeman, Richard B. "The Effect of Unions on Worker Attachment to Firms," 1 *Journal of Labor Research* 29 (1980).

Freeman, Richard B., "The Effect of Unions on Worker Attachment to Firms," *National Bureau of Economic Research Working Paper Series,* Working Paper No. 400 (Cambridge, MA: NBER, 1979).

Freidin, Jesse and Lloyd Ulman, "Arbitration and the War Labor Board" 58 *Harvard Law Review* 309 (1945).

Freidson, Eliot, "Labors of Love in Theory and Practice: A Prospectus," in *The Nature of Work* 149 (Kai Erikson and Steven Vallas eds., New Haven, CT: Yale University Press1990).

French, Michael, *US Economic History since 1945* (Manchester and New York, NY: Manchester University Press and St. Martin's Press, 1997).

Friedman, Lawrence M., *A History of American Law* (New York, NY: Simon and Schuster, 1985).

Frierson, James G., "How to Fire without Getting Burnt," 67 *Personnel* 44 (1990).

Fudge, Judy, "The Spectre of Addis in Contracts of Employment in Canada and the UK," 36 *Industrial Law Journal* 51 (2007).

Gaines, Larry K. and John L. Worrall, *Police Administration* (Clifton Park, NY: Delmar Cengage Learning, 3rd edition, 2012).

Gerber, Larry G., "Shifting Perspectives on American Exceptionalism: Recent Literature on American Labor Relations and Labor Politics," 31 *Journal of American Studies* 253 (1997).

Gintis, Herbert and Tsuneo Ishikawa, "Wages, Work Intensity and Unemployment in Competitive Labor Markets," 1 *Journal of Japanese and International Economics* 195 (1987).

Glater, Jonathan D. "Layoffs Herald a Heyday of Lawsuits," *New York Times*, January 30 (2009).

Glendon, Mary Ann and Edward R. Lev, "'Changes in the Bonding of the Employment Relationship," 20 *Boston College Law Review* 457 (1979).

Goldberg, Stephen B., "Mediation of Grievances under a Collective Bargaining Contract: An Alternative to Arbitration," 77 *Northwestern University Law Review* 270 (1982).

Goldfield, Michael, *The Decline of Organized Labor in the United States* (Chicago, IL: University of Chicago Press, 1987).

Gomberg, William, "Featherbedding: An Assertion of Property Rights," 333 *The Annals of the American Academy of Political and Social Science* 119 (1961).

Gordon, David, Richard Edwards and Michael Reich, *Segmented Work, Divided Workers* (Cambridge: Cambridge University Press, 1982).

Gorman, Robert A., *Basic Text on Labor Law, Unionization and Collective Bargaining* (St. Paul, MN: West Pub., 1976).

Gould, William B., *A Primer on American Labor Law* (Cambridge, MA: MIT Press, 1986).

Gould, William B., *Agenda for Reform: The Future of Employment Relationships and the Law* (Cambridge, MA: MIT Press, 1996).

Gould, William B., "Stemming the Wrongful Discharge Tide: A Case for Arbitration," 13 *Employee Relations Law Journal* 404 (1987).

Gould, William B., "The Idea of the Job as Property in Contemporary America,"' 1986 *Brigham Young University Law Review* 885 (1986).

Greenman, Russell L., *The Worker, the Foreman and the Wagner Act* (New York, NY: Harper Bros.,1939).

Gregory, Charles O., *Labor and the Law* (New York, NY: WW Norton, 1946).

Grenig, Jay E., "The Dismissal of Employees in the United States" 130 *International Labor Review* 569 (1991).

Haber, William and Harold Levinson, *Labor Relations and Productivity in the Building Trades* (Ann Arbor: Bureau of Industrial Relations, 1956).

Hansman, Henry B., "Towards A General Theory of Corporate Ownership," *Yale Law School Program in Law and Organization Working Paper* No. 74 (1988).

Hicks, Frederick, *Material and Methods of Legal Research* (Rochester, NY: Lawyers Cooperative Publishing, 1923).

Hilgert, Raymond L., "How At-Will Statements Hurt Employers," 67 *Personnel Journal* 75 (1988).

Holmes, Rebecca, "The Impact of State Labor Regulations on Manufacturing Input Demand During the Progressive Era, Dissertation Summary," 65 *Journal of Economic History* 531 (2005).

Hoover, J. Edgar, "Comment on the Article Loyalty among Government Employees," 58 *Yale Law Journal 401* (1948-1949).

Hopson, Dan, "Kansas Labor Law and District Court Injunctions," 6 *University of Kansas Law Review* 1 (1957-1958).

Horwitz, Morton J., *The Transformation of American Law, 1780-1860* (Cambridge, MA: Harvard University Press, 1978).

Hoxie, Robert F., *Trade Unionism in the United States* (New York, NY: Appleton, 1923).

Huggins, William L., *Labor and Democracy* (New York, NY: Macmillan, 1922).

Jackson, Janice and William T. Schantz, "A New Frontier in Wrongful Discharge" *Personnel Journal* 101 January (1990).

Jacob, Giles, *The Modern Justice: The Business of a Justice of the Peace* (London: Printed by the assignee of E. Sayer for B. Lintott, 1716).

Jacoby, Sanford M., "The Duration of Indefinite Employment Contracts in the US and England: A Historical Analysis," 5 *Comparative Labor Law* 85 (1982).

Jain, Hem C., "Recent Developments and Emerging Trends in Labour-Management Relations in the USA. and Canada," 20 *Relations Industrielles/ Industrial Relations* 540 (1965).

Jarsulic, Marc "Protecting Workers from Wrongful Discharge: Montana's Experience with Tort and Statutory Regimes" 3 *Employee Rights and Employment Policy Journal* 105 (1999).

Jenners, Lisa, "Employment-At-Will Liability: How Protected Are You," 71 *Human Resource Focus* 11 (1994)

Johnson, George E., "Work Rules Featherbedding, and Pareto-optimal Union-Management Bargaining," 8 *Journal of Labor Economics*, 237 (1990).

Johnson, Julia E., *The National Labor Relations Act; Should it Be Amended?* (New York, NY: Wilson, 1940).

Jung, David J. and Richard Harkness, "The Facts of Wrongful Discharge," 4 *The Labor Lawyer* 257 (1988).

Jung, David J., "Jury Verdicts in Wrongful Termination Cases," *Report by the Public Law Research Institute at Hastings College of the Law* (San Fransisco, CA: UC Hastings, 1997).

Juris, Hervey A., "Union Crisis Wage Decisions," 8 *Industrial Relations* 247 (1969).

Kahn-Freund, Otto, "Blackstone's Neglected Child: The Contract of Employment," 93 *Law Quarterly Review* 508 (1977).

Karsten, Peter, "'Bottomed on Justice': A Reappraisal of Critical Legal Studies Scholarship Concerning Breaches of Labor Contracts by Quitting or Firing in Britain and the US," 34 *The American Journal of Legal History* 208 (1990).

Kassalow, Everett M., "Concession Bargaining: Towards new Roles for American Unions" 127 *International Labour Review* 573 (1988).

Kaufman, Bruce E., "Labor Markets and Employment Regulation: The view of the 'old' Institutionalists," in *Government Regulation of the Employment Relationship* 11 (Bruce E. Kaufman, ed., Ithaca, NY: Cornell University Press, 1997).

Keller, Leonard A., *The Management Function a Positive Approach to Labor Relation* (Washington, DC: The Bureau of National Affairs, 1963).

Keppler, Mark J., "Halting Traffic on the Road to Wrongful Discharge—Avoiding Wrongful Discharge Suits," 67 *Personnel* 48 (1990).

Kerr, Clark, John T. Dunlop, Frederick Harbison, and Charles Myers, *Industrialism and Industrial Man: The Problems of Labor and Management in Economic Growth* (Harvard University Press, Cambridge, MA: 1960).

Kim, Pauline T., "Cynicism Reconsidered," 76 *Washington University Law Quarterly* 193 (1998).

Kiselev, Igor, *State Monopoly Capitalism and Labor Law* (Moscow: Progress, 1988).

Klare, Karl E., "Judicial Deradicalization of the Wagner Act and the Origins of Modern Legal Consciousness, 1937-1941," 62 *Minnesota Law Review* 265 (1978).

Kochan, Thomas A., Harry C. Katz, and Robert B. McKersie, *The Transformation of American Industrial Relations* (Ithaca, NY: Cornell University Press, 1986).

Kolko, Joyce, *Restructuring the World Economy* (New York, NY: Pantheon, 1988).

Korpi, Walter and Michael Shalev, "Strikes, Power and Politics in the Western Nations, 1900-1976," 1 *Political Power and Social Theory* 117 (1980).

Korpi, Walter and Michael Shalev, "Working Class Mobilization and American Exceptionalism," 1 *Economic and Industrial Democracy* 31 (1980).

Krauskopf, Joan M. "Employment Discharge: Survey and Critique of the Modern At-Will Rule" 51 *University of Missouri Kansas City Law Review* 189 (1983).

Krueger, Alan B., "The Evolution of Unjust Dismissal legislation in the United States" 44 *Industrial and Labour Relations Review* 644 (1991).

Labatt, Charles Bagot, *Commentaries on the Law of Master and Servant, in Eight Volumes*, Volume 1 (Rochester, NY: Lawyers Cooperative Publishing, 1913).

Labatt, Charles Bagot, "State Regulation of the Contract of Employment," 27 *American Law Review* 857 (1893).

Lawson, Joseph, *How to Develop an Employee Handbook* (New York, NY: AMACOM, 2nd edition, 1998).

Lebergott, Stanley, "Labor Force and Employment, 1800-1960," in 30 *Output, Employment, and Productivity in the United States After 1800: Studies in Incomes and Wealth* 117 (Dorothy S. Brady, ed., Cambridge, MA: NBER, 1966).

Lee, Barbara A., "Something Akin to a Property Right" (1989) 8 *Business and Professional Ethics Journal* 63 (1989).

Levenstein, Aaron, *Labor Today and Tomorrow* (New York, NY: Knopf 1946).

Levine, David I., "Just-Cause Policies When Unemployment is a Worker Discipline Device," 79 *American Economic Review* 902 (1989).

Levy, Leonard W., *The Law of the Commonwealth and Chief Justice Shaw* (Cambridge, MA: Harvard University Press, 1957).

Lewis, Edward R., *A History of American Political Thought From the Civil War To the World War* (New York, NY: Macmillan, 1937).

Lieberman, Jethro K., *The Litigious Society* (New York, NY: Basic Books 1981).

Linzer, Peter, "The Decline of Assent: At-Will Employment as a Case Study of the Breakdown of Private Law Theory," 20 *Georgia Law Review* 323 (1986).

Lofaso, Anne Marie, "Talking is Worthwhile: The Role of Employee Voice in Protecting, Enhancing, and Encouraging Individual Rights to Job Security in a Collective System," 14 *Employee Rights and Employment Policy Journal* 101 (2010).

MacDonell, John, *The Law of Master and Servant: Part I-Common Law and Part II-Statute Law* (London: Stevens and Sons, 1883).

Magdoff, Fred "The Jobs Disaster in the United States," 63 *Monthly Review-An Independent Socialist Magazine* 1 (2011).

Maltby, Lewis, "The Decline of Employment At Will—A Quantitative Analysis," 41 *Labor Law Journal* 51 (1990).

Manley-Smith, Charles, *A Treatise on the Law of Master and Servant* (London: Sweet and Maxwell, 7th edition, 1922).

Manley-Smith, Charles, *A Treatise on the Law of Master and Servant, including therein Masters and Workmen in Every Description of Trade and Occupation* (Philadelphia: Blackstone Pub., from the 4th English edition, 1886).

Matheiny, Ken and Marion Crain, "Disloyal Workers and the Un-American Labor Law," 82 *University of North Carolina Law Review* 1705 (2003-2004).

Mauk, William L., "Model Termination Act is Flawed," 27 *Trial* 28 (1991).

McWhirter, Darian A., *Your Rights at Work* (New York, NY: Wiley, 1989).

Medoff, James L., "Layoffs and Alternatives Under Trade Unions in US Manufacturing," 69 *American Economic Review* 380 (1979).

Mendelsohn, Susan, "Wrongful Termination and its Effects on the Employment Relationship in the United States," *Organisation for Economic Co-operation and Development, Labor Market and Social Policy Occasional Papers,* No. 3 (Paris: OECD, 1990).

Miller, Glenn W., *American Labor and the Government* (New York, NY: Prentice Hall, 1948).

Mitchell, Broadus, *General Economics: An Introductory Text* (New York, NY: Holt, 1936).

Moglen, Eblen, "Taking the Fifth: Reconsidering the Origins of the Constitutional Privilege Against Self Incrimination," 92 *Michigan Law Review* 1086 (1992).

Moon, Richard G., "Wrongful Termination—New Claims and New Theories for Plaintiffs and Defendants," in *Labor Law Developments 1988* Chapter 9 (Southwestern Legal Foundation, ed., New York, NY: Matthew Bender, 1989).

Moon, Richard G. "Attack/Counter Attack: The Continuing Evolution of Wrongful Discharge Claims," in *Labor Law Developments 1990* Chapter 7 (Southwestern Legal Foundation, ed., New York, NY: Matthew Bender, 1991).

Morgan, David Hoseason, *Harvesters and Harvesting, 1840-1900: A Study of the Rural Proletariat* (London: Croom Helm, 1982).

Murray, Philip, and Morris L. Cooke, *Organized Labor and Production: Next Steps in Industrial Democracy* (New York, NY: Harper Bros., 1940).

Myers, Randy "Protecting Against Employment Perils," 82 *Nation's Business* 65 (1994).

Nelson, William, *The Office and Authority of a Justice of the Peace* (London: Sayer, 1710).

Nevile, Sandford and William Montagu Manning, *Reports of Cases Argued and Determined in the Court of King's Bench, in Hilary, Easter and Trinity Terms, In the Fourth Year of Will IV*, Volume III (London: Sweet and Maxwell 1835).

Kulish, Nicholas, "Defying Others, Germany Finds Economic Success," *The New York Times,* August 13 (2010).

Norwood, Stephen H., *The Third Reich in the Ivory Tower: Complicity and Conflict on American Campuses* (Cambridge: Cambridge University Press, 2009).

Okun, Bernhard and Richard W. Richardson, "Regional Income Inequality and Internal Population Migration," 9 *Economic Development and Cultural Change* 128 (1961).

Oneal, James, *The Workers in American History* (St. Louis, Missouri: National Rip-Saw, 1912).

Orren, Karen, *Belated Feudalism: Labor, the Law and Liberal Government in the United States* (Cambridge: Cambridge University Press, 1991).

Osterman, Paul and Thomas A. Kochan, "Employment Security and Employment Policy," in *New Developments in the Labor Market* 155 (Katherine Abraham and Robert B. McKersie eds., Cambridge, MA: MIT Press, 1990).

Ostrom, Brian J. and Neal B. Kauder, *Examining the Work of State Courts, 1994: A National Perspective from the Court Statistics Project* (Williamsburg, VA: National Center of State Courts, 1994).

Patterson, James, *A Compendium of English and Scotch Law Stating their Differences* (Cambridge: Macmillan, 2nd edition, 1865).

Payne, John, *Reports of Cases Determined in the English Courts of Common Law*, Volume XXV (Philadelphia, PA: T. and J.W. Johnson, 1835).

Peck, Cornelius J. "Unjust Discharges from Employment," 40 *Ohio State Law Journal* 1 (1979).

Peritt, Henry H. JR., *Employee Dismissal: Law and Practice* (New York, NY: Matthew Bender, 2nd edition, 1987)

Person, Carl E., "Fired, Laid Off or Demoted? Your Legal Options," *Law Mall* revised June (1994) <www.lawmall.com/pamphle1.php> accessed February 2012.

Phelps, Orme W., *Discharge and Discipline in the Unionized Firm* (Berkeley and Los Angeles, CA: University of California Press, 1959).

Picot, Arnold and Ekkehard Wenger, "The Employment Relation from the Transaction Cost Perspective," in *Management under Differing Labor Market and Employment Systems* 29 (Guenther Dlugos, Wolfgang Dorow and Klaus Weiermair eds, Berlin: De Gruyter, 1988).

Pingree, Darius H., "The Anti-Truck Laws, and Some Other Laws—A Legal Criticism," 3 *The American Lawyer* 386 (1895).

Pope, James G., "Labor's Constitution of Freedom" 106 *Yale Law Review* 941 (1997).

Pound, Roscoe, "Liberty of Contract," 18 *Yale Law Journal* 454 (1909).

Prichard, J. Robert, "A Systematic Approach to Comparative Law: The Effect of Cost, Fee, and Financing Rules on the Development of Substantive Law," 17 *Journal of Legal Studies* 451 (1988),

Pritt, Denis Nowell, *Law Class and Society. Book I: Employers, Workers and Trade Unions* (London: Lawrence and Wishart, 1970).

Prosser, William L., *Handbook of the Law of Torts* (St. Paul, MN: West Pub., 1941).

Raffaele, Joseph A., "The Changing Status of Management Prerogatives," 8 *The American Catholic Sociological Review* 170 (1947).

Reder, Melvin W., "The Rise and Fall of Unions: The Public Sector and the Private," 2 *The Journal of Economic Perspectives* 89 (1988).

Rees, Albert, *The Economics of Trade Unions* (Chicago, IL: University of Chicago Press, 1973).

Reich, Charles, A., "The New Property" 73 *Yale Law Review* 733 (1964).

Renshaw, Patrick, *American Labor and Consensus Capitalism, 1935-1990* (London: Macmillan, 1991).

Roelfs, David J., Eran Shor and Karina W. Davidson, Joseph E. Schwartz, "Losing Life and Livelihood: A Systematic Review and Meta-analysis of Unemployment and All-cause Mortality," 72 *Social Science and Medicine* 840 (2011).

Rogers, Joel, "Divide and Conquer: Further Reflections on the Distinctive Character of US Labor Law," 1990 *Wisconsin Law Review* 1 (1990).

Ross, Arthur M., "Labor Organizations and the Labor Movement in Advanced Industrial Society," 50 *Virginia Law Review* 1359 (1964).

Rowley, Keith A., "A Brief History of Anticipatory Repudiation in American Contract Law," 69 *University of Cincinnati Law Review* 565 (2001).

Scalia, Eugene, "Ending Our Anti-Union Federal Employment Policy," 24 *Harvard Journal of Public Policy* 489 (2000).

Schatz, Ronald W., "From Commons to Dunlop: Rethinking the Field and Theory of Industrial Relations" in *Industrial Democracy in America: The Ambiguous Promise* 87 (Nelson N. Lichtenstein and Howell Harris, eds., Cambridge University Press: Cambridge, 1993).

Schouler, James, *Treatise on the Law of Domestic Relations; Embracing Husband and Wife, Parent and Child, Guardian and Ward, Infancy, and Master and Servant* (Boston, MA: Little Brown, 1870).

Schulman, Harry, "Reason, Contract, and Law in Labor Relations," 68 *Harvard Law Review* 959 (1955).

Schwartz, Mindy, "American Federation of Musicians: An Unearned Encore for Featherbedding," 47 *Wayne Law Review* 1339 (2001).

Schwoerer, Catherine C. and Benson Rosen, "Effects of Employment-At-Will Policies and Compensation Policies on Corporate Image and Job Pursuit Intentions," *74 Journal of Applied Psychology* 653 (1989).

Scrutton, Lord Justice Thomas E., "The Work of the Commercial Courts,"1 *Cambridge Law Journal* 6 (1921).

Seager, Henry R., *Introduction to Economics* (New York, NY: Holt, 1904).

Seccombe, Wally "Contradiction of Shareholder Capitalism: Downsizing Jobs, Enlisting Savings, Destabilizing Families," 35 *Socialist Register* 76 (1999).

Sedgwick, Henry Dwight, *A Selection of American and English Cases on the Measure of Damages* (New York, NY: Baker Voorhis, 1878).

Selznick, Philip, *Law, Society and Industrial Justice* (New York, NY: Russell Sage, 1969).

Selznick, Philip, *The Moral Commonwealth: Social Theory and the Promise of Community* (Berkeley, CA: University of California Press, 1992).

Shapiro, Peter and James F. Tune, "Implied Contract Rights to Job Security," 26 *Stanford Law Review* 335 (1974).

Shawet, Stephen D., "Concession Bargaining: Legal and Practical Considerations in Light of Recent NLRB and Court Decisions," 12 *University of Baltimore Law Review* 233 (1982-1983).

Shultz, George P. and Charles A. Myers, "Union Wage Decisions and Employment," 40 *American Economic Review* 362 (1950).

Slichter, Sumner, "Lines of Action, Adaption, and Control," 22 *American Economic Review* 41 (1932).

Sloane, Arthur A., and Fred Whitney, *Labor Relations* (Englewood Cliffs, NJ: Prentice-Hall, 1972).

Smith, John W., *A Selection of Leading Cases on Various Branches of the Law*, Volume II (London: Maxwell, 3rd edition, 1840).

Smith, John W., *A Selection of Leading Cases on Various Branches of the Law*, Volume II (Philadelphia: Johnson, 4th American edition 1852).

Smith, Russell A., Leroy S. Merifield, Theodore J. St Antoine, and Charles B. Craver, *Labor Relations Law: Cases and Materials* (Ithaca, NY: Cornell University Press, 1984).

Speed, John J. and James J. Bambrick, "Seniority System in Non-Unionized Companies," *Studies in Personnel Policy,* No. 110 (New York, NY: National Industrial Conference Board, 1950).

Spriegel, William R. and Alfred G. Dale, "Personnel Practices in Industry," *Personnel Study,* No. 8 (University of Texas Dallas, TX: Bureau of Business Research, 1954).

St Antoine, Theodore "Changing Concepts of Worker Rights in the Workplace," 473 *Annals of the American Academy of the Political and Social Sciences* 108 (1984).

Steele, H. Ellsworth and Homer Fisher, Jr, "A Study of the Effects of Unionism in Southern Plants" 87 *Monthly Labor Review* 258 (1964).

Steinberg, Marc W., "Capitalist Development, the Labor Process, and the Law," 109 *American Sociological Review* 445 (2003).

Steuben, John, *Strike Strategy* (New York, NY: Gaer,1950).

Stone, Morris, "Why Arbitrators Reinstate Discharged Employees," 92 *Monthly Labor Review* 47 (1969).

Story, William W., *A Treatise on the Law of Contracts* (Boston, MA: Little Brown, 1851).

Strauss, George, "The Shifting Power Balance in the Plant," 1 *Industrial Relations* 65 (1962).

Summers, Clyde W., "Individual Protection against Unjust Dismissal: Time for a Statute," 62 *Virginia Law Review* 481 (1976).

Summers, Clyde W., "Trade Unions and Their Members," in *Civil Liberties in Conflict*, 65 (Larry Gostin, ed., London: Routledge, 1988).

Sumner, William Graham, "Industrial War," 2 *Forum* (1886).

Sutton, Ralph, and Norman P. Shannon, *Sutton and Shannon on Contracts* (London: Butterworth, 4th edition, 1933).

Swisher, Carl B., *American Constitutional Development* (Boston, MA: Houghton Mifflin, 1943).

Taft, Philip, *Organized Labor in American History* (New York, NY: Harper Bros., 1964).

Tannenbaum, Frank, "The Social Function of Trade Unionism," 62 *Political Science Quarterly* 161 (1947).

Taussig, Frank W., *Principles of Economics* (New York, NY: Macmillan, 4th edition, 1921).

Taylor, Albion G., "Technological Change and Unemployment," *American Economic Review*, March Supplement, 60 (1932).

Taylor, Albion G., *Labor Policies of the National Association of Manufacturers* (Urbana, IL: University of Illinois Press, 1928).

Taylor, Albion G., *Labor Problems and Labor Law* (New York, NY: Prentice-Hall, 1940).

Taylor, Albion G., *Labor Problems and Labor Law* (Upper Saddle River, NJ: 1938).

Terkel, Studs, *Hard Times: An Oral History of the Great Depression* (New York, NY: Avon, 1971).

Theodossiou, Ioannis and Efi Vasileiou, " Making the Risk of Job Loss a Way of Life: Does it Affect Job Satisfaction?" 61 *Research in Economics* 71 (2007).

Thompson, Andrew, "A View from Abroad," in *US Industrial Relations 1950 to 1980* 297 (Jack Stieber, Robert B. McKersie, and D. Quinn Mills, Madison, WI: Industrial Relations Research Association, 1981).

Tomlins, Christopher L., *Law, Labor and Ideology in the Early American Republic* (Cambridge: Cambridge University Press, 1993).

Tower, Charles H., "Law and Labor Relations in the Broadcasting Industry," 23 *Law and Contemporary Problems* 62 (1958).

Troy, Leo, "The Rise and Fall of American Trade Unions: The Labor Movement from FDR to RR," in *Unions in Transition*: *Entering the Second Century* 75 (Seymour M. Lipset ed., San Francisco, CA: Institute for Contemporary Studies Press, 1986).

Van Wezel Stone, Katherine, "The Legacy of Industrial Pluralism: The Tension Between Individual Employment Rights and the New Deal Collective Bargaining System," 59 *University of Chicago Law Review* 575 (1992).

van Wezel Stone, Katherine, "The Post-War Paradigm in American Labor Law," 90 *The Yale Law Journal* 1509 (1981).

Warren, Charles, "*Volenti Non Fit Injuria* in Actions of Negligence," 8 *Harvard Law Review* 457 (1895).

Warren, Charles, *The Supreme Court in United States History,* Volume 3 (Boston, MA: Little Brown, 1922).

Williamson, Oliver E., "Transaction Cost Economics: The Comparative Contracting Perspective," *Yale Law School Program in Law and Organization, Working Paper* No. 55 (1987).

Williston, Samuel, "Note—Repudiation of Contracts" 14 *Harvard Law Review* 421 (1900).

Willoughby, William F., "Public employment offices in the United States and Germany," in *Trade Unionism and Labor Problems* 602 (John R. Commons, ed., Boston, MA: Ginn, 1905).

Wolcher, Louis E., "The Privilege of Idleness: A Case Study of and the Common Law in Nineteenth Century America," 36 *American Journal of Legal History* 237 (1992).

Wood, Horace G., *A Treatise on the Law of Master and Servant, Covering the Relation, Duties and Liabilities of Employers and Employees* (San Francisco, CA: Bancroft Whitney, 1877).

Zolberg, Aristide, "From One Exceptionalism to Many: American Working Class Formation in Comparative Perspective" *Why is There no Socialism in the United States* 101 (Jean Heffer and Jeanine Rovet, eds., Paris: École des hautes Études en Sciences Sociales, 1988).

INDEX